D1355879

HOLY IGNORANCE

COMPARATIVE POLITICS
AND INTERNATIONAL STUDIES SERIES

Series editor, Christophe Jaffrelot

This series consists of translations of noteworthy manuscripts and publications in the social sciences emanating from the foremost French researchers, from Sciences Po, Paris.

The focus of the series is the transformation of politics and society by transnational and domestic factors—globalisation, migration, and the postbipolar balance of power on the one hand, and ethnicity and religion on the other. States are more permeable to external influence than ever before and this phenomenon is accelerating processes of social and political change the world over. In seeking to understand and interpret these transformations, this series gives priority to social trends from below as much as to the interventions of state and non-state actors.

OLIVIER ROY

Holy Ignorance

When Religion and Culture Part Ways

Translated by
Ros Schwartz

HURST & COMPANY, LONDON

First published in the United Kingdom in 2010 by
C. Hurst & Co. (Publishers) Ltd.,
41 Great Russell Street, London, WC1B 3PL
© Olivier Roy 2010
Translation © Ros Schwartz, 2010
All rights reserved.
Printed in India by Imprint Digital

A Cataloguing-in-Publication data record for this book
is available from the British Library.

ISBN 978-1-85065-992-1

This book is printed using paper from registered sustainable
and managed sources.

www.hurstpub.co.uk

Peramuna, JVP (an unsuccessful Marxist youth rebellion that claimed 15,000 lives). I also found myself, a year later, handing out leaflets in Paris supporting the very beautiful Chandrika Bandaranaike, who was standing against her mother, the then Prime Minister, in Colombo (my motivation here was infra-political, or, depending how one looks at it or where one stands, metapolitical). Chandrika ended up as President and appointed her mother Prime Minister—life is full of surprises. But that's another story. I also smuggled nearly the complete works of Mao Tse Tung in Persian (after picking them up from the Chinese Vice-Consul in Kabul, who wondered what on earth I wanted with them) to a vaguely Maoist friend in Tehran, under the Shah. In those days, it wasn't the Islamists who had a blind belief in violence.

What does this have to do with religion? Millenarianism, the death of the old man within oneself, absolute and transcendent truth, universalism, fear of never being on the right side—that of the pure... and in the most radical milieus, like the Khmer Rouge, culture was the very thing that was preventing the birth of the new man. This morbid, pathogenic, often criminal or suicidal concern to eliminate the old man within the self (and within the other) is also a hallmark of the Jihadists' religious radicalism. The idea of man as a *tabula rasa*: this was indeed a case of holy ignorance.

The religious dimension of communism has long been recognized, but it was even more pronounced among the Maoists; it is no coincidence that my former group leader, the man of formal logic and the class struggle, is now the great expert on Persian mysticism (at least this comes under neither logic nor ignorance—as for holiness, that is not my field). If our our beloved ex-leader, "comrade Jean", alias Pierre Victor, alias Benny Lévy, who believed he was God until he met someone with a better claim to the title, ended up as director of a *yeshiva* in Jerusalem, regularly bemoaning the time he wasted "not knowing". Was it in fact a matter of knowing? That's another story. But our careers have continually been haunted by the darkness of holiness rather than its light.

This brings me to the third stage of my student life. I pondered Châtelet's remark. If Mao Tse Tung's thinking was so weak theoretically, why did it "stir up the masses", as people said at the time? Why had it led to an event as improbable as the Cultural Revolution in China? Perhaps Maoism had a cultural dimension that was specifically Chinese—which would invalidate the reasons that prompted us to adopt it in the name of proletarian internationalism. After the intellectual conundrum of religion, I was faced with the enigma of culture, encountering it anew each time I crossed a border. So I decided to learn Chinese. After three years of evening classes at Paris-VII University, our teacher informed me that I had reached the minimum level required in China for the average peasant from the lower category, i.e. 750 characters (out of 49,000), which coming from him, trained in Communist China, was a compliment. Knowing more would probably have denoted class arrogance. As for our classical language teacher, who had followed a similar career path and had become a slavish Red Guard, he had us working on the writings of the Great Leader (accessible to an average peasant from the lower category) instead of those of Confucius (but I made up for it in the libraries). The conclusion (mine, this time) was definitive: the language of *The Little Red Book* was full of clichés, proverbs and sayings that echoed popular Chinese wisdom, comparable to allusions to the fables of La Fontaine in a political discourse in France, but there was no secret wisdom, alchemy of Chinese characters, mystery of Taoist dialectics or the intellectual subtleties of a Go player. There is also age-old ignorance which religion does not explain!

The problem was, my exams were approaching and in order to obtain my Masters thesis, I had to find a link between my philosophy studies and the years spent learning Chinese and Persian and travelling. Studying under Yvon Belaval, master mariner turned philosopher (or vice versa), I discovered that G. W. Leibniz (1646–1716) had been fascinated by China. He was a rationalist, Lutheran (and German) philosopher who supported Italian and French Jesuit missionaries facing harassment from the Vatican over religious rites in Manchu China. The same philosopher sought the keys to universal language in Chinese writings, a rational theology in the Chinese "religion", and finally, the first binary calculation table in the Taoist I-ching. In studying his work, I was guaranteed to find plenty of food for thought.

The quarrel over rites was the beginning of a modern argument. The Chinese imperial authorities were not interested in Christian theology any more in the seventeenth century than in the twenty-first, they simply wanted everyone to worship the Emperor—worship here to be understood as a simple "civic religion", in other words a moral adhesion to the political order and to the values of the empire; that had nothing to do with defending an official religion. What was at stake

CONTENTS

FOREWORD

This book is not necessarily what it appears to be: the work of an expert on Islam who has moved away from his specialist field into comparatism, with all the attendant implications of amateurism.

As a matter of fact, my interest in Christianity goes back much further than my interest in Islam. In 1972, I tackled the question of relations between Christianity, universalism and culture in my Master's thesis entitled "Leibniz and China". But in this foreword, I would particularly like to mention the three "pre-book" stages, prior even to this first publication in 1972, which prepared the ground for *Holy Ignorance*.

It all began in the spring of 1965 in the town of La Rochelle. I was fifteen years old and a member of a Protestant youth group. This milieu offered me a balanced mix of all the interesting things in life. We studied the Bible in an atmosphere of great intellectual freedom; the ministers were cultured, they took us to the theatre, introduced us to books (and politics, in the case of the younger ones); we went to summer camps where sports went hand in hand with intellectual pursuits. And, above all, in those days it was one of the few places where teenage boys and girls could mix, which was much better than the secular school and its Catholic rivals. Of course, our ministers were responsible for ensuring that this fraternizing did not result in transgression. They appealed, in good Protestant tradition, not to prohibitions, but to our sense of responsibility ("Save yourself for the girl who's saving herself for you", and vice-versa for the girls). Naturally, we used all sorts of ploys, some more subtle than others, to bend the rules without questioning either the values or the explicit norms of a Protestant sub-culture in which we felt at home. For example, we formed a folk dance group which, over the course of the year, surreptitiously switched from *kibbutz-kolkhoz* dances to the Israeli tune of *Hava Nagila*—the minister's favourite—to the Argentine tango (no, this has nothing to do with my current stance on the Israel-Palestine conflict).

In the spring of 1965, we planned a camping holiday in Brittany: cycling during the day, camping at night, Bible studies, singing, discussions—and the rest. My best friend and I had smuggled a smaller, cosier tent into the communal camping kit and planned to rendezvous therein with our girlfriends once the ministers were asleep. As we were top of the class in Bible studies, curiously they assumed we had a higher sense of morality than our fellow students—that's Protestant intellectualism for you. Then, two months before our departure, the minister announced the arrival of a new boy. He was sixteen years old, came from the town's working-class parish and had matinee-idol looks. One Thursday he entered the club where we were clustered around a ping-pong table, and zealously shouted "Christ is risen!" It was not so much the words themselves—inscribed in our membership agreement—that felt incongruous, as the way he uttered them. There were times for that, and this was not one of them: "To everything there is a season, and a time to every purpose under the heaven". But the new boy, with his radiant smile and luminous blue eyes, was not daunted by our silence: "Brothers and sisters, say with me: Hallelujah! Christ is risen!"… The holiday was off to a bad start, because a boy like that was bound to be an insomniac, like all those who are inspired. Even more worrying, there was a gleam in the minister's eyes: at last, he had found someone who truly shared his faith.

I had just encountered my first evangelical Christian. At the time, La Rochelle was home to an American military base and acted as a bridgehead for the Mormons, Jehovah's Witnesses, evangelicals, Baptists, Pentecostalists, Adventists and the Salvation Army. The American missionaries had found the working-class districts of Laleu and the industrial port of La Palice particularly fertile ground. The Gypsy (or "Travellers" as we'd say today) Mission pitched its tent every summer. In other words, the spread of evangelicalism and "sects" was occurring right in front of me, twenty years before it became a social issue. It was, in a way, my first experience of participative sociology.

After a brief discussion, a delegation of us went to see the minister with a very simple ultimatum: "It's him or us". The minister very wisely chose to accompany the lost sheep on his bicycle rather than walk with the only sheep that had found the path to the narrow gate. Unless he too was afraid of having his holiday ruined, which is unlikely as he was a man of the cloth. And thus I can boast of having been involved, at the age of fifteen, in Protestant culture's tradition of resistance against the evangelist offensive.

And now, forty-five years on, I am forced to conclude that it was a rearguard battle. The newcomers reconciled not so much faith and reason as faith and logic—which are much more effective. In fact, Paul the Apostle was badly translated when he spoke of *latreia logikê* (reasonable service) in the epistle to the Romans (12:1): it did indeed mean *logical service*, and not *rational* and even less *reasonable*, as the King James Bible says. If we have faith, then it must be at the centre of our lives. And knowledge and culture are of little importance if we are deaf to the call of Christ. I could put away my Greek dictionary with which I tried in vain to impress the girls during Bible studies. After the rational believer (my minister grandfather), came the existential believer (very hip among theology students in the 1950s), the pedantic believer (yours truly, at least at the time), and now it is the time of the logical believer. And of holy ignorance.

The reader may infer from the above anecdote that the purpose of this book is to settle scores with evangelicalism. Not so; I was more puzzled than resentful. Besides, the holiday went as planned: every night the ministers fell asleep very early, or pretended to (these were the good old days of the implicit; nowadays we utter the unsaid, but only as a manner of speaking).

Quite simply, that boy whose name eludes me continued to baffle me: that he could die thus seemed conceivable to me, but how could a person live as a Christian with such a faith? And live forever? To which I would now add another question: these days, do his children—for he must have had some—greet their friends with a loud "Christ is risen"?

The second encounter was with Marxist universalism.

It was of course the student Paris of the late 1960s, and my arrival in the first year of preparatory school for the École Normale Supérieure in a lycée where the Maoists ruled the roost (while the Trotskyists dominated the streets). In the school year of 1967–68 (the year of May 1968), preparatory class 2 of the Lycée Louis-le-Grand had François Châtelet as its philosophy teacher. A colourful character and a Hellenist, an earnest left-winger, he observed our revolutionary protests with an ironic sympathy. He was prepared to brave the riot squad's batons to come and collect us from the police station, and had no hesitation in jeopardising his career to embark on new pedagogical experiments, all the while mouthing a few fashionable slogans in keeping with the mood of the day, like the Greeks offering libations to the local deities; but there was one thing he never compromised on: philosophical rigour.

And so, one day, when the most brilliant student in the class (not me, I should add) began his presentation on "Formal logic and the class struggle" with the following declaration: "Chairman Mao teaches us that just ideas do not come from the sky, they come from the people", Châtelet sighed, adjusted his glasses, gazed at us and interrupted the speaker: "Listen, kids, don't forget that Mao Tse Tungian thought is pre-Baconian!". It was said politely and it had a devastating effect on me at any rate (others took several years to come to the same conclusion). Mao pre-Baconian? Mao "a crappy philosopher"? But then, does that mean that the poorer and more dogmatic the thinking, the more influential it is? This explained, before its time, the success of television philosophers, following Marx's maxim that history, in repeating itself, goes from tragedy to farce. But at that time, I couldn't accept such a pessimistic conclusion.

Then I developed the habit of taking off for the East to get away from this world of imminent revolution that had become unreal. But it was only to encounter the same activists and the same discourse almost everywhere, sometimes punctuated by bursts of Kalashnikov fire— a sound that was to serve as background music to my philosophical musings.

It was between two failed revolutionary movements that I met variously, in little villages in the Afghan province of Nuristan and in the Yemeni Hadramaut, an exiled primary school teacher, an officer who wasn't sure whether he should arrest the passing backpacker or invite him in, and a student back in his parents' village for the school holidays. They and I reinvented the world, compared our strategies for taking power and discussed the revolutionary capabilities of the peasantry. The difference between us was that they really were risking their lives, and that many like them have lost theirs.

Then there was my encounter, in an old propeller-driven crate flying me from Aden to Bombay, with a Sri Lankan student telling us in advance about the bloody and suicidal 1971 uprising led by the Sinhalese Sri Lankan People's Liberation Front, or Janatha Vimukthi

INTRODUCTION

Modernity, Secularization and the Revival of Religion

Why do tens of thousands of Muslims in Central Asia become Christians or Jehovah's Witnesses? How can an evangelical Protestant Church establish itself in Morocco and Algeria? Why has Protestant evangelicalism built up a huge following in Brazil (twenty-five million adherents in 2007) and West Africa? What is the explanation for the fact that the world's fastest growing religion is Pentecostalism? Why does radical Salafism attract young Europeans, both black and white? How come Al Qaida is the "Islamic" organization that has the highest percentage of converts? And conversely, why is the Catholic Church finding it so hard to retain its flock, with priestly vocations plummeting in the West? Why is it that today's custodians of the conservative Anglican tradition are Nigerian, Ugandan or Kenyan, whereas Rowan Williams, Archbishop of Canterbury and head of the English Church has spoken out in favour both of allowing British Muslims to use *sharia* law in civil cases and the ordination of gay priests? Why have the Slavic Orthodox Churches, contrary to Protestantism, fallen back on national identities, likewise Hinduism?

Why is Buddhism catching on in the West? Why has the ideological emphasis on religion in Iran led to a secularization of civil society? Why does South Korea supply the highest number of Protestant missionaries in the world in proportion to its population (in absolute figures, it ranks just behind the United States)? The theory of the clash (or dialogue) of civilizations does not explain these tectonic movements which confuse the issue, blur territories and identities, and sever the traditional links between religion and culture. What happens when

1

religions break away from their cultural roots? Or, to put it simply, why do religions seem to be engines that drive such reformulations of identity?

Two conflicting theories emerged in the last quarter of the twentieth century: one contends that secularization is an inevitable process, both a condition and consequence of modernity, the other acknowledges or welcomes the comeback of religion, perceived either as a protest against an alienating or illusory modernity, or as a different way of entering modernity. This discussion is not purely intellectual: in France, it is central to the argument about secularism. Should secularism be imposed at the expense of individual freedom, to combat religion if need be, or is the revival of religion simply a reflection of diversity, cultural richness and human freedom?

But there is a huge misapprehension in this debate: secularization has not eradicated religion. As a result of our separating religion from our cultural environment, it appears on the other hand as pure religion. In fact, secularization has worked: what we are witnessing today is the militant reformulation of religion in a secularized space that has given religion its autonomy and therefore the conditions for its expansion. Secularization and globalization have forced religions to break away from culture, to think of themselves as autonomous and to reconstruct themselves in a space that is no longer territorial and is therefore no longer subject to politics. The failure of political religion (Islamism as a theocracy) comes from the fact that it tried to compete with secularization on its own ground: the political sphere (nation, state, citizen, constitution, legal system). Attempts to politicize religion in this way always end up secularizing it, because it becomes mixed up with day-to-day politics and because it presupposes both allegiance from each person and individual freedom. Political religion is quite simply torn between two imperatives: non-belief is unthinkable, but faith can only be individual; a collective faith is therefore inconceivable, whereas previously there had been a collective system of norms. This political religion works on the principle that everyone must be a believer, but it cannot guarantee this belief, and must therefore impose a conformity reduced to appearances, which makes it impossible for it subsequently to present itself as the expression of a faith shared by an entire community.

There is a close link between secularization and religious revivalism, which is not a reaction against secularization, but the product of it.

Secularism engenders religion. We are not witnessing a religious come-back, but a transformation. This transformation is probably only tem-porary: it will not necessarily lead to a new religious age.

A preliminary question does however arise: does religion's increasing visibility and the amount of media and political attention paid to it really equate to an increase in religious practice? In Europe, this is not obvious at all: John Paul II's papacy embodied religion's media-friendly modernity, but over the past twenty years, while growing numbers of young people have flocked to meet the Pope on World Youth Day (WYD), the number enrolling in Catholic seminaries has fallen continu-ously. Should we conclude that the more young people see of the Pope, the less inclined they are to become priests? Or rather, to put it more delicately, that their need for spirituality no longer corresponds to what the traditional Church can offer? Europeans' religious practice has declined steadily during the decades of the "religious revival". In Spain, a law passed in 1987 and approved by the Church allows the state to levy directly a voluntary religious tax (0.52 per cent of income tax) which is paid to the Church; but the number of tax-paying households ticking the box fell from 42.73 per cent in 1993 to 34.32 per cent in 2002.[1] In Great Britain, there has been a general decline in religious practice except among three groups: Poles (50 per cent attendance at mass), Pentecostalists and Muslims.[2] But a large proportion of Pente-costalists are from African or Jamaican backgrounds: thus religious "revivalism" is associated with population categories (in particular immigrants), not with the nature of religions themselves. Religion recruits on the fringes, in the same way that the major eighteenth- and nineteenth-century religious revivalist movements (Methodism) concen-trated on the geographical fringes (Wales, Scotland) and ignored the heart of England. In Spain, the astonishing spread of Protestantism, which rose from a few tens of thousands of followers in 1995 to some 400,000 in 2005, is chiefly due to the conversion of immigrants from Ecuador and other Latin American countries. In the Christian Ortho-dox countries, the rush to the Churches that followed the fall of com-munism seems to have fizzled out.

Those who claim there is a religious revival stress that Europe is the exception and that on other continents the return to religion is much more pronounced. In actual fact, even though it is difficult to measure religious practice, what we are seeing today may be new forms of reli-gious visibility rather than an outbreak of religiousness. In the United

3

States, the percentage of people stating they are non-believers rose from 7 per cent to 13 per cent between 1990 and 2001, while the number of Catholic seminarians plunged from 49,000 in 1965 to 4,700 in 2002, even though the number of Catholics was rising as a result of the Hispanicization of the population:[3] likewise, although there are growing numbers of students in Protestant theological colleges, the percentage of those wishing to become ministers is diminishing.[4] In Israel, the increase in the number of orthodox Jews is due to natural population growth rather than to a sudden surge in the number of *bal teshuva* (born again).

Some observers have noted a parallel between a decline in Christianity and Islam's expansion. But it is Christian Pentecostalism that is growing fastest the world over, along with Mormonism. The religious practice of the Muslim minority in Europe seems much more visible, but that is because public practise started from nothing, whereas in fact regular individual observance of the rites (prayers) appears to be not much greater than that practised by other religions.[5] The spread of Islam has been linked to the expansion of Muslim populations rather than to a conversion trend. However, Muslim population growth is experiencing a sudden slowdown: nearly all Muslim societies are currently seeing a demographic transition which places them on a par with or below European fertility levels.[6]

Furthermore, the expression "religious comeback" implies a revival of religions as they formerly were, like after an eclipse. Are the religions that are successful today the same, apart from their labels (Christianity, Islam), as those on which the great civilizations were founded? We are witnessing a shift of the traditional forms of religious practice—Catholicism, Hanafi Islam, classic Protestant denominations such as Anglicanism and Methodism—towards more fundamentalist and charismatic forms of religiosity (evangelicalism, Pentecostalism, Salafism, Tablighi Jamaat, neo-Sufism, Lubavich). But these movements are relatively recent. Salafism derives from Wahhabism which was founded at the end of the eighteenth century. The Hasidim and Haredim were born in the seventeenth and eighteenth centuries. The various evangelical movements belong to the tradition of Protestant "awakenings" which began during the eighteenth century, while Pentecostalism dates from the early twentieth century. Similarly the forms of Buddhism and Hinduism which recruit and export themselves are recent reformulations from the late nineteenth to the late twentieth century (Soka

Gakkai, Falun Gong and Hare Krishna, as well as the political Hinduism of the Indian Bharatiya Janata Party (BJP) and Sri Lankan *theravada* Buddhism). The movements which the French call sects and the Americans cults, or more academically "NRMs" (New Religious Movements) are thriving: the Mormons and the Jehovah's Witnesses, which also began in the nineteenth century, expanded hugely worldwide at the close of the twentieth century.

In this sense, religious "comeback" is merely an optical illusion: it would be more appropriate to speak of transformation. Religion is both more visible and at the same time frequently in decline. We are witnessing a reformulation of religion rather than a return to ancestral practices abandoned during the secularist hiatus. These tendencies go hand in hand with a desire for greater visibility in the public sphere, even an ostensible break with mainstream practices and cultures. Religion exhibits itself as such, and refuses to be reduced to one symbolic system among others.

It is the relationship between religion and public life that is changing, for religious revival in the public sphere no longer takes on the form of cultural visibility but becomes a display of religious "purity", or of reconstructed traditions. Religious conversions in all directions are a sign of this muddying of the link between culture and religion. But one thing is undeniable: in all cases it is the so-called "fundamentalist" or "charismatic" forms of religion that have seen the most spectacular growth, be it Protestant evangelicalism or Muslim Salafism. There has been a similar increase in hardline orthodoxy in the Catholic Church and Judaism, and even in Hinduism. Fundamentalism is the religious form that is most suited to globalization, because it accepts its own deculturation and makes it the instrument of its claim to universality.

Deterritorialization and Deculturation

Clearly it is not the first time that religions have exported themselves and converted beyond their cultural heartlands, but religious change triggers deculturation/acculturation processes where religious and cultural markers attempt to reconnect, often in the context of conquests or some form of political supremacy. The territorialization of religions resulted in their acculturation, or inculturation to use a more recent term (they establish themselves within an existing culture). Christianity and Islam respectively had an undeniable Westernizing and Arabizing effect, even if new syntheses between religion and culture gradually emerged which made it possible to divide the world into cultural regions (Persian or Ottoman culture, Latin American Christianity). Moreover, some claim that the territorialization of religion is the root cause of the clash/dialogue of civilizations, a theory which suits political ends.

Anthropologists have come up with a whole array of concepts to express these connections: acculturation, hybridism, syncretism, mixing... Marxists of all stripes have bandied around the concept of alienation to explain how political or ideological supremacy could implant beliefs whose purpose was to maintain this supremacy by internalising it: this explained why the dominated embraced the religion of the dominators, the most typical example being the African-American slaves' adoption of Protestantism despite the lack of a systematic conversion policy among slave owners (but how do we explain the fact that their counterparts in the Catholic areas of the Americas turned instead to syncretist religions such as Voodoo?).

But nowadays, "religion" circulates outside all systems of political supremacy. Of course, many see the growth of Pentecostalism as a new avatar of American ideological imperialism, but things are more complicated: how then can the spread of Islam, the proportion of Africans in modern-day Catholicism or the expansion of Buddhism be explained? Does the conversion of many African-Americans to Islam make Islam the new form of alienation or the opposite, anti-imperialism in a new guise?

Two factors play a key part in the transformation of religion today: deterritorialization and deculturation. Deterritorialization is not only associated with the movement of people (which only affects a small percentage of the global population), but also with the circulation of ideas, cultural objects, information and modes of consumption generally in a non-territorial space. But in order to circulate, the religious object must appear universal, disconnected from a specific culture that has to be understood in order for the message to be grasped. Religion therefore circulates outside knowledge. Salvation does not require people to know, but to believe. Both, of course, are far from being incompatible in religions which are embedded in culture and where theological reflection is stimulated by contact with philosophy and literature. But not only is this connection no longer necessary, it also becomes an obstacle when it is a matter of circulating in "real time" in a space where information has replaced knowledge.

INTRODUCTION

The separation of religious and cultural markers is not a result of deterritorialization: it goes with it, but it also happens *in situ*, driven by variable factors both internal and external. Secularization prompts religion to distance itself from a culture now perceived as indifferent, even hostile. This is where the argument between "fundamentalism" and "accommodationism" is played out; these are two positions rather than two theologies: the first assumes a breakaway from culture, the second considers that the embodiment of religion in a culture (established or developing) is a pre-requisite for its existence. For the fundamentalist, the criterion of separation is faith: you only share with a person of the same faith. For the accommodationist, the believer can share a common culture and values with the non-believer. We can speak of a Jewish atheist or of a culturally Catholic nonbeliever, and today we are witnessing the appearance of the concept of the "Muslim atheist"; on the other hand it is hard to conceive of an atheist Pentecostalist, an agnostic Salafist, or an intellectual Jehovah's Witness.

So religion then turns against the surrounding culture that is no longer perceived as simply secular, but as pagan (from Pentecostalist preachers to the Taliban and Wahhabis). The space in-between, that of accommodation, disappears. The temptation is then to define a "religious purity". This religious purity can be constructed in diverse contexts. It can be a crisis in social relations that leads to the rebuilding of identity on the basis of a religious marker (immigration, a dramatic crisis in tribalism). It can be the explicit construction of a religion "for export": the missionary urge in the face of a standardized global market, taking a marketing-type approach, tailoring the product to the market, playing on demand but also stimulating a demand. Deterritorialization is also a consequence of the crisis of the territorialized nation-state, to which political secularism still clings. And political secularism attempts to restrict the autonomy of religion and resist the influence of globalization (from France to Turkey) by taking authoritarian measures.

If religions are able to extend beyond their original cultures, it is because they have been able to "deculturate" themselves. The religious marker circulates without cultural markers, even if it means reconnecting with floating cultural markers—*halal* fast food, eco-*kosher*, cyber-*fatwa*, *halal* dating, Christian rock, transcendental meditation. Political correctness has abandoned Christmas in favour of Winterval, thus helping not only to neutralize religion, but also to reinforce it by arresting its metamorphosis into culture, thus preventing it from becoming "embedded" in culture

The deculturation of religion has some fundamental consequences: first of all it transforms the gap between the believer and the non-believer into a barrier, since now they no longer share either religious practice or common values. So all the intermediary spaces of non-practising believers, nominal followers, culturally religious non-believers are vanishing. In the eyes of the believers, the lukewarm, the cool or those who have not been born again belong to the secular—or even pagan—world. Conversely, to the non-believer, the believer appears incongruous, even fanatical. Deculturation is the loss of the social expression of religion. Believers feel themselves to be minorities surrounded by an atheist, pornographic, materialistic, secular culture which worships false gods: money, sex or man himself. This sentiment holds true even if statistically believers are in the majority, as in the United States.

On the other hand, the simultaneous presence in the market of different "religious products" results in both competition and standardization, not of theology but of religiosity. This standardization is also apparent in the sociological profile of followers of new religious movements, who display certain traits specific to so-called neo-fundamentalism: modern family structures (i.e. couples of a similar age and background) but conservative values; political lobbying to promote moral values, but indifference to political ideology and to the form of the state; campaigning, professionally active women who demand traditional roles (women wearing the headscarf for the first time claiming that it is a personal choice); modern professionals (engineers, civil servants) whose discourse is rooted in "tradition"; insistence on the norm rather than on love and compassion; a closed community but a universalist vision of religion; indifference to traditional culture and art but a fascination with modern technology. All religiosities are similar, even if their religious identities are divergent. The standardization of lifestyles, norms and values is a corollary of globalization.

As people are seeking identical things (self-affirmation, fulfilment, happiness, salvation), religions format themselves according to these demands. Market-driven formatting is heightened by the role of institutions, either through legislation or through legal processes which tend to treat all religions in the same way and therefore to mould them in similar categories. Gradually a common template of "religion" is emerging, since institutions need a one-size-fits-all definition that applies to all religions. But this formatting does not simply obey a desire to control, dominate and acculturate, as was traditionally the case when the state intervened in spiritual matters. Nowadays, the formatting of religion occurs for precisely the opposite reason: it is done in the name of freedom and equality. In order for religions to be treated in an egalitarian manner, they must be part of a shared paradigm: for example, allowing a religion to have chaplains in the army assumes that the religion in question has a category of professional ministers of religion, and if that is not the case, it will be invented. Although the principle of the separation of Church and state in democratic countries is there precisely to ensure that the state does not define religion, it nevertheless seeks to use a common paradigm. The paradox is that in the past, religion was formatted so as to reinforce domination in the interests of territorial and political uniformity generally based on a national programme, but nowadays it occurs in the name of "human rights", religious freedom and multiculturalism. Far from being the acknowledgement of primary differences, multiculturalism is no more than the expression of the formatting of cultures and religions within a common paradigm of the lowest common denominators: a few religious markers, divorced from their context, "made equal" by legal process and established as cultural markers. Multiculturalism boils down to obliterating cultural depth and placing under the name of culture a reduced set of religious markers, all of which are similar to each other (dietary and dress requirements reduced to a few paraphernalia, like the headscarf). Multiculturalism is the communal estate comprising only the property acquired after marriage.

What is Pure Religion?

What is the meaning of "pure religion"? A tension has always existed between faith and culture, especially when there is a breaking away (revelation, conversion). Breaking away from the surrounding culture therefore leads to a fundamentalist-type assertion (a demand to return to explicit religious norms and only to these) or integralist (i.e. every aspect of my private life must be governed by my faith, even if I don't impose it on others).[7] New or born-again believers and converts will not allow their faith to be categorized by anthropologists as one cultural symbolic system among others. For them, it is an absolute. This is what the Protestant theologian Karl Barth terms the "leap of faith" that makes religion what it is. There can be no theology without faith. The argument between faith and knowledge is certainly inherent to all the revealed religions. The "moderate" currents, like Thomism, have always argued that there is no contradiction between the two: faith and knowledge mutually reinforce each other. But deculturation destroys this dialectic relation: the sacred texts must be able to speak outside any cultural context. And so we are witnessing the deculturation of the sacred texts. We are aware of the extent to which the Bible is a cultural text, and yet the evangelical Protestants follow it "to the letter", but a letter freed not only from the original language, but from language itself, in order to see no more than a simple message. The ultimate process of this deculturation is the very thing that accounts for the Pentecostalists' success today.

The hallmark of Pentecostalism, in addition to the characteristics specific to what we call evangelicalism (the emphasis on being born again, and the literal belief in the Bible), is glossolalia, speaking in tongues. Under the influence of the Holy Spirit, in imitation of the Apostles, some believers start "speaking in tongues", and people with whom they have no common language are able to understand what they are saying. Admittedly there are several schools within Pentecostalism: they do not all see glossolalia as a condition for salvation, but "speaking in tongues" is indeed a key feature of Pentecostalism. The Pentecostalists who preach in "tongues" do not preach in any specific language and have no knowledge of foreign languages. Glossolalia is no more than a series of sounds, and yet the "message" is transmitted: God's word no longer needs to be enshrined in a particular language and culture; it is detached, like tongues of fire. There is something extraordinary here: the language that is spoken is no longer a real language, the Word of God is no longer embodied in a given language. There are two simultaneous approaches to taking the Scripture literally: Pentecostalism is "literalist", i.e. it does not question the veracity of the letter of the scriptures, but nor is it interested in the actual language of the text, nor, incidentally, in any specific language. But the Biblical text, we suspect, poses a problem: written in Hebrew, Aramaic or Greek, it poses problems of translation, of the cultural environment of the language of the time, for there is no such thing as a neutral language: all languages are rooted in a complex cultural context, every language has a history. In ignoring real language, Pentecostalism resolves the question of the contextualization of the sacred text: God speaks outside any context.[8]

How Can Faith be Passed on to the Next Generation?

How can a person be born from a born-again, how can a person be the child of a convert? A radical breakaway cannot be transmitted; it turns into a new tradition. That is why religions have always acculturated or inculturated themselves. But this severing of the connection between religion and culture today persists precisely because globalization challenges cultures' durability and territorialization. The knowledge society being advocated is that of a deculturated knowledge, reduced to information that circulates. The autonomy of religion and the separation of cultural and religious markers are congruous with this process. That is modern religiosity.

But this permanent tension between religion and culture is unstable. Two recurrent problems arise for converts and the born again—how do you pass on to your children and how do you reach out to others? The buzzword today is reconnection, the only alternative to the ghettoization of religion. The all-or-nothing attitude to faith is not tenable, especially for a new generation which sees the "revival of religion" as a phenomenon that is both established and outmoded.

Reconnection is therefore a recurrent problem in the Catholic Church, for the centrist Muslims, the Jews threatened by assimilation and American evangelicals shaking off the idea that the return of Christ is imminent. Believers do not spend their time praying: they also expect something from politics and from the economy. The American Christian right has run out of steam, as evidenced by the fact that in 2008, it no longer recognized itself in the Republican presidential candidate.[9] The battle against abortion and gay marriage makes it impossible to dodge the concerns of many believers over issues like global warming, healthcare or growing poverty. From Iran to Saudi Arabia, including Pakistan's North-West Frontier Province (NWFP), the implementation of *sharia* law has done nothing to resolve economic and social problems. The growing poverty of the ultra-orthodox community in Israel is an economic problem for the state. Furthermore, a number of young Jewish Haredim are losing their faith, without necessarily becoming socially integrated secular beings.[10] The social and cultural question is resurfacing to haunt faith communities.

So religions are trawling for new cultural markers, in particular borrowed from youth culture:

Heaven may not be too far away if you're a teenager. On the south-western outskirts of Savannah awaits a new 33,000–square-foot facility soon to be filled with games, parties, friends and rock concerts. It will all be free at Savannah Christian Church's new youth centre called The Link. The two-story centre will be unveiled tonight during a three-hour grand-opening celebration. Prizes, including free iPods, will be given away every hour to junior high and senior high school students who register at the door.

The Link includes a plethora of pop-culture diversions rarely found in one place, much less a church. There's a rock-climbing wall, nine Xbox 360s, a basketball cage, skateboard ramps, a cafe, a lakeside patio and lots of comfy couches.[11]

In Lourdes, France:

The bishopric of Tarbes and Lourdes is organising a night of partying and prayer on New Year's Eve. Codename: 3D, the Discothèque of God. The programme includes a concert by the Christian rock band Exo, followed by a procession top at the grotto of Massabielle, where there will be a mass celebrated by Monsignor Jacques Perrier. The young people will then have the choice between a night of worship or an all night café.[12]

With ice cream sundaes, iPod giveaways, spa days and yoga classes, a group of Orthodox rabbis in the Washington area is employing decidedly unorthodox methods to address a growing problem: the fading involvement of Jews in local Jewish life.[13]

American evangelicalist literature, like that of conservative or orthodox Jews, is full of these frantic attempts to reconnect, the proof that the pure religion position is not tenable for much longer.[14] But what is at issue here is definitely the cultural dimension of these new markers, since code is probably being confused with culture. Encoding religion in youth-speak is likely to remain transient and temporary. That in fact is often the view of the religions in question, for which it is a matter of using a sales pitch to attract customers, but not of adopting their world view. But that does not answer the question of what a religious culture is. Meanwhile, Holy Ignorance prevails.

The New Converts

Conversions have always existed, but mass conversions have generally been collective and in specific political circumstances (conquests, assimilation strategy, expression of local identities). What is new today is the high number of conversions undertaken as a result of individual choice and in very different contexts. They have the character of mass conversions and go hand in hand with the rapid boom in new religious movements spawned either by existing religions (charismatic and evangelical movements in Christianity at the expense of more liberal or traditional forms, the rise of Salafism in Islam), or emerging as new religions, often described as "cults". But the key factor in conversions is the lack of a connection between religion and culture; in other words, religions are recruiting outside the cultures with which they are traditionally associated, or are having a deculturation effect which is not followed by acculturation: they distance themselves from each of the surrounding cultures, which are seen as too secular, pagan even, without necessarily promoting new cultures.

The boundary between new forms of religiosity, new religions and cults is not very clear. Where should the Mormons and Jehovah's Witnesses be classed? They consider themselves to be Christians, but are rejected as such by the other Churches. That is why sociologists of religion have coined the term "New Religious Movements" (NRMs), which allows us to go beyond genealogies and affiliations and reflect together on these new movements, be they Pentecostalist, Jehovah's Witnesses or Hare Krishna.

Converts are first and foremost nomads, even if they do not move around physically: they shop around, test out and experiment, surfing the web. A large number of conversions are self-conversions: people choose their religion for themselves, declare they are members and then seek out a religious authority to confirm their choice. Conversions to Judaism, other than for pragmatic reasons (in order to marry or to acquire Israeli nationality), are particularly striking. The Jewish faith does not proselytize, and yet, each year, hundreds of would-be converts knock on every possible door in order to be recognized as Jewish.[15] Conversion here is neither the result of political pressure, nor of the influence of a mainstream culture nor of voluntarist proselytism.

Converts' stories are curiously similar: they generally involve a very personal journey, beginning with a feeling of dissatisfaction and failure, followed by an investigation of various systems of thinking and ending in suddenly finding Jesus, Allah or a guru. Muslim websites abound in stories of conversion, all the more valued if the neophyte was previously Christian, and preferably Western and cultured. Evangelicals prefer a public confession in front of an audience of the faithful: "I used to drink, take drugs and steal, and then one day I found Jesus".[16] Conversion can also be internal, within the same religion, but people are "born-again"; this is a fundamental principle for the evangelicals and Pentecostalists: it is not enough to be baptized, you personally have to return to Christ. The believer is a "confessant": he or she must express their faith in every aspect of their lives. This is equally true of the Salafis and the Jewish Haredim. All the charismatic Christian movements, including among Catholics, follow this pattern, even if there is no specific ceremony. In their own way, the Muslim Salafis and Tablighis consider that a true return is necessary and therefore the traditional conception of Islam must be renounced. (Re)conversion is a personal experience, an illumination, more rarely the result of reasoning. There is no room here for theological debate: it is the "life story" that counts.

Converts and the born-again are central to our study, since they epitomize the phenomenon of the deculturation of religion. Converts and the born-again share common characteristics, even if there are clear differences in style and substance (in particular between groups that tend to be ascetic and those advocating ostentatious wealth as proof of God's blessing).

Conversions and reconversions within the same religion are not evenly matched. There are winners and losers. In Christianity, it is Protestant evangelicalism that is on the rise, with Pentecostalism in the lead. They encroach on all other religions, Catholicism being the primary victim. The figures show that in Brazil the number of Catholics dropped from 90 to 67 per cent of the population between 1965 and 2005; in Spain, between 1995 and 2005, the number of Protestants rose from tens of thousands to hundreds of thousands due to the conversion of immigrants from Latin America; in less than two decades (1980–1998), 10 per cent of the population of Cape Verde switched from Catholicism to Protestantism. But the Christian Orthodox countries (such as the former Soviet Union) and Muslim countries (e.g. in Central Asia) have also been affected. Pentecostalist communities can be found in places as unexpected as Sicily, Greece and Lebanon. This breakthrough by evangelical Protestantism has long been studied by American scholars, but has received little attention in France.[17]

But it is not appropriate to speak only of an internal transformation within Christianity, since evangelicalism is also spreading in China and in the Muslim world. Changes of religion are no longer confined as they once were to areas of tectonic contact, where a new political power imposed its religion. It is a global phenomenon. Nowadays, there exists a real religion market which means that there is a very wide range of choices available. This does not mean that religious freedom exists everywhere, but that the traditional link between a religion and a culture has been eroded: an Algerian is no longer necessarily Muslim, a Russian Orthodox or a Pole Catholic. Choices once unimaginable have become conceivable, if not easy. A typical example is Christian proselytism in a Muslim milieu. Why were there so few conversions to Christianity in the days of colonialism, when conversion was encouraged by the authorities? The secular French Republic supported the missionary activities of the White Fathers. It is no coincidence that the founder of the White Fathers, Cardinal Lavigerie, was also the rallying force who sought to reconcile the Catholic Church with the Republic. In Algeria, a French territory, applicants were not required to abandon the Muslim religion in itself in order to obtain French citizenship, but, as it involved the renunciation of personal status, it is clear that conversion to Christianity facilitated assimilation, so there was a strong incentive to convert. However the results were very disappointing. Apart from a few families of Berber intellectuals (Amrouche, Reghi), the White Fathers' proselytizing activities were astonishingly ineffectual. The Catholic Church gradually abandoned its attempts to convert Muslims and settled for "witnessing" instead (like, for example, at the Tibehrine monastery in Algeria); Father Christian Delorme went so far as to declare that they should not convert Algerians because Islam was integral to Algerian identity.[18]

However, in February 2006, the Algerian Parliament passed a law banning religious proselytism. Why? Previously, such a law would have been pointless as such occurrences were rare. But now, conversions to Christianity are affecting the man and (especially) the woman in the street, without pressure from any external form of domination. In 2008, for example, several Algerian converts to Christianity were put on trial.[19] Explanations in terms of acculturation or of political supremacy do not hold water in this case. Nor did this spate of conversions occur because there was suddenly religious freedom combined with an abundant religious offer. On the contrary, societies, like governments, are hostile to missionary activity. This is primarily true of authoritarian Muslim countries, but in different circumstances many other states are hostile to proselytism. In Russia and India for example, laws were introduced in the first decade of the twenty-first century to curb conversions (in 2006 in Rajasthan): the Hindu nationalists targeted conversions of the lower castes either to evangelicalism or Buddhism in particular. In France, the Miviludes, a parliamentary mission, is explicitly monitoring all the NRMs. Paradoxically, the proliferation of laws and anti-conversion campaigns bear out the success of the new missions.

In recent decades, much has been written about conversions of Christians to Islam, which have swelled the ranks of fundamentalist tendencies (Salafism, Tablighi) and Sufi movements. But it is not so well known that Al Qaida is the "Islamic" organization that counts the highest number of converts (10 to 20 per cent among its internationalist wing) and is the only one which gives them responsibilities (so converts are far from being merely a backup force to dupe security checks and stymie "profiling"). Both Islam and Protestantism are making inroads among North America's Latino immigrants.[20] Islam is gaining a strong foothold among African-Americans, illustrated in 2006 by the election of Keith Ellison, a convert, as the first Muslim American to Congress. As a matter of fact, it has been observed that conversions in all directions affect the same social milieus: second-generation immigrants, the destabilized working classes, "visible minorities", rebellious youths in search of a cause. In France, there is an 80 per cent overlap between the map of mosques and the map of new evangelical churches (Northern France, the Paris region, Alsace, the Rhône corridor and the Mediterranean rim). Attending an evangelical or a Jehovah's Witness' service affords a glimpse of the vast range of ethnic groups involved.

Less trumpeted is the conversion of Muslims to Christianity, namely Protestantism, of course, even if the statistics of the Catholic Church in France show that in these early years of the twenty-first century, around 400 Muslims seek baptism each year, compared with 200 in the 1990s. But, whereas the Catholic Church tends not to proselytize much, the evangelicals have adopted a very aggressive conversion policy.[21]

The most famous case in France is that of the minister Said Oujibou, born in Morocco and President of the Fédération des Nord-Africains Chrétiens de France (FNACF)—the Federation of Christian North Africans in France—which claims to have 10,000 members. Mention should also be made of Azedine Bentaiba, the head of Oasis Toulouse (a local Christian converts' association) as well as the minister of Saint-

Ouen, Amor Bouaziz (of Algerian origin). They are all evangelicals, but a glance at the directory of the French Reform Church also shows a number of names of Muslim origin (Rachid Boubégra, minister in Lunéville in 2005).

I encountered the phenomenon of Muslims converting to Christianity in Central Asia during the 1990s. It is difficult to obtain an exact figure,[22] but it is in the region of tens of thousands. When I was on a mission for the Organization for Cooperation and Security in Europe (OCSE) in Tajikistan (1993–1994) "monitoring" human rights abuses, religions were clearly ethnic: the Muslims were Tajiks, Uzbeks or Kirghiz, the Jews were from Bukhara and the Protestants bore Slav, Armenian, German or Korean names ("indigenous" Koreans deported by Stalin to Central Asia 1940s). Generally they were Baptists, whose communities were long established. But at the end of the 1990s, there was a noticeable change: the majority of the names of the ministers or followers arrested were Muslim, and the Churches tended to be Pentecostalist, of Korean *obedience* (now South Korea); at the same time, Jehovah's Witnesses had a more dominant presence.[23] The Churches mentioned most frequently, as well as the Baptists, were: Grace of Christ Pentecostal Church (minister Felix Li in Tashkent), Good News (ex-Sun Bok Ym), Love Presbyterian Church, Full Gospel, Church of Jesus-Christ, Sonmin Grace Church in Khojent (where the minister was named Alisher Haydarov: an example of a Korean Church with an ex-Muslim minister). Most often they belong to major international Pentecostalist movements which sprang up in California at the beginning of the twentieth century or in the Sixties.

And so we are witnessing a mass movement of conversions to Protestantism among those born Muslim, a phenomenon that is affecting traditionally Muslim countries. In Turkey, where Christianity is historically associated with minority ethnic and linguistic groups (Armenians, Greeks, Syriacs), the first ethnically Turkish Protestant Church was recognized in 2005: the temple of Altintepe, a district of Istanbul, was accepted as a *vaqf*, the legal structure for religious associations. During the same period, after a lengthy application process, several converts succeeded in formally changing their "religion" on their identity papers from Muslim to Protestant. In 2007, in Adiyaman, the first bishopric since the fall of Constantinople in 1453 was established on present-day Turkish soil. The New Syriac Orthodox bishop, Malke Ürek Gregorios, does not practise conversions, but receives requests from dozens of Turks speaking only Turkish but claiming they had a Syriac or Armenian grandmother. This causes some tension: Christian converts were murdered in Malatya in 2007 by people affiliated to the nationalist rather than Islamist movement (the AK [Justice and Development] party is much more open on the issue of Christian religious practice in Turkey than the nationalists of the left and the right, for whom Christianity is the religion of the enemy). In 2008, in Malaysia, the Federal Court refused to recognize the conversion of Lina Joy, née Azlina Jailani. On the other hand, in Egypt, the courts were prepared to recognize the return to Christianity of a Coptic woman who had converted to Islam.[24]

In Morocco, as in Algeria, but also in most Arab countries, clandestine Christian Churches are springing up. The Algerian authorities have reacted strongly: converts are put on trial, priests arrested and missionaries expelled.

Over and above the demographic issue (the number of conversions), the very fact that there are conversions from Islam to Christianity breaks a taboo. Until now, the prevailing wisdom was that of a conquering Islam which is supplanting Christianity in sub-Saharan Africa and gradually expelling the traditional Christian Arabs. But things are more complex than that: although the traditional Christian Churches are suffering a crisis, both demographic and spiritual (the withdrawal of the Christian community from the Middle East excluding the Maghreb), Christianity on the other hand is expanding, but under new Protestant and fundamentalist forms.

Of particular note are the breakthrough of Buddhism (Zen, Soka Gakkai) and forms of neo-Hinduism (the Sri Aurobindo and Hare Krishna movements) in the West as these movements have tended to affect the middle and upper classes. But the spread of a "globalized Buddhism" is interesting as nowadays it is happening in very varied milieus, from among the Indian lower castes to African-Americans. The first American congressman who converted to Buddhism, (not counting the representatives from Hawaii of Japanese origin, for whom Buddhism is a "cultural religion"), Hank Johnson, from Georgia, is an African-American, a member of the Soka Gakkai; incidentally, the first Muslim elected in the same year, Keith Ellison, is also African-American. But on the other hand Buddhists are converting to Protestantism: in the Russian republic of Tuva, where Buddhism is the official religion, the ministers Bair Kara-Sal and Buyan Khomushku of the Sun

Bok Ym Church, founded by South Korean missionaries belonging to the Full Gospel Pentecostalist movement, are stepping up their activities in the Tuva language. And lastly, conversions of figures in the public eye are making newspaper headlines (after leaving office, former British prime minister Tony Blair converted from Protestantism to Catholicism).

In the current climate, it is the question of apostasy in Islam which appears to be the issue most likely to lead to crises and tensions. Many militant secularists, who are outraged at the fate of "apostates" in Islam, are the first to be suspicious of all converts in the other direction, whether their conversion is genuine or assumed. But the question of apostasy is only one aspect of this general transformation of religion in modern times. It is not just a human rights issue; conversion is central to the disconnect between religion and culture. There is no longer an automatic link between culture and religion. The religious marker is free and floating. Tensions will be aggravated by the growing number of conversions and switches between religions in today's world, until people have come to terms with the divorce between religions and cultures. Conversions are a key to understanding what is happening, but their inevitable increase will also be a sign that religions now operate outside cultures, and that the famous clash/dialogue of civilizations, which implies a permanent and reciprocal link between culture and religion, is a futile illusion.

PART 1

THE INCULTURATION OF RELIGION

1

WHEN RELIGION MEETS CULTURE

Is Religion Part of Culture?

The question of the relationship between religion and culture is not new, nor is the phenomenon of globalization. History has already witnessed periods when particular cultures and societies have found themselves suddenly overtaken by communication systems, markets and/or political forces that have led to a deculturation process which has gone way beyond absorption into the mainstream culture, itself re-shaped as a result of its own universalization. Former examples of globalization include the Roman Empire and the various colonial periods, from the Age of Discovery to the triumphant imperialism of the nineteenth century. Universalist religions like Christianity and Islam spread thanks to these upheavals, which they helped to provoke.

Modern-day globalization, however, goes further: it systematizes all the elements of the process and pushes them to extremes, particularly deterritorialization. And there is a new dimension: that of a permanent separation between religions, territories, societies and states, with the outcome that religions enjoy greater autonomy. But in this new configuration not all religions are equal. Protestant evangelicalism, for example, is spreading worldwide. There are two conflicting interpretations. The first makes a connection between a religion's influence and its relationship to the dominant or dominated culture: the growth of Protestantism is thus associated with American supremacy while the radicalization of Islam is seen as the protest of a subjugated culture, that of the Global South.[1] The second interpretation contends on the other hand that a religion is able to appear universal if it is "culturally neutral" (emancipated from cultural elements or compatible with any culture). And so this leads to the key question: does the expansion of a religion go along with the spreading of a new culture (evangelicalism with the American culture, for instance) or does it expand, on the contrary, precisely because this religion has nothing to do with any specific culture? While the success of American Protestantism lends credence to the first argument, the spread of Islam and the new religious movements reinforces the second.

This inequality between religions with regard to globalization largely explains the focus of this book. It is not a general treatise on the relations between religion and culture—to achieve such an exhaustive ambition would require an erudition beyond my own—but is rather an attempt to examine how the relations between religion and culture are being re-forged today, based on a number of case studies, and what this can add to our understanding of the religion phenomenon. We refer primarily of course to the "major religions", the ones which historically have expanded through conquests or conversions, have been grafted into different cultures and experienced territorialization and deflection into secular culture (Christianity, Islam, Buddhism, Hinduism and Judaism); this could also apply to historic cases such as Manichaeism and Mithraism, which we will not be addressing here. But it also concerns today's new religious movements. I am particularly interested in the phenomenon of conversions, not because they are more widespread than in the past (there have been phases of mass conversions in Christianity, Islam and Buddhism, and even in Judaism, on a far higher scale than today for the latter), but because today's conversions are a direct result of individual choices and are therefore good indicators that there is a "religion market" which is, in the main, removed from political constraints.

On the other hand, civil religions (as the Roman and Greek religions were), the cosmologies, the so-called "primitive" religions (systems of myths and rites that are inextricably bound up with the group's culture), and lastly ethnic religions (explicitly associated with a single ethnic group), do not reformulate themselves of their own accord outside the culture to which they belong. They can of course be borrowed from the outside as pure religious markers, but the relationship with the original cultures is then purely nominal, as evidenced by the modern-day development of Celtic, Germanic or Indian neo-paganisms, astrology, Madonna's Kabbala divorced from Judaism, *feng shui*, alchemy, etc. Judaism is a special case: it is a religion which was originally ethnic, since it is identified with a people, but a people that has become diasporic and therefore subject to cultural variation. Judaism therefore encounters the problem of regular disconnections between religious and cultural markers (for example, in the secular Yiddish culture of Central Europe or Americanized Reform Judaism). Ethical or philosophical systems (Confucianism) are another example: they only claim to be "religions" by mirroring the explicitly religious systems with which they compete.

We could be accused of going round in circles: only the religions recognized by today's mainstream culture are defined as religions. That would destroy the argument that religion has become divorced from culture, since, in fact, cultural determination would sneak back in (the concept of "religion" then being a product of Western culture, not in its content, which is variable, but in its form: transcendence, revelation and faith). It is undeniable that the effect of the growth of a "religion market" is standardization, paradoxically reinforced by all the legislation designed either to consolidate a religious monopoly or to guarantee religious freedom; the law ends up creating a "legal status" for a religion, defining it not by its content (for example, it is very often through its fiscal status that a community is recognized as religious, whether this status is negative—in the case of the *dhimmis* (Christians according to traditional Muslim law)—or positive—with tax exemptions, as obtained by the Jehovah's Witnesses in France in 2004. This is what we called the "formatting" of religion by the market. And so there is no doubt that this paradigm owes a great deal to mainstream culture, in other words Christianity, or rather, nowadays, Protestantism.

This standardization of religion is a consequence of globalization: it also transforms Christianity, which is prevalent in form but its traditions and content are being challenged, since globalization allows other religions to enter this new configuration. The debate on the ethnocentrism of the religious sciences was raised by Talal Asad in his critique of Clifford Geertz.[2] He accuses Geertz of using a Christian definition of religion to analyse "religions" with a different relationship to the sacred, the community and mediation. While extremely pertinent in the fields of anthropology and history, this critique has been superseded: globalization standardizes and formats religion, it results in religions being pigeonholed according to common categories which are imposed on their followers.

This is the nagging question: is this formatting not simply the result of the cultural predominance of the North-American model? In short, when we see a "Halal McDonald's" or a "Mecca Cola", which is the winner, *sharia* or fast food, Mecca or Atlanta? This standardization also imposes itself on mainstream culture and creates an autonomous product: evangelicalism in Africa is not merely the exportation of American imperialism. A political vision of supremacy, even hegemony, does not account for the phenomena of re-appropriation and reversal (it is odd that today's progressive thinking, defined by anti-imperialism, has become essentialist).

One of the things we intend to explore in this book is the way legislation creates religions (both in the United States and in purportedly secular France), as well as the normative practices which force diasporic religions to submit to the prevailing religious model of the West. We could, however, also turn the question on its head and demonstrate that the contemporary religious paradigm is not the product of a Protestant Anglo-Saxon culture, any more than globalization in itself is the product of a specific culture, but that on the contrary, this paradigm illustrates how religion has adapted itself completely to deculturation and deterritorialization (a corollary then would be to see American culture as the end of culture, a view that chimes with certain French anti-American thinking);[3] less controversial would be to demonstrate how globalization is most successful when the protagonists assume the separation between cultural, economic and religious markers. American culture then becomes the culture of departure from culture.

But let us begin by first defining the framework of the discussion. I am using the word "culture" in two senses:

1) the productions of symbolic systems, imaginative representations and institutions specific to a society;
2) the symbolic productions valued socially as an independent aesthetic category (art).

Taking the first sense, which is the subject of this book, religion is treated by anthropologists and sociologists as one of several symbolic systems; it is therefore seen as an integral part of a given culture; it is of the culture. And many "religions" do not claim to be anything else, or, to be more precise they are constructed as a "religion" only from the outside, with the associated anachronism and ethnocentrism. For example the great French sinologist Marcel Granet, in the time of Jesuit missionaries, wrote a book entitled *The Religion of the Chinese People*,[4] whereas the word "religion" has no exact equivalent in Chinese and the phrase "school of thought" (*jiao*) is more appropriate.

But this definition comes up against the religious exception: that of the religion that refuses to be a mere system of beliefs among others, because it claims to be, or to state, the truth. These religions consider themselves to be the bearers of a universal message, transcending cultures: for them, faith is not a simple belief or social conformism. They lay claim to a relationship with the truth that does not come under the heading of "culture", since faith sets down a truth beyond the cultural relationship. Even when they preach loyalty, these religions reject the notion of the state or the nation as the inevitable main determinant of the social order. Here we move to religion based on the believer, rather than the imaginative universe or the institutions specific to a society. The social sciences tend deliberately to ignore the position of the believer, attempting to reduce it to a statistic, to group behaviour, even to alienation (the believer is saying something different from what he claims to be saying). The alienation theory is central to the delegitimization of what religion says about itself (Feuerbach, Marx, also Voltaire and even Maurras: it is the social function of religion that matters); French-style secularism ("laïcité") is only the political form of this suppression (not necessarily repression) of what the believer says (by confining it to the private sphere). The issue is precisely that the "religious revival" is primarily about the believer's refusal to see his word reduced to the private sphere. Regrettable as this may be, it is a fact.

If we concentrate on the religions which refer to a transcendent order, that of the truth and the absolute, the relationship between religion and culture is fortuitous and coincidental. A religion thus conceived aims to be above any culture, even if it considers that it is always embodied in a given culture at a given time (Catholic inculturation, the application of the concept of Christ's incarnation to culture), or that it creates a culture, which is the transformation of religious norms into *habitus*, i.e. internalized, stable behaviours which are nothing to do with either faith or even belief. This second conception appears in Muslims' frequent use of the concept of "Muslim culture", where it is a question of cultural norms relating to the family, segregation of the sexes, modesty, food, etc.; it is not what Western Orientalists mean by "Islamic culture", which includes art, architecture, urban life, etc. We also speak of "Protestant culture" in differing contexts (from American Puritanism, which supposedly explains everything, to French high Protestant society, typified by restraint, discretion and successful business dealings). In both cases, what is termed culture does not have the distinction of being a religion.

Fundamentally, religion only asserts itself as a religion when it explicitly dissociates itself from culture, even if it is in a fragile, momentary and, ultimately, abstract effort. The concept of religion suddenly no longer works in systems where what is otherwise associated with religion (devotion, the sacred) is perceived as totally cultural (civil religion); the problem of irreligiousness is a modern issue, since it assumes this separation (hence a recurrent theme among historians: "did the Greeks believe their myths", "Rabelais' religion").[5] Socrates' irreligiousness was not his lack of "faith" (it is an anachronism to describe it thus), but what was perceived as a lack of public spirit, subversiveness, contempt for the city's religion; the real accusation against him is the second one: Socrates "corrupted the youth". Worshipping the gods was a question of practice, not of faith.[6]

A religion that claims to be the "true" religion is one which at a given moment explicitly posits culture as otherness, even though it may attempt to appropriate this culture or to create one. The Protestant theologian Richard Niebuhr vehemently argues that there is an inherent tension between Christianity and any culture, including Western culture; furthermore he is suspicious of any cultural spin-off from Christianity, since it betrays the initial religious impulse.[7] In Niebuhr's view, culture cannot be avoided, it is a human production and also the condition itself of human life on earth, except that the relationship between Christianity and culture is inevitably fraught.

But it is only when religion claims, even abstractly, to be acultural that it can fulfil the conditions of globalization and become universal. There is no theological determinism governing why one religion or another should miss the globalization boat; the reasons why some miss out are much more complex and linked to other factors. The oscillation between deculturation and inculturation is part of the expansion process of any religion that finds itself regularly confronted with culture as otherness, be it the culture of others or the culture it has produced but which is becoming secularized and independent.

So there are three possible positions for religion, and these are to consider culture as profane, secular or pagan. Profane means culture that is indifferent to religion: it is trivial, insubstantial and inferior, because, if it is not inspired by the spirit or faith, its independence is an illusion. Secular is non-religious but legitimate culture: it achieves dignity and acquires a legitimacy and an autonomy, but one which is determined by religion, since it concerns the good governance of society, not ultimate ends; religion delegates a sector to an independent authority, the "secular arm" (the expression is of legal origin); then there are two orders of time and space, there are two orders of the norm: the theological and the legal. Conversely, pagan culture can claim the label of religion, but in opposition to the mainstream religion: the culture is consistent and coherent, it enshrines values (for example, absolute human freedom, the sanctification of nature or of a social group) which not only conflict with religious values but take their place. It is the time of false gods (man, revolution, race, the state).

This configuration has little to do with the theology specific to any particular religion. It is strongly expressed in Christianity, albeit with different values and in different proportions depending on different thinkers (the controversy over the degree of autonomy of the secular in the medieval Church was violent and ultimately provided the intellectual and legal instruments to define secularization). But, contrary to popular belief, the same configuration is also found in Islam. The profane occurs in the grey area between *halal* and *haram*: *mandub* (recommended), *makruh* (advised against) and especially *mubah* (neutral), three categories which escape the religious norm, without having a real positivity. In Islam, the existence of the secular is illustrated by the autonomy of politics and of customary law, even if legal scholars tend to deny or restrict this autonomy which they are forced nevertheless to accept; the secular also applies to the *ta'zir*, i.e. sanctions that the prince can impose, on his own initiative, for the common good. In all religions the discussion focuses not so much on the categories as on managing and extending them. Fundamentalist and integrist movements tend to reduce the space allocated to the three areas, and, conversely, secularized or mystic religions will tend to see the divine everywhere in the cultural sphere. Some Christian theologians (Teilhard de Chardin, Tillich, Bonhoeffer, Cox) were critical of this devaluation of the profane and attracted the opprobrium of conservative circles for dissolving religion within culture in their own way.

In the articulation between culture and religion, four elements are in play: the relationship between religious markers and culture, the norm, religiosity and theology:

- *The religious marker*: this is the sign, the action, the name, the heading that endorses the *sacredness* of an object, area or person: *halal*, *kosher*, blessings, rites, unction. This marker is moveable: a sacred song can be consumed in a profane manner, an ordinary dish can be blessed, a McDonald's can be *halal*, a headscarf can either be religious or a fashion statement.

- *The norm*: first of all this means norms that are explicitly specific to a religion, which come within the province of law or ethics. But, a religion's normativeness is always subject to revision, depending too on the social and cultural understanding of these norms. A norm can be central at one point and marginal at another (the segregation of the sexes or abstinence, for example). Here there is interaction between religious norms and social norms: they can converge (Jules Ferry's secular morality, defining the content of "morality" lessons in French secular schools after 1881, was not fundamentally different from that of Christianity, but the sexual liberation of the 1960s—sex outside marriage, women's sexual liberation, homosexuality etc.—led to a growing gulf between secularism and Christianity). However, certain social practices are considered anathema by the faithful. But the definition of what is anathema is fluid. After a period of censure mixed with relative indulgence, from the mid-nineteenth century the Catholic Church condemned birth control practices with increasing inflexibility, leading to very rigid opposition by the end of the twentieth century, when combating abortion became the focus of the Church's battle against modern culture. Social and religious patterns both influence and oppose each other. Acceptability is the criterion in the relationship between norms and culture. But this relationship is complex: in Egypt, homosexuality became a subject of public scandal in the 1990s, without the explicit religious norm changing, as did paedophilia in the Catholic Church: it has always been condemned by Church leaders, who used to treat it as a minor issue, but within the space of a few years, it became unacceptable in public opinion. The question of "scandal" is also eminently social and cultural.[8]

- *Religiosity*: in other words, the faith as it is lived: the manner in which believers experience their relationship with religion, it is the lived, inner experience, religious feeling, but also the way believers define themselves in the outside world. What is at stake? The "threat", salvation in the next world, salvation on earth, one's neighbour, self-fulfilment, the honest man, mortification, religious humanism? What does it mean to be oneself? Religiosity has many and varied forms and can be accompanied either by tremendous theological conformity or by variations.[9] Once again, religiosity is not theology, but it can be identified with what Niebuhr calls a "religious culture".

- *Theology*: a discursive corpus of beliefs rationalized and methodically exposed, the subject of debate and reinterpretations. The theological corpus is built up and discussed: it is sufficient to look at the debates among the early Christians who had difficulty redefining faith within the categories of Greek philosophy, which could not embrace the concept of the Incarnation of Christ, for example. The same question arose for Islam and Judaism, with Spinoza's radical critique of religion: the theological can in turn transform itself into a philosophical system which excludes the "living God".[10] Conversely, for religions which do not claim to be theological, in other words which refer rather to myths than to a dogmatic exposition of beliefs, it is possible to witness the *post hoc* construction of the theological event, following the example of the religious paradigm set up by the major monotheistic religions, which demands that each religion be associated with a theology (as we shall see with Hinduism).

Converts and Missionaries: the Clash Between Culture and Religion

a) The Term "Culture" and its Prefixes

Before tackling the question of globalization, we must take a step back for a moment and examine how universalist religions, i.e. those which by definition claim to supersede human cultures, have concretely managed their relationship to culture.

Once again, our aim is not to offer a treatise on the history of religions, but to discuss the theoretical and often practical management of the cultural question by some of the major religions in order to help us decipher and understand current developments in world religions. First of all, we note that there is no permanent configuration specific to each religion. Christianity related to culture in different ways, depending on whether it was a "sect" of the Roman Empire or the official religion of that same empire. The relationship changed again when Christianity was adopted by the "Barbarians", or when it embarked on the Crusades, accompanied the Conquistadors or, much later, became established in Europe's colonial empires. The same applies to Buddhism, depending on whether it was supplanting Hinduism, being imported into China and Japan or exported to the Western middle classes. Islam became the very expression of Arabness when from the outset it dismissed all profane forms of this Arabness as "ignorance"; however, it became both secularized in the Arab culture of the classical age—the mid-eighth to the mid-thirteenth centuries—and "inculturated" in Persian and Indian culture.

The question of the other's culture took a long time to emerge in the Christian world. Admittedly, the concept of culture in the anthropological sense is modern (dating from the nineteenth century), but the lack of a name for it does not mean that the missionaries and preachers were unaware of the problem; they generally pigeonholed culture under "beliefs, superstitions and rites". It was a matter of determining *what religious register* cultural markers encountered in other societies belonged to: profane, secular or pagan? The central issue in the dispute over rites in China was to establish whether worshipping the emperor was unacceptable paganism or whether it was simply the expression of political loyalty to the secular order of the day? The Catholic Church never questioned the legitimacy of the Chinese emperors, and Rome never criticized the Jesuit priests for being their loyal servants: the secular legitimacy of the ruling power was recognized, but the issue was that of the priests' loyalty being expressed in an official ritual. The issue was whether there was something religious in this ritual, in which case it would amount to the practice of paganism. The quarrel was interesting because it crystallized the question of the normativeness of the concept of religion: is Confucianism a religious system or simply the ideological expression of a conception of power?[11] As soon as Confucianism was construed as a religion by the Vatican, it was seen as paganism. But it was from the outside that it was defined as a religion.

For a long time, the missionaries saw pagan culture as an obstacle to the propagation of faith; it could not survive as pagan, it could only become profane, but always with the suspicion that, behind its mask of religious neutrality, it could convey pagan values (indecent dress, music etc.). It did not come to be seen as something positive until much later. It was the definition and popularization of the concept of "anthropological culture" (which became widespread after 1945) that led some religions to take up the term for their own ends: recent examples include the Vatican Council II and the dialogue of cultures advocated by the Muslim authorities after 11 September 2001. Moreover, today's Islamists widely use the term culture. But even at other times, when the missionaries had no operational concept of what a culture is, their practices implicitly adapted themselves to the cultural question.

Each time there has been a questioning of the relations between religion and culture, prefixes have been added to the word "culture": to *de*culturate, *ac*culturate, *in*culturate, *ex*culturate.[12] Religion deculturates when it attempts to eradicate paganism (conquering Christianity in America, orthodox Islam on the Indian subcontinent); it acculturates when it adapts to the mainstream culture (the Jews of the *Haskala* (Enlightenment),[13] Christianity and Islam in India); it inculturates when it tries to establish itself at the centre of a given culture (the theologians of Latin America's "indigenous" Christianity), and it exculturates when it thinks of itself as standing back from a mainstream culture of which it was part, but which suddenly or gradually took on a negative, "pagan" or irreligious—and therefore destructive—aspect (Catholic and evangelical reaction at the close of the twentieth century, the Tablighi Jamaat movement within Islam). But religion also manufactures culture: it enshrines languages, develops scriptures and inspires religious art which may become secularized. It can be identified with a people and thus becomes a quasi-ethnic religion, as is the case with some orthodox Churches in Eastern Europe. Religion can identify itself with a particular culture or even operate solely as a culture (this was the case, for example, with Catholicism according to Charles Maurras: for him, faith was no longer of any importance).[14] Religion can go so far as to lose any religious dimension and be reduced solely to an identity-marker (a key example is the Muslim Communist Party, briefly set up by Sultan Galiev in Bolshevik Russia in 1918, but it also applies to the Protestants and Catholics of Northern Ireland, since there it is possible to be an atheist Protestant or a Communist Catholic).

The relationship between a religion and culture is expressed in transfers and transitions, whereas conversely, when there is a long history of permeation between a religion and a culture, the differences in aspirations of the two are eroded, both for adherents and observers. The first transition is, of course, conversion, which marks the separation between culture and religion, since the convert is seeking a religion, not a culture. Admittedly here we are excluding conversions through

33

conformism, which are linked to upward social mobility and to the wish to leave a religion associated with a minority culture so as to become part of mainstream society, as was the case for Christian Ottoman officials who converted to Islam, or the Jews of the *Haskala* between the end of the eighteenth and the beginning of the nineteenth century, who became Protestant in the Northern European countries (like the Mendelssohn family in Germany) and Catholics in the South. Likewise, forced converts (Jewish and Muslim *conversos* in Spain after the *Reconquista*) had no interest in mainstream culture, seeking rather to maintain their tradition (*Marranos* and "cryptos" of all sorts). In this book, we are essentially interested in conversions through conviction.

The word "conversion" is reserved for changing religion. People do not convert to a culture: they may adopt it or learn it. The suddenness of conversion marks a clear distinction between culture and religion. That is why conversion is often viewed with suspicion: for his former coreligionists, the convert is a "traitor" (heretic, renegade, *murtad*, apostate), and a neophyte's zeal sometimes arouses suspicion among his new brothers. This guardedness is based on two contradictory perceptions. On the one hand, religion is always associated with culture, and so the converts are often suspected of still belonging to their former religion because they are thought to have held on to its culture: for example, detractors of Jean-Marie Lustiger, Archbishop of Paris (1979–2005), routinely alluded to his Jewishness, while in Spain during the *Reconquista* attempts were made to root out any vestiges of "Arab" (and not just Muslim) culture among the *Moriscos* (converts were banned from using bath houses, since it was an "Arab" custom). A remarkable Islamic author, Mohammed Asad, who was appointed ambassador to the United States from the newborn state of Pakistan, before falling from grace, is hardly mentioned these days: he was born Leopold Weiss. Meanwhile, secular militants are often wary of converts: in debates on Islam in France, it is not uncommon for experts to be under suspicion of having secretly converted.[15] Furthermore, if the convert is evidence of the universality of religion, he is also the proof of its separateness from culture and is therefore always suspected of fanaticism, in other words of being the expression of a religion that is unpoliced, untempered and unhoned as it is not rooted in culture. His faith is not disciplined by culture. The convert is not acquainted with the "unsaid" and is always surprised at what appears to be a lukewarm welcome from his new friends. In 2008, Mansur Escudero, a

Spanish convert, chained himself to a pillar of Cordoba's Great Mosque, now a cathedral, as part of his campaign for Muslims to be allowed to pray there: he did not receive the support of Spain's Union of Islamic communities, which recruits among Muslim immigrants. Faith without culture is an expression of fanaticism.

Admittedly, there is a considerable difference between the mass conversions carried out as part of a campaign for political supremacy (conquests, colonialism, empire), and the voluntary individual signing up to a religion that is not necessarily dominant in the "religion market" of the day. The question of primacy is therefore central, and we shall address it later. But between these two extremes, there is a whole range of attitudes. The success of conversions is not necessarily due to pressure. Islam has rarely forced people to convert, as is evidenced by the large numbers of Christians who have remained in Arab or Ottoman lands; even though one of the reasons could be fiscal—Christians pay higher taxes—compared with the Spanish *Reconquista*, which converted by force then expelled numerous *Moriscos*, is illuminating. Does a Muslim Algerian who converts to Christianity in the twenty-first century do so in order to break away from the mainstream national culture (Islam) or out of fascination with the prevailing global culture (American Protestantism)? Nor is sincerity incompatible with the fact that a convert is following the trend of the day: for instance, the conversion of Aaron Lustiger to Christianity at a time (1940–45) when there was a strong incentive to convert Jewish children (Jewish parents trying to avoid persecution for their children and families, and institutions which hid Jewish children during the German Occupation, refusing to hand baptized Jewish children back to their families),[16] casts no doubt on the future prelate's sincerity. Domination does not reduce conviction to a mere form of submission.

However, here we are examining not the point of view of the convert, but that of the missionary: how do you approach the other's culture, be it the pagan in your own society, or the stranger who speaks a foreign language? The disjunction/conjunction between culture and religion is our core concern.

Within Christianity and Islam there are theological reasons for converting others. To convert is to help hasten salvation, either individual (it is a pious act which will be rewarded in heaven), or from a millenarist point of view (to hasten the second coming of Christ, which will only come to pass when the entire world has been transformed by preaching). The drive to establish "missions", which is self-evident for Christianity, Islam and, to a lesser extent, Buddhism, appears to be non-existent in Judaism and Hinduism, since both seem to be linked to a specific people and society, and consequently have little interest in spreading the Word to the world beyond. But, once again, things are more complicated: Judaism has carried out mass conversions (among the Berbers, Khazars and Karaites) and, still today, while proselytism is no longer fashionable, the myth of the lost tribes of Israel "rediscovered" in various corners of the world makes it possible to smuggle fresh converts into Israel, thanks to the efforts of forgotten missionaries or the desire of a group to recreate an identity for itself.[17] And lastly, various forms of Hinduism have been exporting themselves to the West since the end of the nineteenth century.

A religion can appear in the midst of a culture in two ways: from within, as the result of a revelation (Jesus, Muhammad), or from the outside through proselytizing in all its forms (conquests, missions). The relationship with culture is not the same: in the first instance, religion is closely bound up with the culture (through the use of a shared language, among other factors), whereas in the second, it is an external relationship. But the problems posed are perhaps not so different.

b) Converting Within a Culture

For many of the early Christians, Christianity, which was not yet called by that name, remained within the framework of Judaism: they were not aware of moving out of a cultural universe, but knew that they were introducing a new religious message, the "good tidings", without being aware that this message was also challenging cultural Judaism (which explains why the Jewish communities of the diaspora were fertile ground for conversion, as the new religion presented itself as the realization of the Jewish religion and not its negation).[18] It was Paul the Apostle who clearly signified the breakaway and the continuity: God's word was addressed to Jews and gentiles alike, it had to be extracted from the formalism of the law. The religious marker was no longer the prerogative of a given people. Universalization requires a severance from culture, but not from religion. This was to be the foundation of Christianity's ambivalence towards the Jews: the religious continuity could not be denied, therefore the emphasis was placed on the Jews' "obscurantism", in other words the religion's eclipse by a sense of identity increasingly perceived as ethnic (which creates a connection between religious anti-Judaism and racialist anti-Semitism).

This declaration of absolute autonomy from culture is a fundamental claim of the major revealed religions, but it proves untenable—unless all the followers withdraw from the world and from quotidian concerns (which would be yet another way of "creating a culture" as well as a society). While first-generation converts (and later born-again devotees) have the sense of breaking away from mainstream culture, subsequent generations belong more to a new culture; they have internalized the newness and experience it as a new tradition: the "cooled down" and acculturated religion, now part of history and taken on by new generations of non-converts or socialized within already converted families, no longer remains outside mainstream culture (unless the group has a radical wish to perpetuate its difference as a community: for example, the Amish in the United States). The new converts could be described as taking up a stance of rejecting the culture rather than actually rejecting it: early Christian converts did not stop speaking Greek or Latin or studying the classics. In the Roman Empire, Christianity did not introduce a new culture of foreign origin (neo-Hebraic, for example). It attempted to convey a message that was explicitly non-cultural within a very strongly marked culture: Christianity could not present itself as superior to or as a competitor with Hellenism from the cultural point of view. Its purported pre-eminence was the religious message, not the cultural challenge. In Corinthians I: 22, 23, Paul even defies the Greeks, claiming Christianity was superior to the wisdom of the philosophers: "we preach Christ crucified, unto the Jews a stumbling block, and unto the Greeks foolishness".

Christianity thus became "inculturated" within the Greco-Roman civilization, operating a "cultural translation", according to the expression coined by V. Limberis.[19] This is an example of what I call "formatting". The position of "pure religion" adopted by a closed community waiting for the return of Christ could not be maintained among the new generations or with Christianity's spread into diverse social categories which had little desire to withdraw from the world.[20] The Emperor Constantine initially proposed a compromise, a cohabitation between Christians and pagans.

The intensity of the Christological quarrels of the first centuries of Christianity (how does one conceive of the dual nature of Christ, both God and man?) can only be understood if they are seen as part of a painful process of formatting the Christian faith within the intellectual categories of Hellenism. The purely theological issues are barely apparent today, other than the intrinsic difficulty in understanding the nature of incarnation. But this recurrent difficultly should not prevent the definition of an orthodoxy, necessary both from the internal point of view (the cohesion of the community) and the external (the cohesion of the empire). Only that orthodoxy presupposes that the principle dogma of Christianity, incarnation, is expressed in the formal language of the mainstream culture. The quarrel over monophysitism, i.e. of Christ having only one (divine) nature, which divided the Church at the Council of Chalcedon in 451 has been generally declared outmoded by the successors of both camps: contemporary religious leaders speak of misunderstandings, of translation problems, of translation from the field of Semitic languages (Hebrew and Aramaic) to Greek and Latin (nature, person, hypostasis). But that is precisely what it was about: a translation means a reformulation. The Christian authors took their inspiration from the heirs of Aristotle and Plato, adopting Greek and Latin philosophy (in particular the Western stoic tradition, through Cicero) and trying to show how it was an instrument for enabling the faith to establish itself. Today, former Jacobites, followers of the Orthodox Church and Catholics find it hard to explain their differences; admittedly the theological arguments masked political and strategic agendas (supremacy of the emperor of Constantinople, hierarchy of patriarchates, the Persian Sassanids' support for the "heresy"), but that does not in any way diminish the magnitude of the quarrel, for it is no coincidence if these political issues found their outlet in a theological argument: there was indeed a difficulty in formatting religious categories within culturally acceptable concepts.

In early Christianity, conversions were carried out on a person-to-person basis, within the framework of a society and a shared culture, using shared vernacular languages (Greek rather than Latin). The first apostles converted people whose (often dual) culture they shared. The pagan was the unbeliever, and not someone from another culture; but this shared culture was both the bond and the main obstacle, since Christianity was not only a newcomer, it also challenged religious pluralism—or rather it imposed a new concept of religion: absolute, revealed, universal, hegemonic and monotheistic. It was not combating a specific religion, but was against even the idea of the religious relativism of the mainstream culture. Christian thinkers had to pit their minds against Greek philosophy rather than against the Greek "religion" (Acts of the Apostles 17 and 18). Culture was not foreign, it was what everyone was steeped in, believers and unbelievers alike. So it was a question then of subjugating it by Christianizing it and demonstrating its incompleteness; and to achieve this, people had no hesitation in using its own language, in taking it as witness, as did Paul in Athens (Acts of the Apostles 17).

This was also the problem of the first Protestants: they shared the culture of those whom they accused of neo-paganism. That is why they were so adamant about the boundaries between culture and religion. It is also a hallmark of the modernity of today's Protestant evangelicals: by interpreting the New Testament literally, they are able to manage a contemporary world that is more akin to that of the Roman Empire than that of the Crusades or of the Catholic foreign missions. It is a matter of Christianizing the world one belongs to, the only difference being that today people speak of re-Christianization, but the surrounding culture is once again perceived as pagan, much more than profane or even simply secular (this is the argument of the book *France, pays de mission*, written by a Catholic priest, André Godin, in 1943 at a time when, for the past century and a half, "mission" had meant overseas mission). The difference is, of course, that early Christianity had the future ahead of it whereas the modern-day reconquest is starting out from a position of loss. But an evangelical preacher who roams around a country with the Acts of the Apostles in hand can have the impression of being part of the here and now.

In Islam, which is more radical on this issue, everything that belongs to Arab culture from before the revelation is termed "ignorance" *(jahilliya)* and is thus in a way nullified, starting with the Arabic language: for the fundamentalists, it is not the language which produced the Qur'an, but the other way around (or, at least, the Qur'an elevated Arabic to perfection, since the Qur'an was inimitable, it even existed without having been created). Suddenly, the Arabic of the Qur'an was at the core of future Arab cultural production, and the religion thus claimed the right to veto cultural production. Pre-Islamic culture is presented by the majority of Muslim Arab commentators as an "anthropological" culture, that of the tribal Bedouin society; which was doubtless an advantage for converting to Islam, with this being presented as an emancipation and an advance, but there was an unspoken question regarding the relationship between language and culture and the autonomy of a cultural corpus. Moreover, the *jahilliya* myth is also used today by liberals and reformists arguing that the problem of Islam emanates not from the religion but from the culture, still in the anthropological sense: God's message has been confused with the way it has been received and interpreted by those it was initially destined for. The Qur'an must therefore be restored to its anthropological context to extricate its true meaning; but, in so doing, the idea of the dichotomy between Islamic culture and Arab culture is reinforced, by devaluing the latter.[21]

The refusal of most of the *ulema*— the body of Mullahs (Muslim scholars trained in Islam and Islamic law)—to place the Qur'an in its cultural environment raises the fundamental problem of how to articulate the relationship between Islam and Arab culture, in other words, how to articulate the autonomy of an Arab culture that is not merely a by-product of the Qur'anic revelation. It is the export of Islam into other cultures that highlights the autonomy of the cultural factor. In the early days of Islam's expansion, it encountered two cultures which it acknowledged: the Greek (philosophy of course, but also fields of lay knowledge, such as "Greek medicine", *tebb-i-yunani*, which is still alive within popular culture), and the Persian (*ajam* is a person who does not speak Arabic but is still a Muslim: here we see the emergence of a category which is not that of the Western Christian—*kafir*, Crusaders—nor of the Arab Christian, but that of a Muslim who is the bearer of another culture). It is no coincidence if today we are witnessing a crisis in the production (and perhaps especially in the consumption) of culture in the Arabic language, whereas the Turkish and Persian linguistic spheres are thriving.

And yet historically, an autonomous cultural sphere (philosophical, literary, artistic) developed in the Arab-Muslim world, but it was regularly the target of an iconoclastic, anti-cultural fundamentalism, from the Almohads to the Taliban, including the Wahhabis and anti-syncretist movements which, justifiably, from their point of view, are suspicious of the very notion of culture. The fear of syncretism is not new in Islam; it has less to do with the absolute demand for unity and divine transcendence than with the tenuous relationship between religion and culture. Anti-syncretist movements appeared both in periods of political hegemony (Aurangzeb's reign in the Moghul Empire) and of subjugation (the Tabligh Jamaat movement for the reawakening of faith in British India). Wahhabism is an interesting case here: to define it as the expression of a resistance movement against either the Ottomans or the British would be an anachronism. Its tendency towards deculturation is definitely inherent and not simply the consequence of foreign domination.

c) Converting to Another Culture

Although preaching and conversion are motivated by theological considerations, the practice of conversion itself is profoundly determined by the cultural and political context and always raises the question of the connection between religion and culture.

It is misguided to claim that "since time immemorial" Christians, Muslims and Buddhists have sought to convert their neighbours; likewise it is erroneous to say that Judaism has never sought to convert. Nowadays conversion is often viewed as the extension of a campaign for political hegemony (*jihad*, foreign missions in the nineteenth century, American evangelicals), whereas this is not necessarily the case: some colonial enterprises did not seek to convert, like the English settlers who went to America. Despite the fact that they were Puritans and were inspired by religion alone, they very rarely attempted to convert the Native Americans or the slaves (it was the latter who turned to Christianity). Tsarist Russia carried out an active drive to convert the Tatars and later the Kazakhs while neglecting the other Muslim peoples of Central Asia and banning missionary practice among the Muslims of Azerbaijan. The fact is that conversions take place only at certain times and among certain population categories. For example, the most active Muslim conversion movement of the twentieth century, Tablighi Jamaat, was devoted almost exclusively to the individual "reconversion" of those who were Muslim only in name, a phenomenon that did not exist in the classical era. Catholicism very rarely attempted to convert Muslims before the nineteenth century (apart from a few exceptions like Peter the Venerable and Raymond Lulle— but the case of the Spanish *conversos* of the *Reconquista* is not an appropriate counter-example since these converts were never recognized as authentic Christians). On the other hand, after a silence of 250 years, there was a mushrooming of Protestant missions at the end of the eighteenth century; in America, these targeted peoples for which America had no colonial ambitions (the first mission set sail from Salem in 1812 for Mauritius), while continuing to ignore the Native Americans and slaves.

Once Christianity had become the official religion throughout the former Roman Empire, missions (usually of monks) sought to convert entire peoples, e.g. the Barbarians, who did not share a common culture. But the question of their culture did not arise: only that of language. Here the approach was pragmatic, and the Church embarked on stabilising the languages (Gothic, Slavonic), setting them down in written form if necessary, in order to translate the Bible. In fact, most of the time, the Barbarians wanted to integrate into the West, which was identified with Roman civilization and then with Christianity. Conversions were collective and instigated by the elite, even by the King himself, as in the case of Clovis. Far from being the expression of supremacy, on the contrary this new legitimacy and access to the services of men of letters (the clerics) made it easier to wield power: the converted "nation" could then mobilize Christianity in its fight against other peoples. Language, as was the case later with the Protestants, was not perceived as the vehicle of a culture but as a simple means of communication. The only culture was that of Rome and Byzantium, and the entire cultured elite, once again, was in agreement.[22]

Once Europe was synonymous with Christianity, in the eleventh century, conversions gave way to Crusades. The problem was not the pagan, but the heretic; now Islam was seen as a heresy rather than as another religion, and it was denounced as a corrupt form of Christianity: Muhammad was a "false prophet". As it was a sort of negative Christianity, there was nothing to learn from it; nor was there any foreignness in it, but rather a monstrousness, in the sense that the monster is he who displays shared traits but out of all proportion, deformed and the wrong way round.[23] Scholars have pointed out Christian Europe's lack of interest in Muslim thought until the sixteenth century, with a few brilliant exceptions (Pope Sylvester II, the Englishman Robert of Ketton, the Archdeacon of Pamplona who translated the Qur'an, Raymond Lulle); there was an interest in the philosophers who transmitted Greek thought, but not in the Qur'an or in *sharia* law. That was because no one could see what value there might be in it (the circulation of technical knowledge, like medicine, weapons and crafts, or that of the Greek writings was something different).

The Crusades sought not to convert, but to eradicate (e.g. heretics on Christian territory, which sealed the fate of the Cathars) or to conquer (the Holy Places); in other words to expel and win, but not to convince. There are a few exceptions which only confirm the rule, for example, the Kingdom of Valencia under James I of Aragon in the thirteenth century, when priests schooled in Arabic attempted to convert the Muslims who had remained in the city after the reconquest.[24] But in general there was no connection between the missions and the Crusades: missions followed in the wake of the Crusades in the case of heretics (for example, the Cathars, with the invention of the Inquisition), they never preceded them. It was a matter of making a territory religiously uniform, not of saving the heretics' souls. During the Crusades, there was no proselytism: there were killings, expulsions and pacts, but no preaching. The Spanish *Reconquista* also had a cautious attitude towards conversions: converts remained suspect (whether they were *Marranos* or *Moriscos*). The point of the *disputatio* (polemic between a Christian scholar and a Muslim doctor of law), a very popular genre, was less to convince the other person than to convince oneself, or it was to make the other person look obstinate, oblivious to reason; the *disputatio* is an incantatory reconciliation of faith and reason through rhetoric. The other is truly other because he is "a mirror image": he is perceived by the prevailing religious order either as an "archaism" and guilty conscience (the Jew), or as the "devil", the opposite to and enemy of the good religion. Those seeking to regain a lost Christianity attempted to bypass Islam geographically (with the quest for the mythical "Prester John's kingdom" throughout the Middle Ages).

The same applies to the Reformation: for the Catholic authorities, rooting out heresy was deemed more important than preaching to Protestants; this made sense at first, insofar as the Protestant, as a former Catholic, knew the Church doctrine which he had deliberately rejected. The Protestant was the "internal" negative other, the Muslim represented the external other. Islam and Protestantism were seen as corrupt forms of Christianity and not as "cultures". Meanwhile, in Catholicism, Protestants saw what remained of customs, rites and errors when the religion was stripped away. For them, Catholicism was not a religion: it was a culture that had hijacked the true religion, it was paganism. The first Protestant operated a separation between culture and religion, and sought not so much to convert as to bear witness. It was only when Protestantism was well established and "cultured" that conversion missions led by the Catholic Church made sense, since the division between culture and religion no longer stood:

these missions, such as that in seventeenth-century Bohemia, made art, Baroque in this case, a preaching instrument.

The question of culture was gradually imposed from the outside. The Catholic Church differentiated internal reconquest missions (the Cathars, Protestants, nineteenth and twentieth-century non-believers) from "foreign" missions, which were the only ones to raise the problem of culture. It was only during the Age of Discovery that, for Catholicism, conversion became a systematic activity to which specialist institutions were devoted, particularly "congregations" or "institutes" (a new name for the traditional religious male and female "orders") destined for "foreign" missions,[25] in other words specifically targeting the other. But this other was not only the non-believer (i.e. the free thinker and the Protestant), it also included those who had never had access to the true religion and yet were steeped in a pagan universe of meaning which was not a corruption of Christianity and therefore had its autonomy: and this was culture.

It is interesting to note that Protestantism, considered today as much more proselytising than Catholicism, lagged 250 years behind Rome in setting up missionary organizations. The burst of Catholic missionary activity from the fifteenth century onwards cannot then be seen simply as a corollary to colonization, because the English and Dutch Protestants who embarked on the path of colonialism a century later carried out very few conversions but were just as "imperialist" if not more so.

Catholic Missions

The first Catholic monks to land with the Conquistadors were simply the chaplains to the troops; however, very quickly (in less than fifteen years), the Church sent missions on the heels of the colonizers to convert the new peoples (Bartolome de las Casas was in Santo Domingo in 1502, he was ordained in Cuba in 1513; by 1508, the Franciscans were in Venezuela, and by 1541 in California). Then the missions began to precede the armies and to explore countries where there was no colonial expedition planned (the Jesuit Francis Xavier arrived in India in 1542 and in Japan in 1549; from 1582 the Jesuits were in China, where Matteo Ricci arrived in 1601, after having already translated the Catechism into Chinese; they were in Ethiopia in 1557). The Jesuit order was set up as a missionary order (targeting both Protestants and pagans). In Canada, the Jesuits opened the first schools to educate and convert the local population in 1615, while 1628 saw the opening of the first school to train an indigenous clergy in Rome (the Congregation for the Evangelization of Peoples). In 1639, the first female religious missionaries, French Ursuline nuns, set sail for Canada. In 1675, Father Marquette entered Illinois to convert the Native Americans: nowhere did he meet a Protestant competitor. And in 1685, the first Chinese bishop was appointed.

At first the missions were conceived as aids to colonization, and the European states jealously kept control not only of their own missions, but also, and especially, of the right to establish Christianity in their new colonies. This was known as *padroado* (Portuguese for patronage): the local bishops were appointed with the agreement of the colonial power and non-authorized missions risked being sent home (one of the reasons for the dispute between most of the European states and the Jesuits was that the latter refused to seek their approval and would only defer to the Pope). In Canada, Colbert gave instructions to the Jesuits on mixed marriages and the baptism of Native Americans. That fitted in with the tradition of French Gallicanism, in which the King's temporal power was considered to be of divine right, but in a very broad conception of that temporal power, since it extended to everything related to public order; it included religion as practice. The colonial states ignored or circumvented the Holy See in the same way as the Christians of the Ottoman Empire were placed under the direct protection of France. The Treaty of Tordesillas (1493), in which the Pope divided the world between the Spanish and the Portuguese, was not the recognition of the Pope's superiority, but on the contrary, the affirmation of the states' primacy. The case of the Jesuit Reductions of Paraguay is interesting in this respect: the Jesuits organized autonomous Native American villages in Paraguay (and also in Quebec); Spain and Portugal obtained from Rome the right to dismantle them; such villages survived only in Canada, under the control of the French monarchy.

But, gradually, the Holy See attempted to manage the missionary movement directly and restrict state control over the Churches, both national and colonial. Rome endeavoured to make the missions independent from the colonial powers. Initially (at the close of the seventeenth century), it circumvented the *padroado*, which it had instigated, by appointing non-territorial apostolic vicars above the bishops who could only be appointed with the approval of the colonial authorities.

But in the nineteenth century, everything changed dramatically: the Holy See succeeded in building a supranational, global Catholic Church, whose foreign missions were a crucial component. This was made possible because of the ongoing conflict between the Pope and the Emperor, that is, between the Pope and the temporal state power, which gradually led to a separation, in practice if not in law. The French Revolution put an end to Gallicanism. The "trauma of the Revolution" turned Catholics, especially French ones, away from the modern state which was the product of the Revolution and from elections, in other words from human power: this power was perceived, if not as atheist, at least as too profane. In a century marked by the instigation of the nation-state, Rome established a principle of "supranationality", but in the name of a spiritual and no longer territorial power. Catholics could then pledge allegiance directly to the Holy See. The same phenomenon occurred elsewhere in Europe: the Italian *Risorgimento* (call for unification) of 1848 was anticlerical, like most nationalist movements. But consequently direct state control of the national Churches was weakened. Ultramontanism triumphed and defended the absolute power of the Pope in the organization of the Church. Direct control became official Vatican policy, as it sought to manage Catholics directly without delegating or deferring to state powers. The nineteenth-century French missionaries, for example, saw themselves as agents of Rome and not of the Republic.[26] The European states' territorial privileges over their Churches grew less stringent, and missionary societies became international both in their recruitment and in where they chose to operate.

Deterritorialized congregations were created which recruited internationally and worked directly with the Vatican to evangelize the pagans, often supported by private institutions and "charitable organizations" such as the *Œuvre pour la propagation de la foi*, set up in Lyon by Pauline Jaricot in 1822.[27] Missionaries travelled the world over: Catholic priests from Alsace evangelized Nigeria and standardized the local languages. The Vatican had firm control over the missions in the nineteenth century. Collective, planned action (congregations) prevailed over individual and often unfortunate heroism, even though a romantic hagiography of zealous suffering missionaries did develop.[28]

This separation between Church action and colonial administration (even if at the local level collaboration was the norm) posed anew the problem of how much autonomy should be granted to the indigenous population, both legally (the Church was opposed to slavery) and institutionally (setting up local Churches), as well as culturally (recognition of local rites and adapting training to the local clergy). The globalization of the Church posed the recurrent problem of the articulation between religion and culture in a different way.

One essential point is that at a very early stage the Catholic Church advocated the indigenization of clerics. The impetus was given in 1622, with the declaration by Pope Gregory XV, who founded the Congregation for the Propagation of the Faith *(De propaganda fide)* and gave instructions to train an indigenous clergy, but with no cultural, let alone doctrinal, concessions to the local cultures and religions. The instruction *Neminem profecto* of 23 November 1845, issued by the same Congregation for the Propagation of the Faith, laid down the conditions for setting up local Churches.[29] It was a matter of territorializing, entrenching and integrating the indigenous Christian communities into the institution of the Church.

The only cultural concession however relates to the Oriental Christian rite (the Christians of the Russian and Ottoman empire). Elsewhere, nothing was said about local cultures; on the contrary, seminaries were to promote a standard training model. Meanwhile the missions were advised not to become involved in trade or political affairs. So there was a two-pronged movement of globalization and Westernization, leading to the institutional independence of the Catholic Church which would be revived in the twentieth century (in the trend towards the political indigenization of liberation movements, and also its counterpart: the conservative reaction, which found a number of bastions in the third world). Catholic universalism triumphed in every way: truly superseding (on the ground) national European identities resulting from secularization campaigns and the separation of Church and state in Europe, which paradoxically strengthened the Church's autonomy; a real global vision (henceforth the Church was interested in all peoples, including those furthest away, without having to take into account geostrategic or political considerations); the standardization of rites and doctrines (the end of Gallicanisms and regional idiosyncracies, with the exception of the Oriental Christians, doubtless for highly political reasons: uniatism[30] only works if it respects traditions); setting up a fully internationalist body of missionaries, etc.

The Church was ready for globalization; and yet this movement occurred particularly within the Protestant Churches. This is because the separation between culture and religion is more marked in Protestantism.

The Protestant Missions

From the outset, the Reformation reinforced the total separation of religion and culture,[31] which largely explains the Protestant Churches' initial reticence with regard to missionary activity.

Contrary to received opinion, at first the Protestants did not seek to convert, either in Europe or in the colonies. In Europe, the Word was spread through texts, in a receptive, "pre-Reformation" intellectual milieu; conversion "of the people" was often collective and was a top-down process instigated by a prince, a king, or quite simply a municipal council. Calvin was called to Geneva, but he did not convert Geneva: on 21 May 1536, it was the General Council of citizens that decided to adopt the Reformation.[32] In fact, the switch to Protestantism was the result not of preaching; rather it was a reversal, or a turnaround, of a section of Catholicism. Many ministers were former monks, priests or seminarians—they were clerics and not just anybody.[33] People "discovered" they were Protestant; they were not converted by someone else. One preaching technique consisted of ascending the pulpit in the churches and organizing *disputationes*. People bore witness, they did not convert. Calvin never in fact called on people to convert, but solely to bear witness. Theodore of Beza declared explicitly that there was no reason to bring into the Church those who were far removed from it, either spiritually or geographically.[34] Subsequently, there was particular concern with providing chaplains to ships' crews or to the Protestant settlers, but not with using colonies as a base from which to convert the indigenous population. Of course, there were exceptions, but those who pressed the case for foreign missions failed to convince the great Protestant Churches of Europe to support the movement.[35]

If there were no foreign missions, it was also because there was no difference between interior and exterior, between home and foreign. The problem was not a foreign culture, it was culture full stop, that of idolatry. Papism was the main form of idolatry, but so was humanism, as were indigenous religions and customs. For a Calvinist, at least at first, there could be no such thing as a noble savage, any more than there could be a good, civilized person, because there were no good men.

There were theological foundations for this reticence towards missionary activities: the theory of culture and that of salvation. Luther's Reformation professed a break not with a religion, but with a religious culture: what was false in Catholicism was not dogma itself, but a whole series of accretions, deviations and customs presented as dogmas that had altered the essential doctrines of Christianity which Luther declared he was re-establishing—not establishing. Culture was conceived in terms of "customs", and the entire Protestant critique portrays Catholicism as a body of customs, in other words it seeks to dissociate religion from "custom". These "customs" are culture.

An interesting case is that of Minister Jean de Léry (1534–1613), an ethnologist, warrior and former shoemaker. He was dubbed the first ever ethnologist by Claude Lévi-Strauss and hailed as the inventor of the myth of the "noble savage", since his book had a profound influence on Montaigne and the philosophers of the Enlightenment.[36] Admittedly, it is always dangerous to generalize from an isolated case, and the history of the Huguenot expedition to Brazil is undoubtedly more complex than has been described to date.[37] There follows a brief summary of this exemplary episode.

In 1555, a French expedition set sail for Brazil. It included a number of Protestants, some of whom at least intended to establish a colony and live there in accordance with their faith, at the time when the wars of religion were starting in France. A group of ministers, including Jean de Léry, sent by Calvin, joined them in 1557 (again, it was to tend to the Protestants in the group, not to convert Native Americans). Following religious conflicts within the French group, Jean de Léry spent several months with the indigenous population. He was not a missionary, but once he found himself among them, he wondered about converting the indigenes. He decided against doing so, and at the same time expressed his admiration for Native Americans' customs—or rather he considered that they were no more primitive or reprehensible than those of Europeans. For Léry, cannibalism was a rite, albeit not a particularly commendable one. And what about Catholic communion, according to which participants eat the body of God, and the anthropophagic acts that had taken place in Europe during the atrocious Wars of Religion (1562–98)? In contrast, the Capuchin monks who had sailed to Brazil with the Portuguese during the same period saw cannibalism as an abomination and a reason to convert the native population as quickly as possible, by coercion if necessary. Léry's cultural relativism was previously unheard of. It was his precise, impartial and unbiased recording of Native American customs that prompted Lévi-Strauss to describe his book as an "ethnologists' breviary".[38]

So we are presented with two seemingly contradictory elements: a sympathetic attitude towards a culture perceived as different but not inferior, and a profound pessimism as to the possibility of converting Native Americans.[39] In fact, there is no contradiction if we understand Léry's thinking as belonging to the school of thought that separates culture and religion, which is profoundly Calvinist. For him, Catholic culture was worse than that of indigenous peoples, in that it corrupted religion, whereas the Native Americans, being unaware of religion, were more "innocent". However, at the same time, and as a good Calvinist, Léry believed in predestination. Only a few are chosen, and that depends entirely on God's grace: converting to save souls was presumptuous and vain, since salvation did not depend on human choice. The otherness of the native evoked that of human nature, not of a specific culture; it only illustrated the duality of human nature: everyone has a "savage" inside them. The antagonism between culture and religion was first and foremost internal to man, including Christian man, so the discovery of an external otherness did not challenge the conception of human nature.[40]

So we find in Léry an ambivalence that would equally justify apartheid (Léry was opposed to sexual relations with the natives) and multiculturalism: all cultures were equal, but there was only one true religion. He did not praise cultures, but considered all cultures to be the sign of man's fall. There was no "noble culture", but there were certainly cultures that were less hypocritical than others, and therefore more laudable, like those of the Native Americans. Léry's position was thus anti-colonial before the notion existed: since, in any case, the Native Americans could not be saved, what was the point of imposing a new culture on them that would destroy their own? As Frank Lestringant says, "the Native American is saved in this world and lost in the next".[41] Andrea Frisch shows that Léry's "modernity" is his Calvinist approach in challenging (Catholic) custom; he supported the idea of the contingency of cultures, much more than that of the apologia of a primitive culture. The "noble savage" reading of Léry is an eighteenth-century one.[42] There is neither paradox nor exception, but a clear expression of the division between religion and culture that is the very essence of the early Reformation.

This principle opposing the "community of the Saints" and "those who will not be saved" is a frequent feature of Protestant colonialism. Protestants did not seek to rule over another people but to live according to their religion. Thus they did not regard the native as a potential "subject of the King" as did the Spanish and the French (who for the most part consistently followed this line during this period): the native was, at best, part of the scenery, at worst a pagan who went against God's design, like the Canaanites who inhabited the Holy Land.

This was also the attitude of the Puritans arriving in America: the "other" was the devil, since they themselves were the "holy" (which partially explains the identification of many contemporary American evangelicals with Israel and the equation between Palestinians and Native Americans: the other is he who wants to prevent God's design from being realized on Earth).[43] In fact, the refusal to accept theories of immanent morality and natural religion mean that even if there is an empirical recognition of the Native Americans' qualities (in Léry), ontological acknowledgement cannot follow.

Anglo-Saxon Protestants refrained therefore from evangelizing Native Americans and slaves, whereas French and Spanish Catholics devoted huge efforts to converting them. It was the Catholics who concentrated on the Native Americans: by the time Rand, a Protestant minister, started to take an interest in the Mi'kmaq of Canada around 1840, they had been Catholic for two centuries.[44] Of course, there were exceptions: the first Lutheran mission among the Native Americans was in 1643 (John Campanius in Delaware); Daniel Gookin (1612–1687) went among the Algonquins, as did John Eliot, who translated the Bible into the Native American Wampanoag language (though the terms *Testament*, *Bible*, *God* and *Jesus* remained in English). In the seventeenth century, Thomas Mayhew established a Native American settlement in Martha's Vineyard.[45] The German Moravian brothers sent missions;[46] in 1726, the Quaker John Wright settled in Pennsylvania to convert Native Americans. However, these converts were never integrated: in 1675, during King Philip's war, the "praying Indians", in other words the converts, were considered as traitors, and either killed or reduced to slavery. These attempts were all exceptional and short-lived.

But things began to change in the mid-eighteenth century. Between 1726 and 1760, the first "Awakening" in the Americas did not give birth to a missionary movement, but laid the foundations for one. In 1726, John Wesley himself sailed from England on a mission among the Native Americans, and in 1728 carried out the first baptisms of slaves in America. In Europe, the Society for the Propagation of the Gospel in Foreign Parts (1697–1701) was founded by English Anglicans (who sent Wesley to America and Thomas Thomson to Ghana in

1726); at the time, the Danes sent missionaries to India and Greenland. But these were one-off initiatives (to which should be added the opening, in 1728 in Halle, Germany, of a Lutheran institute to convert the Jews). In 1759, the Mohegan Indian Samson Occom was ordained a Presbyterian priest: he was the first Native American to write books in English. In 1766, the first ordination of a non-European Anglican priest took place (Philip Quaque, from Ghana).

But these were in fact the beginnings of the huge missionary wave associated with the second Awakening. The burst of missionary activity began at the end of the eighteenth century with the establishment of specialist institutions to train professionals. In fact, it was between 1790 and 1810 that the major Protestant mission societies were established; they were "low church", working class and "emotional". In 1789, William Carey (born in 1761), a self-taught Englishman who had switched from Anglicanism to Baptism, published *An Inquiry into the Obligation of Christians to use Means for the Conversion of the Heathens*, which resulted in the creation of the Baptist Missionary Society (1791–1792). In 1786, Thomas Cook (a Methodist) began his missions to the Caribbean. Founded in 1795, the London Missionary Society sent its first mission to Tahiti in 1796, chosen because there was no colonial power there. Then followed the establishment of the Church Missionary Society (Anglicans, 1799), the Netherlands Missionary Society (1797), the New York Missionary Society (1800), the British and Foreign Bible Society (1804). In 1807, more than two centuries after the Jesuits, the first Protestant missionary (Robert Morrison) arrived in China. In 1810 the American Board of Commissioners for Foreign Missions was set up, and in 1822, the Société des Missions évangéliques de Paris was born.

What explains this late eighteenth-century mushrooming of Protestant missions? There are two obvious reasons. First of all, most Protestant trends, including Calvinism, moved from a belief in predestination to an "Arminianist" view of salvation (God has granted sufficient grace for the entire human race to be saved, if men so wish). It was no coincidence that John Wesley was both the promoter of "prevenient grace",[47] as opposed to the Calvinist belief in predestination, and missions to convert. Protestantism then became "inculturated". The separation of culture and religion did not last; it became a source of internal tension, but the faithful practised their religion as if it were embedded in a culture, and it was this Anglo-Saxon culture, forged by the religious awakenings of the eighteenth and nineteenth centuries, which would develop into missionary zeal. But underlying Protestant missionary activity was always a tension between "pure" religion and culture, which was not an issue for the Catholics who were much more focused on inculturation. Catholicism confronted the question of culture head on, whereas Protestants experienced it in an implicit way, or denied it.

From the mid-nineteenth century onwards, for the Protestants, conversion was now explicitly linked to civilizing ambitions: the cultural model had to be disseminated. Hence the establishment of Protestant schools and universities (Beirut, Cairo). Conversion was not sufficient: there also had to be assimilation. But this came up against the question of race which, contrary to what had happened in the Catholic world, was often subject to theological rationalization (the race cursed by God). For a Puritan, the culture of the Native Americans was an obstacle to salvation, as seventeenth-century Protestants were now culturally embedded. After having relativized the question of culture, probably when they saw that they themselves were minorities in a culturally Catholic society, the triumphant Protestants made their new culture the condition of access to the religion: John Eliot, one of the rare seventeenth-century Protestants keen to evangelize the Native Americans, declared that the indigenous population "must have visible civility before they can rightly enjoy visible sanctities in ecclesiastical communion"; in short that they had to be physically and culturally Englishmen (hence the importance of the race question).[48] But, at the same time, rampant apartheid meant that it was almost impossible for the indigenous population to assimilate first, if at all. Consequently, the policy of "separation" generally prevailed.

The Protestants did not attempt to convert their slaves either: faced with the reluctance of Anglican missionaries, it was instead the slaves themselves who embraced Christianity.[49] While it is questionable to contrast a non-racist Spaniard with a racist American (for in fact racism played an important role in Latin America), the construction of racism was totally different in each case: based on a continuous skin colour spectrum in the Latin world where through mixed marriage (which was never prohibited, even though it might have been frowned upon socially) it was possible to move from one category to the other (the whiter a person was, or rather the less dark, the higher they were on the social ladder, but in a continuum), whereas in the Calvinist world colour was a very powerful discontinuous barrier (often associated with the prohibition of mixed marriages): a person was either black or white. A single drop of black blood made a person black. Once again, the fight against racism did not change this definition, even if it changed its manifestations: white and black remained legal categories both in the United States and in South Africa, even if negative discrimination was transformed into positive discrimination. In June 2008, the Chinese of South Africa celebrated a great victory: they were finally classified as black! Which gave them access to positive discrimination benefits.

However, some Protestant sectors continued to refuse to convert blacks, particularly in the American south.[50] Similarly in South Africa, the Afrikaners did not embark on missions to convert the blacks (but the German Moravians preached among the Hottentots from 1738, in the Genadendal mission; they were banned from there for nearly fifty years by the Calvinist Protestant Church of Cape Town). In the United States, Protestant places of worship were generally segregated before the 1960s' Civil Rights movement.

In tandem with colonial missions, the Protestants began establishing institutions and missions for the conversion of the Jews. Although it was contemporaneous with it, the process was the opposite of colonization. In this case, it was effectively the Jews who came out of the ghetto and entered mainstream society, which immediately gave rise to the debate on assimilation: should assimilation mean the abandonment of Judaism (i.e. conversion) or should it be a matter of separating the religious marker and the ethnico-cultural marker (Judaism as a "mere" religion, on the model of the French Israelites). Examples include: The London Society for Evangelizing the Jews in 1808, and The American Society for Meliorating the Conditions of the Jews in 1820 (the word "evangelizing" has been replaced by meliorating, for legal reasons to do with respect for religious freedom, which only serves to underline the real aim further). Meanwhile the Kingdom of Prussia founded a Mission for the Jews in 1822. Here too, the idea was that conversion is a condition for assimilation: this is both contrary to the French model at the time (separating the religious marker from the cultural marker) and to the model that would prevail in the second half of the twentieth century which was to make a new connection between the religious marker and the cultural marker (Jews for Jesus, the Hebrew Catholic Church in Israel: both combine a Christian religious marker and a Jewish cultural marker). On this model, the Mission to the Jews, founded in 1894 by Leopold Cohn, was renamed the American Board of Missions to the Jews in 1923; but riding the beatnik and hippie wave, a splinter group led by Martin Rosen (who converted to Christianity in 1953 and reclaimed his name of Moshe in the 1970s) founded Jews for Jesus, based on the idea that there truly is an independent "Jewish culture"; he also started a band, The Liberated Wailing Wall. Their music was aimed at young, deculturated Jews and claimed to reconnect them to their Jewishness by bringing them to Jesus. This played on ethnic pride; for them, conversion meant returning to their true Jewish roots.

This is a completely different paradigm: in the course of this retrospective account, we have gone from the devaluation of the cultural marker in favour of the religious marker to the re-evaluation of the former, raising issues of identity and culture which have once again stifled the purely religious moment. The ongoing tension between religion and culture and the notion of pure religion constantly resurface in very different contexts, but by the twentieth century the tendency was to follow the model of American Protestantism and identity fundamentalisms, be they Christian, Jewish or Muslim.

To sum up, after the period of dissymmetry between a non-converting Protestantism and a conversion-centred Catholicism, the transition from the eighteenth to the nineteenth century saw a massive proliferation of very similar missionary movements: these tended to be bottom-up rather than top-down, depending heavily on private initiatives (Pauline Jaricot) or individuals (François Libermann, a French priest who founded l'Œuvre des Noirs, an association for converting Africans, which we will discuss in Part 2), but were legitimized and approved at a senior level. The clergy, both Protestant and Catholic, recruited largely among the most popular milieus (and often predominantly on the fringes of the nation-state: Alsace, Brittany and Northern France; Wales, Scotland and Ireland in the United Kingdom; and among the Basques in Spain). The missionaries set sail often full of romantic zeal, before the missionary movement was rationalized and "technocratized". Emotion and public relations had a part to play: through compassion, one moves from anxiety over one's own salvation to that of others, which developed in its secularized form into the great passion for humanitarian values at the end of the twentieth century. The missionary impetus was linked to a change in religiosity.

Funding came from collections and donations. People signed up for missions in a militant manner, and these missions were supranational. The mission was a two-way street: parishes or churches sponsored a mission, they organized a series of talks to raise the money, inviting local missionaries and novices. There was an element of colonial exoticism, as at the Colonial Exhibitions of 1907 and 1931 in Paris. Women played a major part in developing the missions, among both Catholics and Protestants.[51] In all cases, it was a globalized movement which had no intention of being the religious arm of a national policy (even if locally there was a great deal of collusion between missionaries and the military. Moreover, the subject of expeditions, military or otherwise, coming to the aid of lost or persecuted missionaries proved constantly newsworthy, from the Stanley-Livingstone encounter to the siege of Peking). Paradoxically, centralizing Catholic Ultramontanism[52] went in the same direction as the privatization/dispersion of Protestant missions: that of globalization, of the supranational, but also of the definition of a Western model. There seems to be an obvious parallel with humanitarian aid today.

But beyond the common features of Western missionary Christianity, which went in the direction of globalization by different routes, Catholicism and Protestantism managed the relations between cultural markers and religious markers differently. The Catholic Church invested heavily in seeking a symbiotic relationship with culture through the concept of inculturation, for example. The issue of culture is central to contemporary Catholicism, in very diverse forms: inculturation, defence of a European culture, reference to Latin, liberation theology, etc. Protestantism chose on the other hand to go far in the opposite direction, that of deculturation, of distinguishing between religious and cultural markers.

2

FROM CIVILIZATION TO MULTICULTURALISM

One Civilization, Many Cultures

Missions were unquestionably an enterprise of acculturation. Until the first half of the twentieth century, missionaries believed overwhelmingly in their civilizing role, and although they accepted the idea that there were different cultures, for them, there was only *one* civilization, and that was theirs. *Civilization* meant Western culture in that it was a product of Christianity and therefore superior to other cultures. Missionaries believed in ethical, moral and social progress, even if many of them acknowledged that indigenous cultures did have some positive elements. Admittedly there was a whole spectrum of views, particularly on the issue of whether Western culture was innately superior, even in its lay form (partly because it derived from Christianity), or whether it was superior solely insofar as it was inhabited and permanently inspired by religion. But the idea of a "pure religion" which was above all culture—since culture is tainted by the Fall of Man, God's creation—a powerful idea that was much in evidence in Calvinism, was absent from the missionary project until the appearance of the evangelicals in the twentieth century. In the nineteenth century, Anglo-Saxon—non-evangelical—Protestantism effectively accommodated the idea of the lay superiority of Western civilization: this Protestantism eventually became extremely liberal, retaining the idea that Christian civilization was morally superior and upholding Jesus as an absolute moral figure,[1] whereas Catholic missionaries believed in the superiority of such a culture only if there was faith. But in all cases, missionaries could only conceive of religion as part of a culture.

At first, the Catholics were more "assimilationist" than the Protestants. In Quebec, Recollet monks and Jesuit missionaries alike dedicated themselves to the Native Americans; they encouraged mixed marriage to promote assimilation, and displayed no racism, either theological or biological. The Duc de Montmorency's instructions, penned in 1603, sum up their aims thus: "to seek to lead the natives thereof to the profession of the Christian faith, to civilization of manners, an ordered life, practice, and intercourse with the French for the gain of their commerce; and finally their recognition and submission to the authority and domination of the crown of France".[2] The Recollets arrived in 1615:

They soon concluded that the success of evangelization depended, in good measure, on the success of efforts by both Church and state to induce the Native Americans to adopt a sedentary way of life. They decided to found agricultural mission stations and to invite the Native Americans to settle around these *bourgs*. They planned, also, to intersperse French families from virtuous Catholic backgrounds in these settlements. In 1616 the Recollets met with Samuel de Champlain[3] and some pious laymen to discuss these plans. It was unanimously decided that it was necessary "to render the Native Americans sedentary and to bring them up in our manners and laws.[4]

Rome energetically encouraged the indigenization of the clergy, but at the price of acculturation:

[The missionaries] often find themselves confronted with the impossible challenge of imposing on the local seminarists a Roman training and discipline which implies a prior complete deculturation of candidates to the priesthood. Programmes, training methods and monastery life are modelled as closely as possible on European seminaries. And yet it would be anachronistic to interpret the Roman position in the light of contemporary debate on the issue of religious acculturation. It was based on a different way of thinking, that of promotion through training, it being understood that the only valid training was that dispensed according to the Roman model.[5]

As Prudhomme states:

The inculturation viewpoint, as it was developed in the 1970s, has nothing to do with the nineteenth-century missions… Missionary literature generally shows a genuine sympathy for the evangelized populations, even if it denounces outright the ill effects of paganism on civilization. The fact remains that no Las Casas, Vitoria or Ricci emerged in the nineteenth century to challenge the issues raised by the universalization of Christianity and the transfer of Catholicism into non-western cultures … In practice the effect of the civilizing mission was also to assimilate the mission with the spread of western modernity embodied by the schools.[6]

However, the Catholic Church's acculturation drive stemmed less from a positive definition of Western civilization than from the determination to defend a standardized, centralized model of a universal Church. It was the defence of the clerical institution that resulted in a single cultural model being recognized, especially at a time, i.e. the nineteenth century, when the Church was distancing itself from a Western culture that was becoming increasingly secularized. François Libermann, promoter of missions in Sub-Saharan Africa,[7] summed up the ambivalence of Catholic policy towards acculturation: "We believe that the faith is unable to take on a stable form among these peoples, and that the burgeoning Churches cannot have an assured future, other than by through the assistance of civilization perfected up to a certain point. [...] The second principle is that civilization is impossible without faith".[8] This was a constant theme in Catholicism, up until the time of Pope Benedict XVI. Western culture has no intrinsic value except in the sense that it has been, and still is, inspired by Christianity. It is not Western culture that the Church is defending then, it is Western Christian culture. Christianization was very much part of a civilizational process (and all the missionaries, Catholic and Protestant, were in agreement), but for the Catholics, there could be no lay, secular civilization.

On this point, the Catholic missionaries did not share the view of many Protestant missionaries for whom Westernization in itself represented progress, and was even a preliminary to conversion. Nor did they share the nineteenth-century idea that acculturation towards Western civilization was a first step: instead they promoted the model of the Church. "Civilization" could only be conceived of within the faith, and the notion of giving recognition to indigenous cultures was unthinkable, but that was because they were pagan, not because they were indigenous.

Now the Protestant missionaries, especially the Americans, identified much more closely with their national culture, which they felt to be superior, even in its secularized form. They almost systematically maintained their Western lifestyle (in terms of clothing, homes and diet).[9] Less well trained than the Catholics before their departure, they emphasized studying spoken languages rather than culture,[10] taking more interest in vernacular forms (dialects) than scholarly written languages. A Catholic White Father was trained in classical Arabic, an evangelical missionary in a Moroccan dialect. In the nineteenth-century

Protestant vision, which was no longer Calvinist and not yet evangelical, civilization meant a less zealous religion, the shifting of the law towards ethics and of the norm towards etiquette. Here secularization was experienced as more of a positive thing (except of course in the Churches of the Awakening), it was moving in the direction of what would become liberal Protestantism, far removed from religious excess. So for these liberal Protestants, Western culture, particularly Anglo-Saxon, was part of civilization in general because it was born of Christianity, even if it was no longer necessarily inspired by the faith. For Catholics on the other hand, civilization only had meaning if it was explicitly informed by the Gospel, and this civilizational model was perfected by the Church and not the different national cultures: the Catholic Church is in fact far more diverse in terms of recruitment, both geographical and social.

Nevertheless, in both confessions, nearly all seem convinced of the superiority of Western civilization and made a link between "civility", Christianization and Westernization, even if they had different views on the relationship between culture and religion. There would not be any true discussion of culture before the mid-twentieth century.

However, attitudes towards other cultures would not escape the slow re-appraisal that came about as a result of more extensive knowledge but also of the questioning of the notion of civilization.

The Christian missionaries had solid experience on the ground and all had, by definition, a certain knowledge of the other's culture and how to manage cultural differences: they learned indigenous languages and, touring around their native countries, tried to explain to the parishes where they were invited to speak that the savages had certain qualities. Many missionaries in fact carried out valuable ethnographic research, documenting customs and rites. There is also evidence throughout the nineteenth century and the first half of the twentieth of a general tendency towards increased sympathy for the indigenous populations and a greater distance from the colonial order; in the twentieth century, social and educational action in the missions took precedence over conversion: the hospital or orphanage counted for more than the stone church. In the many school and university networks, conversion was no longer a pre-requisite, and these networks often became the training centres for the new elites, Christian or otherwise. The fact that the new generation of twentieth-century third-world nationalist leaders was more often than not Christian (Chang

Kai Chek in China, for example) also led many missionaries to advocate more egalitarian political relations between colonial powers and indigenous movements. Racial prejudice was frowned upon by the missionaries (which posed a problem, for example, for Baptist missionaries from Alabama when they went home to their segregationist state).[11]

The fact remains that the approach to culture here is empirical and pedagogical: what is there that is positive and can be used, following the example of Paul in Athens with the altar dedicated to the "unknown God"? When François Libermann coined the slogan: "Become Negroes with the Negroes", he did not mean take an interest in Negro culture: here, the Negro is the pauper, the excluded, the rejected, and not the bearer of another culture. Even if there is evidence of an increased sensibility towards local cultures, there was hardly any willingness to find a compromise with these cultures, and the debate still focused on rites: how far could one go in making concessions to rites and customs?

Advent of Cultures and the Crisis of Civilization: the Inculturation of Religion

After 1945, a new concept emerged among the general public and politicians: that of cultural relativity and parity between cultures that were equal in dignity but also in complexity, which automatically led to the concept of "civilization" conceived as the material and moral accomplishment of a given culture being put into abeyance. Value judgements disappeared. It was the end of evolutionism and the philosophy of history as far as cultures were concerned. In France, Claude Lévi-Strauss was the most vigorous proponent of this idea,[12] which crystallized the major twentieth-century trends in anthropology. But it is especially interesting to note that this theme of the autonomy and dignity of cultures, divorced from its scientific origins, was picked up politically. There are a number of reasons for this.

First of all, there was an urge to combat the racial prejudice which had given birth to Nazism, and then there was the need to rationalize the exit from colonialism by attacking what was probably its major ideological justification: propagating civilization. The recently created UNESCO played an important part in popularizing these two ideas. Subsequently, immigration, the civil rights movement in the United States, the problem of "minorities" (ethnic, cultural, religious and latterly sexual) would prompt people to think of differences in terms of "cultures". This sudden advent of the issue of "multiculturalism" profoundly changed the relationship between culture and religion—by placing religion on the side of culture. The term "multiculturalism" first seems to have been used officially in Canada in 1960: at first, the word referred only to the respective positions of the two "peoples", English-speaking and French-speaking, but it was very quickly applied to all the minorities which appeared as a result of immigration.

This raises several fundamental problems: how can universalism and authenticity be reconciled? What is the place of human rights and democracy? And especially, what is the place of cultural diversity and religious universality? Either religion is reduced to culture, or it has to separate itself from culture (in any case from Western culture) to assert its universality.

Catholic theologians then forged the concept of "inculturation", which was the touchstone for Catholic thinking throughout the period following the Second Ecumenical Vatican Council, even though it was adopted by a few Protestant thinkers.[13] The different forms of Protestant evangelicalism did not consider the issue because they resolved it automatically in separating the cultural marker from the religious marker, in other words in ignoring the debate about culture. The Catholic Church meanwhile focused on this question, adopting a whole range of positions, from an extreme multiculturalism (in which cultural biases are flushed out from the very heart of theology, for example, the fact that God is defined as male) to the reaffirmation of an intrinsic link between Western culture and Catholicism. The conservative Catholic reaction to the liberation theologians remained bound up with the problem of the centrality of the cultural question. In this case the concept of civilization is upheld—i.e. the idea of an absence of cultural relativity: civilization is culture that has incorporated religion's ethical norms.

The debate around inculturation relies on a simple principle: religion is not culture, but it cannot exist outside culture. The link between the two realities is of the same order as that between the Word and the flesh in incarnation: "The Gospel does not identify with a culture, even though it can never exist outside a cultural expression, be it that adopted by Jesus in the Jewish world or that expressed by Paul within the parameters of Hellenism and diaspora Judaism, or that of the Christians of the early centuries in the womb of Greco-Roman and later Barbarian culture".[14] The problem nowadays is twofold: Christianity's ethnocentrism and the de-Christianization of European culture, which led to the division between culture and religion. As Pope Paul VI stressed in his apostolic Exhortation *Evangelii Nuntiandi* on "Evangelization in the modern world" (1975), "The split between the Gospel and culture is without a doubt the drama of our time, just as it was of other times".[15] It was a Belgian Jesuit, Pierre Charles, who introduced the word "inculturation" into missiology:

but [he] gave it the same anthropological meaning as "enculturation", i.e. the process by which a person acquires his or her own culture. It was Joseph Masson, S.J., who coined the expression "inculturated Catholicism" in 1962. It would take another fifteen years before the word inculturation was used in its current theological sense. The term was reportedly used for the first time at the 32nd General Congregation of the Society of Jesus, from December 1974 to April 1975, and it was Father Pedro Arrupe, Superior General of the Jesuits at the time, who introduced it in 1977 to the Roman Synod of bishops on catechesis. Pope John Paul II picked it up officially in his apostolic letter *Catechesi Tradendæ* of 1979 and this led to its being used universally.[16]

The term is repeated in John Paul II's encyclical *Redemptoris Missio* (1990), but with a whole series of reservations:

The process of the Church's insertion into peoples' cultures is a lengthy one. It is not a matter of purely external adaptation, for inculturation "means the intimate transformation of authentic cultural values through their integration in Christianity and the insertion of Christianity in the various human cultures". The process is thus a profound and all-embracing one, which involves the Christian message and also the Church's reflection and practice. But at the same time it is a difficult process, for it must in no way compromise the distinctiveness and integrity of the Christian faith. Through inculturation the Church makes the Gospel incarnate in different cultures and at the same time introduces peoples, together with their cultures, into her own community. She transmits to them her own values, at the same time taking the good elements that already exist in them and renewing them from within... Groups which have been evangelized will thus provide the elements for a "translation" of the gospel message, keeping in mind the positive elements acquired down the centuries from Christianity's contact with different cultures and not forgetting the dangers of alterations which have sometimes occurred.[17]

It is less a question of adapting the gospel to cultures than of transforming cultures through religion.

Subsequently, these reservations only grew stronger, and Pope Benedict XVI has returned to a more ethnocentrist standpoint, or, to be more exact, one which favours the religious culture of the period before the Second Vatican Council (particularly authorization to hold mass in Latin); he thus automatically promotes the Western dimension of Christianity. But this conservative reaction is also justified by a certain drift in inculturation, on two specific points.

First of all, in retranslating the fundamental concepts of Christianity into foreign cultures, the theology becomes modified. The indigenist tendency here is very often linked to liberation theology, which criticizes Christianity for having been an instrument of domination and dispossession, first of all in the hands of the colonial powers and then of the postcolonial ruling classes, especially in the case of Latin America where the indigenous culture was associated with the dominated masses and Western culture with the ruling elites. The upholders of "Indian theology" went so far as to question whether God was male (a tendency that is also found in feminist theology). They tried to define God through the *Pachamama* or "Earth-Mother"; the figure of Christ merges with a much wider entity: "We believe in Jesus Christ who lives, dies and is resuscitated in those who fight to build a historic life project starting with the poor. We believe in Jesus Christ God of closeness and unity, who gave us life and strength through the sacrifice of Quetzalcoatl who was, is and will continue to be by our side, to seek a new *pachakuti*, through, community, solidarity, reciprocity and brotherhood, for all that is the actualization of his immense love which guides us towards the new Earth and the new Heavens".[18] And finally, inculturation questioned the obligation of celibacy for the priesthood, in the name of indigenous notions of the family. It was in fact over the issue of the ordination of indigenous deacons that the Catholic hierarchy of Mexico opposed this extension of inculturation.[19]

Rarer among the Protestants, this theology of culture can be found, for example, in the writings of the Tongan theologian, Sione Amanaki Havea:[20] the Revelation spread immediately throughout the world thanks to the Holy Spirit (other authors cite the case of the Three Wise Men to justify the affirmation of an immediate universalization of the Revelation). The missionaries simply came to confirm a message that had already been received, but they distorted it according to their own culture; it is then legitimate to turn towards traditional Polynesian culture to find the authentic Revelation. The cultural argument is turned against the missionaries. Other authors go even further and, as in Native American theology, the figure of Christ is relegated to the background as being too "historical" to be superseded by the *Fenua*, divine, maternal Nature, as in the work of the Tahitian poet Turo Raapoto.[21]

Furthermore, valuing non-Christian cultures means valuing the religions associated with them, and here we move from cultural relativism to religious relativism which ends up becoming the main focus of interreligious dialogue. Arguing against inculturation, the Catholic conservatives invoke the critique against "natural theology" advocated by Leibniz, because, just like the theory of implicit revelation, it relativizes the historicity of the revelation and merges the specificity of Christianity into a lukewarm ecumenism, reduced to a hollow spirituality.

And so it is logical for critiques of inculturation to go hand in hand with a reticence regarding ecumenism. The Catholic theologians penalized by the Vatican from 1980 are those who appear to challenge this universality of Western Catholicism (for example, Claude Geffré, a French theologian and author of an *Essai de théologie interreligieux* [essay on interreligious theology], who was banned from receiving an honorary doctorate in Kinshasa[22] or the Spanish theologian Juan José Tamayo Acosta whose writings were condemned in 2002).

In both cases, religion is "swallowed up" by culture and is reduced to a vague form of religiosity. Once again we encounter the tension between religion and culture, but here it is culture that has absorbed religion. Can religion regain its autonomy by saying goodbye to culture? But before addressing this question, it should be stressed that the dominant religions were powerful machines for manufacturing culture.

3

RELIGION, ETHNIC GROUP, NATION

In many societies and ethnic groups, the link between culture and religion seems obvious: the Polish are Catholics as are the Irish, the Bretons and the Vendéens; the Russians are Orthodox, the Malays Muslim, the Tibetans Buddhist, etc. Religious allegiance is not considered to be a question of personal choice; it is a community identity and individual belief does not come into it. The cultural marker and the religious marker coincide, and even if societies become secularized, they still bear the cultural imprint of the founding religion. This world view is at the root of Huntington's famous "clash of civilizations" theory, and also of the notion of dialogue between civilizations.

However, the two markers are linked in a way that is more complex than simply merging into each other; the relationship fluctuates over time and space, and the received facts barely survive historical events or geographical displacements. In some cases, the religious marker is only one of several identity markers, such as language and literature (the Danes speak Danish and are also Lutheran Protestants): or it can become a cultural marker devoid of all religious significance (in the above example, now that Denmark is one of the most "secularized" societies in Europe, to define the Danes as "Lutherans" no longer makes sense from a religious perspective). The ethnic and cultural identity is more deep-rooted than the religious identity.

The religious marker can, however, also become the key identity marker, without necessarily being tied to an authentic religious practice, although it may be conducive to such practice. Catholicism appears to be a fundamental trait of modern Irish identity, all the more so since the ethno-linguistic marker (use of Gaelic) has disappeared.[1] And yet, in the nineteenth century, the first Irish nationalists (including Charles Parnell) were Protestants, as were the nobility of Vendée before the revocation of the Edict of Nantes: the amalgamation of a cultural marker and a religious marker (Catholicism) is recent in this case. But once the connection between the religious marker and national identity is established, the religious dimension can disappear and the religious marker transforms itself into a cultural, even national marker: in Northern Ireland, it is not religious practice that distinguishes Catholic from Protestant, because one can be atheist, Marxist and still a militant Catholic—as was true of an entire faction of the IRA. It is possible to be a Catholic politically despite having been excommunicated by the Church (on several occasions in 1920, the Bishop of Cork, Daniel Cohalan, excommunicated members of the IRA, who nevertheless did not repent). In this case, the religious marker is almost ethnic, going beyond simply defining a political camp.[2]

There are comparable situations where the connection is very different. As in Ireland, at certain times Welsh and Scottish identity has found expression through forms of territorial or purely linguistic nationalism; in Scotland, again as in Ireland, the linguistic marker also disappeared to be replaced by English. A specific religious marker then emerged to reinforce a sense of identity that was struggling to assert itself; in Wales it was Methodism, while for Scotland it was the Presbyterian Church, which, being Calvinist, is institutionally and theologically independent from the Anglican Church. And yet, in both cases, contrary to Ireland, religious identity has never been invoked to consolidate a political identity. The religious awakenings of the United Kingdom affected the ethnic groups on the periphery (Welsh and Scottish), in an original way, yet this religious marker was never associated with a cultural identity marker. On the contrary, the awakenings developed within the framework of a universalist and often missionary proselytism, in the same way as, in the nineteenth century, Welsh, Irish and Scottish expatriates remained within the framework of the British imperialist ideal: they provided the majority of overseas officials and soldiers.[3]

Anthropologists are familiar with the use of a religious marker as an ethnic marker: for example, the Hemshin of Turkey are linguistically Armenians and religiously Muslim; they are therefore cut off from an essential trait of Armenian identity, which is Christianity (even if the proposition could be inverted to state that the Armenians are first and foremost people who speak Armenian and only secondarily Christians). This religious marker resulted in the Hemshin being perceived as a separate ethnic group.[4] The same applies to the Druze and the Sikhs, for whom the ethnic designation is that of the religion, since the other ethnolinguistic markers do not distinguish them from their Arab or Punjabi neighbours.

In other cases, however, the religious marker transforms a disparate population into an identity group, to the point where it becomes a quasi-ethnic group. For example, those who are beginning to be designated, especially in the Anglo-Saxon countries, as the "Muslim minority" in Europe: although they come from very different linguistic and cultural groups, they are identified according to their lowest common denominator: Islam. This also applies to "Pakistanis", citizens of a country which is only differentiated from its Indian twin by religion. This assignation of a group to a religion often derives from a political or even simply administrative construct, rather than from an actual religious practice (this was true of colonial Algeria, and also of the Bosnians of former Yugoslavia).

The association between a religious marker and a cultural marker is therefore transient, since it is linked to a given historical moment. This tie works both ways, either through reinforcement of the religious marker or, conversely, of the ethnic one. It thus has a significant impact, since it can help intensify religious practice and make the group's natural spokesmen "religious", as we are witnessing in present-day Pakistan, which then breeds a purely religious, internationalist militantcy. But a consequence of this real impact can also be the fabrication of a quasi-ethnic group constructed solely from the religious marker (like the "Muslim minority in Europe", or the Bosnians), even of a nation (Bosnia-Herzegovina). In any case, this association between the two markers is structurally tenuous, since it shatters when religion asserts itself as "pure religion", either in the form of revivalism or fundamentalism, as a reaction against secularization, either through emigration or conversions. Globalization is a major factor in the separation of the two markers.

The Interplay Between Religious and Cultural Markers

The following points are analyses of the see-sawing between religious and cultural markers with reference to some examples.

a) The Syriacs of Turabdin: From a Religion to a Neo-Ethnic Group

The Syriacs of Turkey's Turabdin region are defined by two character-istics: a neo-Aramaic language and their allegiance to the Syriac Ortho-dox Church. For this faith community of Turabdin, being Syriac means being Christian, speaking Syriac and being neither Turkish nor Kurdish.[5] Their religious identity correlates to an ethnic identity (and likewise for the Turks, a Christian is by definition a member of a non-Turkish ethnic group). Hence, intermarriage with other Christian groups (Armenians and Greeks) is very rare.

But shift to the Middle East, and the two criteria no longer coincide. The Syriacs of Turabdin who live in or who have emigrated to Arab countries become Arabized, linguistically and culturally, and intermar-riage with other Christian faiths is frequent, since the category "Arab (ethnic) Christian" makes sense, contrary to the category "Turkish (ethnic) Christian". The Syriac Orthodox Church of Antioch (which emerged directly from the Patriarchate of Antioch after breaking away from the "imperial" Church at the Council of Chalcedon in 451), which had its patriarchal see in Damascus, counts many more Arabic than Syriac speakers; Mor Ignatius Zakka I, Patriarch since 1980, is an Arabic speaker and defines himself as "Arab": he considers Syriac identity as purely religious and not ethnic.[6] For the Church, being Syriac means being a follower of the Syriac Church, which defines itself first and foremost by its history: the patriarchate of Antioch, the schism of 451. The liturgy is in Church Syriac (a dead language that is hard for speakers of modern Syriac to understand). The link between cultural marker and religious marker is all the more tenuous as a large number of Syriac speakers have become Catholics (Uniate), and even Protestants. It is further weakened by the fact that, under the influence of the Chaldeans of Iraq, who also speak a neo-Aramaic dialect but are Nestorians or Catholics, young Syriacs born of immigrant families now claim an ethnic-type Assyrian-Chaldean identity, divorced from religion but based on the language and culture and the dream of a "shared land" in a mythical Mesopotamia. This then makes them a group that has no common ground with the Arabic speakers who are followers of the Syriac Orthodox Church. It is not a simple reforging of a group's identity, but the construction of a new ethnic group start-ing from the rejection of two purely religious identities: Orthodox and Nestorian. Although divided in their religious history, these people all speak neo-Aramaic, whereas Arabic-speaking and Syriac-speaking Orthodox are united by religion but speak two different languages.

Here we have competition between a purely religious identity, constituted around a Church which refuses to consider itself as ethnic—despite being mainly Arabic-speaking—as opposed to an ethnic identity founded on the use of modern neo-Aramaic and referring not to a specific Church, or even to Christianity, but to a territory and a history that is both pre-Christian and pre-Islamic, i.e. that of the Assyrian and Babylonian empires of antiquity (hence the choice of the Assyrian eagle as its emblem—even though the Church objects to it as being "pagan").

At the local level in the Middle East there is no contradiction between all these identities: the clergy celebrate the liturgy in Church Syriac and preach in the vernacular language. But the mass immigration of the 1970s and 1980s changed things: the vast majority of followers of the Syriac Church of Antioch now live in the West (Germany, Sweden, the Netherlands, Switzerland, Belgium, France, the USA, Australia). And, as is often the case, immigration has played a considerable part in the recasting of identity.

For the Church, the diaspora remains a faith community that must above all organize itself around the clerical institution. Once reticent on the subject of migration, which deprived the Church of its territorial base in the Middle East, since the investiture of Mor Ignatius Zakka I the patriarchate has supported migration and is setting up new bishoprics and new parishes in the West, with a centre (both monastery, cemetery and seminary) in Losser in the Netherlands. But the patriarchal see remains in Bab Tuma (St Thomas's gate), Damascus.

Lay members, on the other hand, play a much greater part in the West due to the Church becoming established later, but also because they set up cultural associations as a means of negotiating their place with the authorities of the host countries, which prefer to deal with lay members of cultural associations than with clerics. The spoken language is becoming an issue, since it is gradually replacing the religious marker as an identity trait. And yet nowhere is modern Syriac encoded or written down, since for the Church there is only one sacred language: Church Syriac, which is used solely in the liturgy, but has no secular function. But many second-generation young people, while remaining loyal to the Church—albeit in a context where multiculturalism and minority rights are a positive aspect of integration—contribute to the ethnicization of the community, which is out of step with a solely religious affiliation. They continue to speak the language, even among the second generation, because it is the only language of communication of a community that is now dispersed but which continues to promote endogamy and therefore needs a shared language (second generation offspring speak German, English, Swedish or French). They have two satellite television channels, which broadcast in neo-Aramaic and a folklore "culture" comprising "traditional" songs and dances. The Swedish government in particular has been receptive to this demand for "ethnic" recognition. The Swedes support a multiculturalist policy based on ethnicity: immigrant children must also learn to read and write their mother tongue. But vernacular Syriac has never been a written language—it is Church Syriac that fulfils the role of a written language. A young Syriac linguist thus obtained from the Swedish government the necessary funding to "set down" the Syriac dialect as a written language using the Roman alphabet, and the language was then used to teach children Syriac. So here we have a typical example of the invention of an Oriental ethnic language by a Western state, and the subsequent transformation of a religious community into an ethno-linguistic group.

This manufacturing of an ethnic language is a typical example of the self-confirmation of Western multiculturalism: it creates ethnicity while being convinced it is only observing, recording and giving a culture the recognition it deserves.

But the reverse process also occurs. In the 1930s, the Turkish government demanded that religious texts should be in Turkish, with the aim of diluting the Christians' ethnic identity. The Syriac religious authorities were cunning: they bought Bibles in Turkish (from Protestant missions, who were the only ones to translate) and displayed them on the tables of the catechism schools for the benefit of the police, should they pay a surprise visit. Nobody used them. But a few adults then began to read the Bible for the first time, since although they were unable to read Church Syriac, they could read Turkish, having been taught to read by the Kemalist Republic. Their access to the sacred text was through the language of cultural alienation. Several families, after reading these bibles, then converted to Protestantism.[7] In this instance, the disappearance of the cultural marker led to the reformulation (and not the disappearance) of the religious marker, towards a deculturated universalism.

Far from expressing a millenarist amalgamation of religious identity and ethnico-linguistic identity, the Syriac example shows that the two markers can always be separated, even if they are closely interlinked. It is not the simple fact that they are connected but the way in which they connect that constitutes the real identity issue.

b) The Pamiris

There are countless examples of the complex relationship between cultural markers (essentially linguistic ones) and religious markers. The Pamiris of Central Asia are identified with Ismaili Islam but in fact there is no systematic relationship between language and religious affiliation: while the majority of the speakers of the so-called Pamiri languages (Shughni, Wakhi, etc.) are Ismailis, they also include Sunnis; and conversely, large Ismaili communities speak Persian (the Ismailis of the Kayan valley in Afghanistan). To complicate matters, during the Soviet period it was the Pamiris of Tajikistan who were the driving force behind a national Tajik identity (therefore Persian-speaking) and who supplied the Republic of Tajikistan with cadres before being supplanted by the Khojentis and the Kulyabis: they then joined the "Islamo-democratic opposition".[8] The Ismailis of Tajikistan thus found themselves in the reverse configuration to that of their brothers in Afghanistan, who were politically close to the Communists and strongly opposed to all Sunni fundamentalists. To complicate matters even further, the question of how to define the religious marker arises: does being an Ismaili mean: 1) belonging to Islam in general, 2) belonging to Shia Islam, 3) belonging to a specific religion, or does it mean 4) identifying with secularism, the most neutral form of religion, given the very low level of religious practice?

Lastly, as is frequently the case, an external, Western factor has recently helped "ethnicize" religious affiliation: since 1990, the Aga Khan Foundation based in France has run education and development programmes which link the different Ismaili groups of Afghanistan, Central Asia, China and Pakistan, thus creating competition with other ethnic and religious groups, and tending to emphasize the neo-ethnic criterion of the Ismaili community (even though the Foundation's programmes reach out beyond the Ismaili community). However, the answer to the above question depends this time not on the local communities but on the supranational institution that speaks in their name.

At this point, the question is twofold: is Ismailism a religion in itself or a branch of Islam? The Ismaili Institute in London, which is the movement's academic think-tank, tends to waver on the issue: before 1979, the emphasis was rather on a de-Islamized version of Ismailism, along the lines of Zoroastrianism and Oriental spirituality, while post the Islamic Iranian Revolution, the community leaders have seemed more anxious to re-integrate Ismailism into the great Muslim family, no doubt so as to avoid the persecution of members living in societies that have become increasingly Islamized, in the way that the Bahai of Iran were persecuted in an Islamic Republic that refused to recognize them.

c) African-Americans

Religion can serve as an identity-marker in particularly violent deculturation contexts, such as the slave deportations. African-Americans have successively embraced Christianity, and then, partially, Islam. Through Christianity they demanded equality, even assimilation, and by appropriating the dominant religion, turned it against their overlords. This appropriation involved developing a particular form of worship, epitomized by Gospel. African-Americans identified with the people that had been enslaved (the Jews in Egypt: *Let my people go!*), they embraced a Messianic view *(Joshua fit the battle of Jericho)* and one of consolation *(Jesus rock my soul)*. The entire "narrative" seeks to exist in relation to mainstream culture, precisely by isolating its religious message from the social and cultural environment: in actual fact, this message breaks the dominant/dominated paradigm. Far from being a syncretist form, Gospel separates the religious marker from the cultural marker in the other, the white, hence the difficultly in imagining "white Gospel" in the United States other than as a political decision to identify with African-Americans. White Gospel as a "technique" of universalist preaching has only been possible outside America, in France as it happens, albeit sung in English.[9]

However, with the growing emergence of a militant black consciousness throughout the twentieth century, identification with the Master through religion was challenged. So the question was: how do you choose a religious identity that is not that of the white, Anglo-Saxon master? Here too arises the possibility of rethinking the two religious and cultural markers (racial for the latter). There is one option: that of choosing another universal religion, Islam for example, but which takes two different forms based on cultural markers. Under the leadership of Elijah Mohammad, Black Muslims chose a separatist black Islam: the Nation of Islam is a religious community for blacks, the religious marker being secondary to the racial one. Other African-American Christian Churches would also define themselves as "black first and foremost" (like for example the minister Jeremiah Wright of the Trinity Church of Chicago, which Barack Obama was very close to). Religious universality is secondary to the ethnic group (ethnic group here being understood according to the legal category defined at the end of the nineteenth century by the American Supreme Court: a person who has a single drop of black blood is considered black), which was basically inspired by the pro-slavery Protestants and led to segregation and apartheid.[10] A "black" re-writing of religious history developed, in the tradition of the indigenous theology discussed earlier. It is interesting to see that some African-American anthropologists tried to give scientific credibility to this hypostasis of the ethnic marker: Gospel was allegedly the expression of a purely African religious practice, which had survived as a substratum and would make "black" Christianity a different religion from "white" Christianity.[11]

But under the impetus of followers who had been to Mecca, in 1975, on the death of Elijah Mohammed, an orthodox current led by his own son, Warith Deen Mohammad, rejected the ethnicization of American Islam, preferring to emphasize the universality of the religious marker. It referred to the *ummah*, the community of believers, and not just to the black community, as the Nation of Islam did. This led to a split in the Nation of Islam. Warith Deen Mohammad's centrist movement is the stronger today, and the African-Americans who convert generally join it. For them, there is no such thing as "black Islam".

And yet we are far from a purely religious community that is beyond race. From the 1980s onward, orthodox American Islam has been represented mainly by immigrants from the Middle East and South Asia, who consider themselves to be "white",[12] belong to the middle and upper classes and are more integrated and better educated than African-American Muslims. The barrier here is no longer so much ethnic as social. The "congregations" (communities around a mosque) follow the social segregation pattern of the wider American environment, and the "black" and "white" mosques (in other words Arab or Indo-Pakistani) do not mix, despite the attempts to close ranks after 11 September and act as a lobby supported by a uniform demographic base.[13] Furthermore, despite the efforts to seek a rapprochement between African-American converts and Muslim immigrants, their strategies remain different. The latter attempt to define themselves as Muslim Americans, where the cultural marker is American and the religious marker Muslim. They format themselves depending on the environment: young Mohammad is nicknamed Mo at school, and Samiullah, Sam.[14] On the other hand, many African-American converts do the opposite, divesting themselves of their "white" names (John as a first name, Smith or Jackson as a surname) and choosing "exotic" names such as Abubakr or Abu Mumia. In other words, while there is agreement on religious orthodoxy, the two groups have a differing relation to cultural markers: African-Americans seek differentiation/integration by Islamizing the cultural marker, the immigrants by Americanizing the religious marker.

Islam therefore is used sometimes to strengthen the African-American sense of identity, sometimes, conversely, like Christianity, to try to dissolve that identity within a wider faith community.

Another interesting case is that of African-American converts to Judaism. As is often the case with isolated groups which suddenly claim to uncover their Jewish origins, it is a case of self-conversion under the pretext of rediscovered origins, that of the ten lost tribes of Israel; they state incidentally that the ancient Hebrews were black and therefore that they are more Jewish than present-day Jews. The most radical group is the Nation of Yahweh (founded in 1979), accused of promoting a racial vision. The oldest movement, Church of God and Saints of Christ, appeared at the end of the nineteenth century, followed by the Commandment Keepers and the African Hebrew Israelites of Jerusalem, founded in 1966 in Chicago. Hundreds of members of these groups have emigrated to Israel, where they are not recognized as Jews but often manage to obtain resident's permits. Here the religious marker is floating, as it is mythical, with no connection to a real religion or culture and is generally linked to a guru figure.

d) Tatars and *Moriscos*

There are other examples of subjugated ethnic groups embracing the conqueror's religion, but this time under coercion. We have already cited the case of the Spanish *Moriscos* and *Marranos*. For them, conversion was an obligation, not a choice. Wrongly or rightly, their conversion was never accepted as genuine by the Spanish monarchy, for whom, blatantly, there could not be any Christians belonging to a culture other than the mainstream culture.[15] But while, in the case of Black American slaves, deculturation was an automatic consequence of being reduced to slavery, the Muslim and Jewish minorities of Spain maintained their link to the land and their family structure, hence their capacity to transmit their culture. Some managed to blend into the Spanish social landscape, often at the price of moving to a different place, but the rest were ultimately expelled.[16]

The less tragic case of the Russian Tatars hinges on the same question: can someone from a non-Christian culture be a Christian? After the capture of Kazan in 1557, the Russians set about converting the Tatars to the Orthodox Church while allowing them to keep their language: conversion was not assimilation. For Muslims, it was the only way to maintain their social status (until the recognition of Islam by Catherine the Great in 1783). The combination of the ethnic and the religious marker is complex in this instance: the descendents of the Tatar converts continued to be called "converts"; their official designation at the end of the nineteenth century was *kreshchenye inorodty*, "foreign converts"; they were still perceived as "other" from an ethnic and cultural point of view, despite the very different philosophy of the conversion policy compared with Spain. In the early twentieth century, many of them sought to revert to Islam—even though the Orthodox Church did not accept "relapsed heretics". However, they did manage to obtain the right to change religion: and effectively the argument used by the authorities was that their culture was not linked to Christianity and therefore their religion remained somewhat artificial.[17] Here again, we have self-confirmation of the pervasive idea that there is no religion without a culture and that all culture is linked to a religion. The outcome was not that all the Tatars reverted to Islam, but that from then on, those who remained Christians defined themselves as Russian.[18]

This paradigm is perhaps echoed in the unexpected judgment of an Egyptian court in January 2008 which granted the request made by Coptic converts to Islam to be allowed to revert to Christianity. The court decreed that, deep down, they had never ceased to be Christians: what appears to be the recognition of religious freedom is perhaps only the assignation to/of a permanent cultural identity. This same argument resurfaces in a column by the priest Christian Delorme in *Le Monde*, in which he rails against attempts to convert Algerian Muslims to Christianity, since in his view, Algerianness is inextricably bound up with Islam.[19]

e) States and the Manufacture of Neo-Ethnic Groups Based on Religious Markers

States are great manufacturers of neo-ethnic categories from religious markers. It is very often the "Muslim" marker that is used to group disparate populations under one label.

The most famous case is of course that of the Ottoman *millet* system. The Ottoman state divided its population into religious groups retaining their own personal status under the control of their religious authorities. There was often a natural crossover between ethnic group and religion as far as the Christians were concerned, but it was always the religious criterion that prevailed, for when there were several "Churches" for the same ethnolinguistic group, then a *millet* ("nation") was created for each Church: there was the Armenian Orthodox *millet*, a Catholic Armenian *millet*, etc. Likewise, people from different ethnic groups could find themselves under the same *millet*: the Arab Orthodox Melchites were put in the Greek Orthodox *millet* (their clergy is Greek). The Maronites' *millet* was defined by the specificity of their Church, and not by their language (they are Arabic-speaking). When the Uniate movement (rallying the Orthodox churches to Rome) spread under Rome's aggressive impetus in the sixteenth century, the "Latins", backed by the Western powers (France), obtained the creation of Latin *millet*s, which were simply Catholic versions of the Orthodox *millet*s. The *millet* system is still in operation today in Palestine, Israel, Jordan, Syria and Lebanon, but also in Greece. People belong to a *millet* whatever their personal convictions: George Habash, the leader of the Popular Front for the Liberation of Palestine (a far left group), was a member of the Greek Orthodox *millet* and was given a church funeral.

The history of the Christian *millet*s is well known, but in contrast to the creation of a whole range of Christian *millet*s, the diversity of forms of Islam was reduced: confronted with a divided Christianity, there had to be one single face of Islam. The Muslim *millet* was therefore defined solely as Sunni orthodox, ignoring the Shia and the Sufis.

By using only the religious marker, the *millet* paradigm helped to standardize identities.

The complex relationship between religious and cultural markers is again apparent in the case of the Muslim minority in Greece. Protected by a treaty, it has its own civil courts that still use Ottoman law, which has not been applied in Turkey since Ataturk's day. The laws are written in Osmanli and apparently have never been translated into Greek. Consequently, the community's official language is Turkish (even if there are non-Turkish-speaking Muslims, like the Pomaks) and it is certainly perceived as an ethnic community, protected by minority rights. But, since the 1990s, a new Muslim presence has been growing in Greece comprising mainly Arabs from the Middle East who are recent immigrants, and they demand to be recognized as a religious group (Greek citizens of the Muslim faith) and refuse to be considered as part of an ethnic minority with which they share only a religion. Here, the wish to create a religious community divorced from its ethnic origins conflicts with the tradition of ethnicization of religious affiliations resulting from the Ottoman *millet* system.

Let us now turn to three cases of Muslim neo-ethnic groups manufactured on the basis of political decisions.

– British India: the "creation" by the Colonial Authorities of the
  Neo-Ethnic Category "Muslim"

Amid India's vast and complex religious and ethnic landscape, in order to carry out a census, the British simplified and classified sub-groups with complex identities as "Muslim", and subsequently treated them as such. This had the effect of confirming some groups as administrative categories and of other groups confirming themselves as such. These groups were pushed into effectively becoming Muslim, whereas their actual religious practices were more complex. From this point on, they were defined only by a religious marker which up until then had been very weak, and they ended up "adhering" to the only marker that was attributed to them. For example, "Muslims" from Bengal who have Hindu names, and who use their own words to say "God", started using Muslim names and saying "Allah".[20] The act of creating separate electorates (1919 and 1935) on the basis of religious affiliation helped to enshrine the religious marker as the determining one, which inevitably led to the Partition of 1947. Admittedly, this religious polarization was not solely the work of the British: it was also a consequence of the reformist and fundamentalist religious movements which tried to substitute a purely religious marker for the cultural markers (Ahl-i Hadith, Deobandi, Tablighi Jamaat). It is precisely this problem that resurfaces in British-style "multiculturalism".

This administrative standardization at the end of the nineteenth century went hand in hand with the development of pan-Islamism among Indian Muslims, including their dress (Muslims started wearing the fez in Aligarh, and "Arab" dress elsewhere).[21] Languages were also fixed to highlight a religious differentiation which had nothing to do with linguistic reality: Hindustani was split into Urdu (the Muslim language) and Hindi (the language of the Hindus) firstly by the choice of a different alphabet, even if the two languages subsequently evolved separately.

– Pakistan: Muslim State or Islamic State?

The logical consequence of the establishment of two electoral colleges and of the division of Indian society into Hindus and Muslims, to the detriment of more complex identities (ethnic, religious and regional), was the birth of the Muslim separatist movement advocating the creation of a state (Pakistan) for Muslims of the Indian sub-continent. But it is interesting to note that for its founder, Muhammad Ali Jinnah, it was not Islam as a religion, but as a culture, that defined Pakistan (for which Abul Ala Maududi[22] severely criticized him).

Pakistan has always wavered between two definitions of identity: whether to become a territorial nation state, which happens to be Muslim, or to be an ideological Islamic state whose vocation is to represent all Muslims of the region, even of the *ummah*. In short: Muslim state (Jinnah, the country's founder) versus Islamic state (Maududi). The army, a pillar of the state, initially supported the idea of a Muslim state, rallying to the concept of an Islamic state when General Zia came to power in 1977. In fact, the merging of the religious and cultural markers to create a Pakistani identity has never succeeded and Maududi's objections have proved well founded. General Zia's re-Islamicization consisted of making the Islamic religious marker alone Pakistan's trademark, ignoring its cultural markers.

This Islamicization policy can work only if it is founded on Islamist or neo-fundamentalist movements which are trying to build a "pure" religion in opposition to, or beyond, existing cultures, and do not recognize the territorial intangibility of the Pakistani state; for them, it is an ideological state, a regional subset of the Muslim *ummah*. Deterritorialization and deculturation are therefore the consequences of this hegemony of the religious marker.

This is the epitome of holy ignorance, since the supremacy of the religious norm kills any attempt to create a culture.

– The Bosnian Example

The Muslims of former Yugoslavia have never constituted an ethnic group.[23] Their religious rights were guaranteed by the Austro-Hungarian Empire on the annexation of Bosnia-Herzegovina (1908). Throughout Yugoslav history (1920–1992), the political elites were divided between pan-Islamists, pro-Serbians, pro-Croatians and supporters of an independent Bosnian identity, which would in fact be reserved for the Muslims living in Bosnia-Herzegovina and not for all the Muslims of Yugoslavia. In 1968, the Communist League of Bosnia-Herzegovina recognized the Muslims of the Republic of Bosnia-Herzegovina as a "nation" (or a "nationality" in the Soviet sense of the word). Here a religious marker, with little bearing on actual practice, which was minimal at the time, was combined with a territorial marker to create a neo-ethnic group, resulting in the movement to constitute a nation; it was these people who seized on the word "Bosnians", or "Bosniaks" to describe themselves. The Muslims of Bosnia were artificially distinguished from the other Muslims of Yugoslavia, like those of the Sandjak (included in Serbia) who are connoted only by a religious marker (they are Muslim Serbs). For the former, the word "Muslims" was written in Serbo-Croat with a capital "M", and for the latter, with a lower-case "m". After the break-up of Yugoslavia, the Serbs attacked the Bosnian Muslims, but did not touch the Muslims of Serbia: they were targeting the Bosnian neo-ethnic group and not those who practised Islam as a religion.

This was not a war of religion, but a consequence of the ethnicization of religious affiliation. Interestingly, the "Islamists" of Bosnia, who supported Alija Izetbegovic's Party of Democratic Action (SDA), appealed to the solidarity of the *ummah* during the war with Serbia, but never claimed to represent all the Muslims of former Yugoslavia: they were indeed an "Islamo-nationalist" party, and not an internationalist religious one. Foreign Muslim volunteers who came to fight alongside the Bosnians during the war against Serbia were sent home afterwards and had their Bosnian nationality, given to them during the war, revoked—an illustration of the nationalization of religious identity, the corollary of which is the difficultly in creating a "Bosnian" definition of citizenship that includes both Serbs and Croats. Religion here has been thoroughly ethnicized.

– In Immigration

The category "Muslim" operates as a neo-ethnic rather than a religious category. There are complex reasons for this; it is not just down to administrative criteria.

Whatever the group in question, the immigration process initially reinforces the religious marker rather than cultural markers (the language spoken, observation of customs), which becomes problematic with the second generation. This tendency is particularly evident in the United States,[24] where Catholicism acts as an umbrella for Latinos, as do the Protestant Churches for Koreans (some Koreans convert to Korean Protestantism on immigration in order to reconcile integration and preserve a Korean identity). In countries where religious practice is part of social life, as in the United States, there has even been a religious revival among the second generation (American Jews became more religious in the 1950s, for example).

But the ethnic character runs into difficulty with the second generation (those that switch to English).[25] The religious marker then acts as an ethnic marker in a highly racialized society, when there is no longer any real linguistic or indigenous cultural content in the practice of the religion in question. The religious marker is effectively often perceived as positive or, in any case (except for Islam after 11 September 2001), honourable; it also allows the individual to escape racialist classifications and move up the social ladder in countries like the United States where this marker is very often negative: it is better to be Hindu than Indian, Buddhist than Asian, Greek Orthodox than Arab. So here there is a subtle game of equivalences between religious and ethnic markers, which has nothing to do with preserving an original culture or at least identity;[26] on the contrary, it reflects the disappearance of cultural markers in favour of the religious marker alone, which will function not in the cultural but in the ethnic domain. The religious marker makes it possible to conceive of ethnicity separately from culture, making it a deculturation factor.

This is the process by which the category of "Muslim" developed in Europe to become virtually interchangeable with that of immigrant. Whereas studies published in French talk of "people of immigrant origin", those carried out by English-speaking institutes routinely speak of "young Muslims", or of "Muslim riots". An example is *Muslim Youth and Women in the West: Source of Concern or Source of Hope?*, a report published in 2008 by New York University's Center for Dialogues between the Islamic world, the United States and the West; in 2007, the Open Society Institute embarked on a major monitoring project entitled "Muslims in EU Cities". Similarly, the campaigns against Islamophobia (whatever one thinks of the general concept) tend to identify Muslim with immigrant populations (because there is often confusion between racism and religious discrimination). In November 2007, during a conference of the Organization for Security and Co-operation in Europe (OSCE) in Cordoba on this issue, most of the official speakers were in favour of the idea that combating Islamophobia requires more dialogue between civilizations.[27] Here we come full circle: Muslims remain foreigners because we dialogue with them through the intermediary of Middle East organizations (the Arab League, for example). The debate in Belgium on Muslim representation also reveals similar ambiguities: in 2004, while voting to select representatives of the Muslim faith, people of immigrant origin who were secular and not observant demanded to have polling stations in schools because they did not want to enter mosques. They wished to be recognized as non-practising Muslims, Muslim atheists even. The vote took place, but the resulting committee was unable to function.

In France, the French Council of Muslim Faith (CFCM) was set up in such a way as to avoid this confusion, in theory, since it addresses only practising Muslims and operates through the mosque network. But there remains frequent confusion on both sides: state officials tend to speak indiscriminately of immigrants, Arabs and Muslims, and the Union of Islamic Organizations of France (UOIF) itself issued a *fatwa* ("Don't burn cars!") against the 2005 riots in the *banlieues*, as if it too saw suburban youths as synonymous with Muslims. This systematic ethnicization of Islam also allows self-proclaimed "community leaders" to justify their position (to lead a community, that community has to exist, at least virtually). The construction of neo-ethnic groups also derives therefore from religious authorities keen to cling to their leadership in a climate of minoritization and deculturation.

f) Judaism: Between Religion and Cultures

Probably nowhere else has the interplay between cultural marker and religious marker been as complex, over such a long period of time, as in Judaism. The expulsion of the Jews from Jerusalem by the Romans in 135 left them in a diaspora, where they were always the minority, until 1948. For the Jews, the contradictory questions specific to minorities have been continuous issues of debate: acculturation-assimilation, or reinforcement of Jewish identity. The common denominator has unquestionably been a religious marker: observance of Jewish law or *halacha*.[28] It is not so much a theological permanence (the religious debates are rich and enduring, the schools very different) as a proclaimed "orthopraxy", i.e. adhesion to the same practical norms, if not always followed to the letter.[29] It is typical that in some cases of forced conversions (among the *Marranos*, for example), the only vestiges of "Jewishness" are practices.[30] Conversely, complete assimilation presupposes the disappearance of all markers; Jewishness then becomes a quality attributed from the outside, either through the racial prism, like the Pure Blood law in sixteenth-century Spain and the Nuremberg laws in Nazi Germany, or quite simply through genealogical research—a number of celebrities are found to have a Jewish grandmother.

So there was a double phenomenon in the diaspora: acculturation (adopting the language and several features of mainstream culture) and reinforcement of the religious marker. The result of the *kashrut* laws was the creation of strict boundaries between Jews and their surrounding society, boundaries at times reinforced by policies of exclusion and territorial confinement regularly implemented by states (ghetto, *shtetl*— the pre-war Jewish village community in Eastern Europe—and the *pal*, the territory assigned to the Jews in Russia). In Muslim lands, on the other hand, acculturation was more prevalent since religious markers were structurally closer to those of Muslims (circumcision, food taboos). Linguistic assimilation was widespread too even though the Hebrew alphabet was used (hence Judeo-Persian, Judeo-Tat, Judeo-Berber, etc.). The German Ashkenazi Jews on the other hand developed a system of prohibitions and standards governing language, clothing, religious norms and food that was much stricter than that of the

Sephardi Jews of the Middle East.[31] In the exclusion areas, a specific culture developed; while Yiddish, a Germanic language, became the Jewish language in non-Germanic contexts (Slav and Romanian).

In all countries, whether Muslim or Christian, assimilation presupposed conversion, at least until the nineteenth century. So it was therefore the religious marker that was dominant in defining Judaism, particularly since the religious authorities often supervised and represented the community: when the city of Amsterdam accepted Sephardi Jewish settlers expelled from Spain in the seventeenth century, it recognized them as a religious group and entrusted the management of the community to religious leaders (who excommunicated Spinoza for his heretical ideas).

When the Jews came out of the ghetto in the late eighteenth century, there were various attempts to redefine a Jewish identity in a manner that was no longer tied to strict observance of *halacha*:

- Judaism conceived of as a "religion" similar to others, in other words modelled on Christianity's institutional workings and religiosity (the transition from Jew to Israelite in France);
- Judaism understood as an ethnic, even racial trait (the construction of the Jewish "race" through a shift from religious anti-Judaism to racial anti-Semitism);
- Judaism seen as a sort of culture, with a Jewish spirit and a humanism divorced from any specific religious belief;[32]
- Judaism perceived as nationalism, either deterritorialized ("nationality" in the USSR, the Bund movement in Russia and Eastern Europe, Austro-Hungarian Marxism), or territorialized (Zionism); Jewishness was then defined within the framework of the nineteenth-century nationalist paradigm (a people, a state, a land, a language).[33]

The religious marker is either reconstructed ("Jewish worship" in the USA or in France, recast as *"Culte Israélite"*), or isolated and strengthened (Hasidim and Haredim), or ignored (by the socialist Bund), or again reintroduced as an ethnico-political marker (to emigrate—make *aliyah*—to Israel you can be an atheist but you must be Jewish).

At the same time, Jewish communities were extensively formatted by the framework provided by the host country: be it the *millet*, ghetto, "Church", ethnic group, or a multicultural situation, each of these paradigms influenced the way all or some of the Jewish population either became integrated or differentiated itself.

If we take the religious marker, the nineteenth century witnessed attempts in Europe and in the United States to define a purely religious Judaism, either voluntarily (the *Haskala* movement) or imposed (establishment of the Great Sanhedrin by Napoleon). That was how the word "*juif*" came to be replaced by "*Israélite*" in French official parlance (up until the Vichy regime), with its only reference being the association with the "*culte Israélite*" (the Israelite form of worship). The French Jewish institutions overwhelmingly adopted this appellation (the Central Consistory of Israelites of France and Algeria, Universal Israelite Alliance, Éclaireurs Israélites de France (the Jewish Scout movement), Representative Council of Israelites in France, founded in 1943).

The Reform Jewish movement in the United States also attempted to "liberate" the religious marker from any ethnic context. It rejected the Orthodox definition of Jewishness as being passed on solely through the mother, abandoned strict *kashrut* law, replaced the synagogue with a "temple", was open to conversions and took its cue from the feminist movement by ordaining women rabbis. Hebrew barely played a part. Quite logically, Reform rabbis felt that once Judaism was de-ethnicized and considered a universalist religion, proselytism made sense. A Jewish missionary movement on the Christian model thus emerged in the United States in the 1930s.[34] The cultural marker disappeared, and the community was now defined solely by a religious marker formatted along the lines of the main religions.

But the reduction of Judaism to a purely religious paradigm, constructed incidentally in parallel with Christianity (especially Protestantism), was challenged by a whole series of movements specific to the twentieth century which foregrounded an ethnic identity again. First of all, anti-Semitism and Nazism, unlike religious anti-Judaism, made Jewishness synonymous with race, thus depriving it of the right to define itself.[35] Then Zionism made the Jews a people, an ethnic group, a nation in search of a state. The present-day State of Israel defines Jewishness by filiation (even though the Jewish Agency, which is in charge of *aliyah*, and the Grand Rabbinate do not use the same criteria, since for the latter, lineage goes solely through the mother) and by non-affiliation to another religion, in other words the strictly religious marker (practice) becomes secondary to an ethnic affiliation. The "liberal" demand that Jewishness should be transmitted through either the father or the mother is tantamount to removing the only religious element in the definition of ethnicity, and therefore automatically strengthens the ethnicity argument.

The third tendency is multiculturalism, which reduces all religious markers to cultural ones. Ethnicization can come from the left. In the United States, it was the involvement of liberal Jews in the civil rights movement that caused many of them to go back to an "ethnic" position regarding their Jewishness, because theory-based, institutionalized multiculturalism does not recognize "religion" as a category but does recognize "ethnicity". Multiculturalism is a powerful ethnicization factor. As well as manufacturing neo-ethnic groups, even more fundamentally it underscores the ethnic dimension of a group that has always defined itself as a people. There is talk of the Jewish vote, like the African-American or Latino vote, the WASP vote etc.; none of this has anything to do with belief or religious practice.

In postwar France, there was a rapid switch from the word "Israelite" to "Jewish", illustrated by the renaming of the CRIF (the Representative Council of Israelites of France) as the Representative Council of Jewish Institutions of France. According to the magazine *L'Arche*, "in a SOFRES survey conducted by Émeric Deutsch in 1976, a third of French Jews still used the word "Israelite" to describe themselves. Nearly eleven years later, in 1988, only 5 per cent used the word, and this percentage had remained unchanged in 2002".[36]

At the same time, Judaism was not impervious to the twentieth century, to the new wave of religious revivalism that sought to place the religious marker on everything that came within the sphere of the profane. Here the Lubavitch movement differed from former trends that were dedicated above all to preserving a faith community: it tried to "reach" all the "cultural" Jews to convince them to present themselves as observant; it campaigned for the visibility of religious markers, such as displaying a *menorah* (candleholder) during the feast of Hanukkah (which celebrates the victory of Judaism over Hellenism, in other words the refusal to assimilate).

So this period witnessed two movements going in different directions. One was a religious revivalism that emphasized the religious marker, while the other tried to develop a Jewish identity for non-believers, along the lines of an ethnic culture. The stress on the religious marker came from revivalist movements like the Lubavitch, but also from the Great Rabbinate of Israel which insisted on the strict criteria governing the definition of a Jew (Jewishness being passed on through the mother) and conversion. The Great Rabbinate protested, for example, against the authorization of the sale of leavened bread during Passover;[37] it pressed for the religious marker to dominate the public sphere; meanwhile, the ultra-orthodox Jews of Jerusalem did their utmost to establish themselves as the norm (demanding segregation of men from women on buses serving orthodox districts).

Meanwhile, a whole movement celebrating Jewish identity and culture without reference to religion was developing. This was a two-pronged movement, sometimes attempting to define a Jewish identity that remained diasporic (in other words not fundamentally tied to political Zionism), and sometimes, after 1948, one that developed into a non-religious Israelism, seeking to define an Israeli culture that was neither that of religious Judaism nor that of the humanism of the diaspora, but that of a secular Israel. It thus fitted into the tradition of nineteenth-century ethnic nationalism with a contemporary multiculturalist slant. As Paul Mendes-Flohr writes, "the struggle between cultural and political Zionists was in a large measure a question of how to code a modern Jewish identity—by a territorial political framework, pure ethnicity or by culture".[38] In the same vein, in 2006 in London "Simcha on the Square"—a sort of "Jewish Pride"—was launched. It was a festive gathering in Trafalgar Square of everything "Jewish" (music, food, handicrafts, culture), but with no religious connotation, attended by the Mayor of London, Ken Livingstone.

There is also evidence of an attempt to create a "secular Judaism" from secularized religious markers. For example, in 1963, Rabbi Sherin Wine (who died in 2007) founded the Humanistic Judaism movement, the driving force behind the International Institute for Secular Humanistic Judaism, the aim of which is to combine "rational thought and Jewish culture".[39] The Great Rabbinate reacted to the opening of a secular *yeshiva* in Jerusalem in 2006 by trying to ban it.[40] The curriculum emphasizes Judaism as a culture and not as a religion, even if this culture involves religious markers (Jewish marriages, *britot milah* and *bar* and *bat mitzvot* are celebrated). There is a parallel with the Paris City Hall's efforts to promote secular Arab culture by setting up, in 2007, an Institute of Islamic Cultures, where religious festivals such as the end of Ramadan are celebrated. The religious marker is then transformed into a cultural marker, but suddenly, inevitably, secular culture is seen from the religious angle. This secularization of religious rites sometimes descends to the level of pure folklore.[41]

In Israel, the gulf between Israelis and the diaspora seems to be widening. Even setting aside explicit attempts to create a distinct ethnic and cultural Israeli identity (like the so-called "Canaanite" movement around the journal *Alef*, from 1948–58), the fact of no longer being a minority obviously changes Israelis' relationship to the world.[42] In a "real" society the connection between religious and cultural markers is more complex than in a minority situation. Cultural markers and religious markers are continually being connected and disconnected, secularized and made sacred, in a see-sawing that is never simple repetition. This is particularly true since the founding of the State of Israel suddenly and radically transformed the concept of diaspora. As a homeland is once more theirs, the diaspora is no longer central, and there are powerful tensions between religious universalism, diasporic Judaism and the territorialized nation-state, even if they are masked by the diaspora's overwhelming support for the State of Israel. But it is clear that an Israeli identity is developing which is not a simple subset of Jewish identity: for example, in May 2008, the Paris Salon du Livre invited Israeli writers to attend, but this meant authors writing in Hebrew (such as Sayed Kashua, who is an Arab and a Muslim) and not Jewish authors writing in languages other than Hebrew, even if they are Israeli citizens. And finally, a growing Israeli diaspora is forming in the United States, but these people do not mix with the Jewish American community.

It could be concluded from the above that the religious marker has been definitively reconnected to the cultural marker, to the detriment of the religious dimension, and that we are indeed witnessing a process of ethnicization of Jewish religion, given Jewish atheists' difficulty in disputing the religious marker. However, there are also examples of a new severing of links and there is evidence of an interesting recent development in the jostling between the two markers. It is this: in the association between the Jewish religious marker and the Jewish cultural marker, the Jewish religious marker is being replaced by a Christian marker. Jewish ethnic identity, signalled here by the practice of Hebrew, is claimed by two diametrically opposite Christian movements. Firstly, Jews for Jesus proclaim themselves to be entirely Jewish and entirely Christian; and then there is the emergence of a Hebrew-speaking Catholic Church, set up by Pope John Paul II, who placed at its head Bishop Gourion, a converted Jew. Breaking with the traditional association in the Middle East between the Latin Church and

Arab identity (embodied by the Latin patriarch of Jerusalem, who leads a Church that is both Catholic and Arab, therefore Palestinian), the Pope wanted to separate Oriental Christianity from Arabness by establishing a Hebrew Church. This eminently political move was possible precisely because there is a Hebrew-speaking Catholic population: spouses of Israeli Jews who have remained Christian, converted Jews and Arab Catholics who have become Hebrew speakers. Even if it is only a matter of a few hundred people, the symbolic aspect is important, and once again, very ambiguous: presented as support for Israel and, for the first time, as a recognition of Israel's territorial rootedness in the Middle East, the decision to found such a Church is tantamount to saying a person can be Israeli, of Hebrew mother tongue and also Catholic. This is a change from the traditional question of a Jew converting to Christianity, for the new convert remains, or at least wants to remain at the heart of the Jewish political and cultural community: the barrier between inside and outside the community created by the observance of Hebraic law disappears. The change of religious marker while retaining the same cultural content is profoundly new and doubtless destabilizing. It was possible to be a Jewish atheist, since that was not a challenge to the religious marker, but is it possible to be a Jewish Christian, a Jew for Jesus?

g) Religious Nationalisms

By religious nationalism, I mean when a religious institution identifies with a state and a people. It is more than simply a close link between Church and state, as was the case between the Spanish Catholic hierarchy and the state under Franco, or a strong link between a people and a religious identity (Irish or Quebecois Catholicism). It is when a religious institution embodies the soul of a people to the exclusion not only of other religions, but also of other peoples; consequently, this institution can only be closely bound up with the political authorities of the people in question, whatever the hierarchical link between the two (in particular religious and political leaders cannot be appointed without the other authority having a say, which has never been the case in Ireland, for example). This association can be virtual, when the people have no political existence; by way of anecdote, we could mention some Protestant Churches that pushed the principle of inculturation and indigenous theology so far that the religious community identified with the ethnic community: the evangelical Church of French Polynesia champions the identity and the culture of the Ma'ohi people and supports their independence movements.[43]

In the hijacking of religion by a an ethnico-political movement, it is often political actors who have "nationalized" a religion already in place, as is the case in Sri Lanka, where Buddhism became the Singhalese religion of identity, and where the clergy took up the Singhalese nationalist cause at the time of independence,[44] or that of Malaysia, where after independence Islam became the identity marker of the Malays and therefore of the new state (despite religious freedom being laid down in the constitution, which, according to jurisprudence, actually only concerns non-Malays, since a Malay cannot abandon Islam).[45]

But unquestionably the most explicit forms of religious nationalism are to be found in Christian orthodoxy, where the identification between Church and people relies on a close link with the state. In Christian orthodoxy, the link between Church and state goes back a long way: well before the end of the Latin Empire of Constantinople, the Byzantine emperors took the leadership of religious affairs in hand, intervening not only in the internal organization of the Church, but also in theological disputes (the one around Christology or during the iconoclast crisis). The Church as an institution then deployed itself within the political sphere.

Admittedly, this does not mean that Orthodox Christianity is "ethnic" in its religious vision: God's grace and the message are announced to the entire world. But concretely, when orthodoxy converted, it did so within the framework of empire: sixteenth- to nineteenth-century Russian orthodoxy conducted a vast missionary effort within the Russian Empire to create a parallel between the political order and the religious order (indigenous languages were set down using the Cyrillic alphabet, local priests were trained), but the missionary movement remained inward-looking towards the empire. In contrast to the Spain of the *Reconquista* however, Russian orthodoxy was not racialist, the convert was welcomed into the framework of the empire, and the Tatar nobility, which accepted baptism, became part of the Russian nobility (the Yusupov family, for example). But the ethnico-national nature of religion eventually prevailed. The autocephalous principle, which provided for each national Church to have its own patriarch even if the symbolic primacy of the Patriarch of Constantinople was

91

recognized, accentuated the identification between Church and nation to the extent that the transition from empire to nation-state (from the collapse of the Byzantine Empire to that of the Soviet Empire) went hand in hand with the proliferation of national autocephalous Churches which thus automatically became ethnic.

Let us take three typical examples:

Firstly, the Middle Eastern "Melchite" Orthodox Church (today the word "Melchite" also applies to Catholic Uniates), which is the Church of the Byzantine Empire ("Melchite" means "associated with the emperor"). Thus from the outset it was a "court" Church whose language was Greek, because Greek was the *lingua franca*, not because it was the language of a Greek "ethnic group". However, with the fall of the Byzantine Empire and the advent of nationalisms in the nineteenth century, Melchite orthodoxy gradually refocused around Hellenism, which prevailed as the national ideology in nineteenth-century Greece. "Greek" orthodoxy was the official religion of Greece. But what about the Melchites of the Eastern Mediterranean, most of them Arab, who suddenly came under the control of an ethnic clergy? Whereas the Greek Orthodox Church of the Middle East became Arabized, the Greek Orthodox patriarchate of Jerusalem remained Greek, and the prelates were all Greek citizens, whereas the worshippers were Palestinian Arabs.[46] But the high clergy of Greece flatly refused any openness to the Arabs, on the pretext of defending Hellenism. The fact that the Greek Orthodox Church was once multi-ethnic in the Middle East now looks like an accident of history in the face of today's closed ethnico-nationalist stance.

After the incorporation of Greece into the European Union, the country's Orthodox clergy waged endless battles for the link between Hellenism and Orthodoxy to be maintained (inclusion of religion on the identity card, refusing to allow a secular civil status, etc.). But this position has become increasingly untenable with regard to EU directives; and yet, the Greek supporters of a de-ethnicization of the Church are in a tiny minority.[47]

The same applies to Russia: the Russian patriarch wields his authority over all Russian Orthodox Churches, including those in exile. The October Revolution resulted in a split between the patriarchates, one remaining in the USSR and the other established in exile (the same split would divide the Armenian Church). But, whereas the so-called "white Russian" communities in the West clung to their Russian identity for a long time, non-Russians converted to Orthodoxy during the twentieth century, in France particularly, with a liturgy in vernacular language, and they do not see why they should have to declare themselves Russian, or choose between the existing ethnic patriarchates.

Lastly, the creation of independent states after the break-up of the USSR exacerbated the problem: as in a set of Russian dolls, each new country, even those sharing an Orthodoxy and sometimes a language, insists on having its own autocephalous patriarchate. The Macedonians and a Ukrainian faction, for example, respectively broke away from the Serbian and Russian patriarchates. The division of the Ukraine into two Orthodox patriarchates mirrors the division of the country into pro-Russians and pro-independence supporters: it is political, and not religious. The fact that the Bosnian Serbs claim to be followers of the Serbian patriarchate of Belgrade means primarily that they do not recognize themselves as Bosnians, but as Serbs. On the other side of the Orthodox world, Eritrea's independence from Ethiopia in 1993 resulted in a split in the Ethiopian Coptic patriarchate and the establishment of an Eritrean Coptic patriarchate in 2003.

Of course states encourage this quasi caesaropapism (whereby the head of state is also the head of the Church and supreme judge in religious matters) as well as the monopoly of the Orthodox Church; following the example of Muslim countries, they try to combat Protestant proselytism with laws on conversions or religious worship.[48] Russia introduced the concept of "national religions" into its Constitution (naming Orthodoxy, Islam, Buddhism and Lutheranism), on the principle of a parallel between ethnicity and religion (the Buryats are Buddhists, the Tatars Muslim, the Estonians Lutheran and the Russians Orthodox). So despite its claims to universalism, national Orthodox Christianity no longer converts, as it considers identity to be a combination of religion and culture. It is therefore fighting a defensive battle, maintaining the osmosis between national culture and religion at all costs. It is not missionary.

Any universalist religion can therefore transform itself into religion-as-identity, as exemplified by the Christians of the Orient, but this also applies to the Singhalese Buddhists, and in Malaysia, as a result of the equation constantly re-asserted by the courts between Malay and Muslim. The slide from universalism towards religion-as-identity is illustrated by a court ruling in December 2007 prohibiting the Catholic Malaysian *Herald* newspaper (which publishes in several languages, including Malay and English) from using the word "Allah" for "God", apparently in all the languages used, including Malay.[49] Out of a universal, a specific has been created regarding the use of the word "Allah". As illustrated by the Muslim profession of faith—"there is no God but God": the same word is used successively as a common noun and a proper noun, it is indeed the Arabic word for God—the one also used by the Christians of the Orient. Copyrighting God is truly emblematic of religion being kidnapped by culture.

Nationalism pushes the appropriation of religion to the extreme by defending a "national authenticity" which is expressed both in terms of culture and religion. We have already pointed out how authoritarian Islamist regimes use the words "culture" and "religion" interchangeably. It is also a way of opposing the values imported from the West, which are branded "American", "Catholic" or "Christian" depending on the situation.

Religion and Language Policy

Language is a fundamental identity-marker. The vehicle of a lay culture, its linguistic status is also connected to the political or social status of the group that speaks it, and it is modified by that group: a national language will be subject to an explicit standardization process, unlike patois. The terms language, patois and dialect are defined by the group's status, and not by the nature of their speech. The transition from dialect to spoken and later written language and lastly to the language of culture, *lingua franca* or sacred language, defines the status of those who speak it in profoundly different ways. Multilingualism nearly always implies a hierarchy between the languages spoken: in the 1950s, a Flemish Belgian or an Afghan Pashtun was bilingual, but their French or Persian-speaking fellow countryman was not. The term "regional language" implies that the speaker is bilingual *vis-à-vis* the national language, but that symmetry is extremely rare (Breton/French; Kurdish/Turkish; Catalan/Castilian). This situation is of course reversible, with some languages, becoming, at certain moments, transnational languages of culture (Greek, Latin, French, English, Arabic).

And finally, the setting down of a language in written form is a key status factor: a language that has no written form cannot become the mouthpiece for a written culture and certainly cannot be a language of political institutions. The status of a language can therefore change to

become a non-spoken sacred language (like Hebrew from the Hellen-
istic period until the creation of the Jewish homeland in Palestine, or
Latin after the fall of the Roman Empire), the language of the mainstream culture (Greek in the Eastern part of the Roman Empire), the
language of culture and state (modern French, English, German), or a
language with different registers (literary and vernacular, like Arabic).
The written form can moreover be accessible in varying degrees: sometimes it is monopolized by a body of scholars (hieroglyphs, Japanese
written in Chinese characters), and sometimes its use is democratic
(phonetic alphabets).

Religions have played a fundamental part in all these processes, but
it is an ambiguous role, since they are torn between the sacralization
of a privileged language (Hebrew, Arabic, Latin, Sanskrit) and the need
to use the vernacular to reach out to the masses. They tend both to
transpose the message into the vernacular languages, setting them
down in written form if need be, but also to retain control of the corpus by preserving it in a sacred language monopolized by the clerics. It
can be that a religion fits in with the state edifices of the time: for
example, the use of the "sacred" language as the chancery language (in
medieval Europe and in the Arab world). In contexts where writing is
taught only in religious schools (before the establishment or in the
absence of a secular education system), the sacred language also tends
to be the language of the scribe, the literati, the scholar, the state official, in other words the language of the state, or at least of its archives
(Hebrew—in competition with Aramaic—Latin in the medieval West,
written Arabic). The jurists of the French kings of the Middle Ages, the
Seljuk and Ottoman vizirs were clerics or *ulemas* (religious scholars):
both Robert de Sorbon (a French theologian, confessor to King Louis
IX, and founder of the Sorbonne) and Nizam ul Mulk (whose name
means "administrator of the realm") founded the "universities" of
their day within a religious framework.

The Catholic Church has been through phases of intensive translation (during the second half of the first millennium) to periods of censorship and back again to translation. Its reticence towards translation
is not related to the sacredness of the text (Latin is not the language of
revelation), but stems from the need to control what people read. The
issue was not the sanctity of the language but the authority of the
Church.[50] In 1199, Pope Innocent III prohibited lay people from reading the Bible. In 1210, the Synod of Paris banned the publication of

religious books in profane language (this measure was against the spread of mysticism among women of the nobility, who read and wrote French but not Latin; there is a similar relationship between Hebrew and Yiddish, which was initially the written language of women of good families who were prohibited from learning Hebrew). In 1408, the so-called Constitutions of Oxford prohibited translations of the Bible into English without the approval of the Church authorities:[51] John Wycliffe, and the pre-Reformation movement more widely, were the intended targets. Later Rome banned the reading of the Bible in common languages through the *Index of Prohibited Books* of 1559 and of 1564.[52]

But at the time when the Catholic Church was insistent in its ban on translations, Rome was forced to rethink, prompted by the wave of explorations and conquests that followed the discovery of America by Columbus and the need to regain the ground won by Protestantism. Conversely, during the same period, Protestants adopted a pragmatic attitude towards languages: for them, there was no longer a sacred language, since the "Word of God" went beyond all languages and could therefore take any language as a temporary and temporal vehicle. Thus, Catholics and Protestants alike opened up to languages, but for different reasons.

The concrete choices made at different times by different religions have had a fundamental impact on politics, ethnicization and cultures. The need to preach presupposes that preachers speak the language of the faithful, which amounts to giving enhanced status to profane languages serving as vehicles. They become written languages which, thus ennobled, are then transformed into channels for constructing a totally secular identity. There are several possible scenarios, veering from one extreme to the other: either the hegemony of a dominant language is associated with the "message" to be conveyed, or the dominated languages are transformed into written languages so they themselves can be a conduit for the message. While the effect on the salvation of souls may be similar, the two different scenarios have a diametrically opposite impact on politics, culture and the status of the elites. In general, religions spread the languages of the ruling powers (Spanish in Latin America, French in Africa, Arabic in North Africa). Present-day Protestant or Mormon evangelical missions often offer English lessons. The dominant language which is spread is not necessarily the "religious" language. This applies to English and also that of the Alliance Israélite

Universelle, founded in France at the close of the nineteenth century to help Oriental Jews: this organization worked in French and helped "Westernize" and Frenchify Oriental Jewish elites, often preparing them for emigration to France rather than to Palestine.

Religions also encouraged the development of non-state languages so as to reach out to new populations; in so doing, they offered these communities both the linguistic instrument of their political identity and a framework for their cultural and even political organization (a new "intelligentsia"). This was a frequent source of tension during the Western colonial period: sometimes the Church spread the language of the colonizer widely (as was usually the case), sometimes it worked to standardize and codify the indigenous languages, or to devise a more accessible alphabet (as with Vietnamese), and this effort in turn fuelled the politicization of national identities. This is how the Catholic Church helped to invent, standardize or simply spread alphabets reflecting the spoken language, whether it was still oral or transcribed in a scholarly form of writing (the Chinese characters of Vietnamese or Japanese). It was the Church that invented Cyrillic, transcribed Vietnamese into Latin, promoted the *kana* in Japanese (namely a more accessible written language, which until then had been the prerogative of women), spread the Korean *Hangul* (the Church adopted it but did not invent it) instead of the Chinese characters used by the mandarins and especially by the Buddhists.[53]

This attitude is governed by pragmatism, like that of Calvin who preferred to write in Latin but continued in French for pedagogical reasons. However, the consequences of these linguistic practices were considerable.

One of the paradoxes of universalist, Western Christianity is that on more than one occasion it has served as a means of empowerment (access to the levers of power rather than to power itself) of indigenous or minority elites, and it has helped create an ethnico-national identity based on resistance against the dominant state or against Western colonialism. The Catholic Church has often served as protection (even a refuge) for local languages and identities (Brittany, Ireland, the Basque Country, Alto Adige). It also provides the instruments for establishing cadres and social and political institutions in minority, indigenous or regional societies. First of all by setting down the language in written form, which results in the development of a category of literati and intellectuals educated in this language (teachers), but also political cadres whose future career is linked to their new ethnico-national identity. Priests and ministers often become the leaders of political movements (even if they have to relinquish their Church duties): in Tahiti, in Haiti, among the Karen of Burma, in South Africa (Bishop Tutu) and in the United States (for African-Americans). The Church helped create spaces for a local elite to develop outside national power networks; this goes from the Christian schools in the colonies to Christian trade unionism (likewise in France with the Jeunesse Ouvrière Chrétienne [Young Christian Workers—JOC] and the Jeunesse Agricole [Young Christian Farmworkers—JAC]). It thus explicitly used the concept of local culture, of popular culture, right across the political spectrum from right-wing Catholic Brittany to left-wing liberation theology.[54]

The Catholics also defended Quebecois identity. The Protestants did likewise in Tahiti: the evangelical Church of French Polynesia promoted the identity and culture of the Ma'ohi people, particularly in developing a theology of culture (championed by the anti-colonialist writer Turo Raapoto).[55]

Paradoxically, the missions therefore encouraged local nationalisms by contributing to the standardization and territorialization of identities, to the development of elites and the spread of a universalism that could be turned against the colonial power. The Vietnamese Marxists seized on the Jesuits' alphabet, which rid them both of the burden of the mandarins and the shadow of the Chinese civilization. Clearly this operation does not always result in the emergence of a new nation. In Nigeria, for example, Anglican leaders were keen to promote vernacular languages whereas the colonial authorities favoured English. But the Igbo dialects which these missionaries set down in written form with a view to creating a standard language, called Union Igbo, did not gain currency in the face of triple opposition (from the colonial authorities, Igbo intellectuals and the Catholic Church). Here again, these were tactical choices. The Catholic Church was effectively represented by the congregation of Fathers of the Holy Spirit, established in France, whose missionaries were very often German-speaking Alsatians, like Father Kirchner. One of its members, Father Aimé Ganot, had even published the first Igbo grammar, in 1899; and yet, the congregation chose English as the vehicle for evangelization.[56] The reason was that many indigenous families only sent their children to the missionary schools in the hope that they would learn English to help them climb the social ladder. In short, the appeal of the colonizer's language was so deeply rooted that it seemed counterproductive to preach in a local language.

Conversely, in India, the choice of a local oral language made it possible to isolate a subjugated group and reconstruct it as a Christian group. In helping to standardize a language common to several tribes by writing it down, the missionaries automatically prevented these tribes from being assimilated into mainstream Hinduism. First of all, through a process of linguistic acculturation, they helped to define a tribal identity that was not only linguistic but also political—for example by publishing newspapers, which was unthinkable before the language was standardized and written down. Besides, nobody could read or write this language and the missionaries took it upon themselves to teach it,[57] which went hand in hand both with the ethnicization process and with reforging the link between cultural markers and religious markers.

In France, during the Reformation, Protestant and Catholic elites both held on to Latin (Calvin preferred writing in Latin to French); however, they switched to the vernacular for reasons that were sometimes identical (to reach the people), intensified by the competition between the two Churches. The Catholic Church gradually lifted the prohibition on translating the Bible into lay languages.[58] The decline of Latin in favour of national languages, marked by the Edict of Villers-Cotterêts (1539), was not a consequence of the Reformation since it was beginning to happen throughout Europe. However, at that time Protestantism played a major part in standardizing and setting down major national languages, in opposition not so much to Latin but to dialects and regional languages; it promoted the spread of standardized national languages which would be helpful for building a central state. In this respect the importance of Martin Luther's translation of the Bible played a paramount role in standardizing literary High German, whereas the English of the King James Bible contributed not to standardizing the language, but to literary production, by providing a fund of literary references and expressions.[59] Less well known is the role the Reformation also played in spreading French in the Occitan-speaking region of France. Church ministers appear to have used French systematically rather than the local patois. The inspired prophets of the Cévennes, the Camisards, prophesied in French, when supposedly they did not speak it.[60] It is no coincidence that even today the Protestant mayors of Marseille (like Gaston Deferre) speak with a Northern French accent and the Catholics (like Jean-Claude Gaudin) with the accent of the south.

Conversely, without making a doctrine of it, the Catholic Church in France increasingly encouraged religious expression in the regional languages. This was principally because, from the 1789 Revolution onwards, these languages represented a refuge for Catholic identity from French, which was centralized and atheist (all of a sudden, whereas the Revolution explicitly condemned regional languages, the local Catholic clergy started promoting them).[61] In the seventeenth century the bishops of Mende and Auch had the catechism translated from French into local Occitan, with the aim of countering the Protestants active in the Cévennes and the Béarn.[62] It was the Jesuits who compiled the first Breton grammars in the eighteenth century, and a number of Basque and Breton grammars and dictionaries were written by canons and priests. The Bishop of Quimper, Joseph-Marie Graveran (1793–1855), approved the use of the transcription of Breton invented by Le Gonidec (who could afford to publish his New Testament in Breton with the support of a Protestant society, which underscores once again the Catholic Church's vacillation between the need to speak the vernacular and its wariness of translations of the Bible). Under the aegis of the Bishop of Quimper, the newspaper *Feiz a Breiz* (Faith and Brittany) was founded in 1865. More recently in September 2003, Bishop Gourvès of Quimper published a pastoral letter entitled "The renewal of Breton culture: a challenge for the Church". He stated in an interview: "When I was making preparations for the Pope's visit—he met each of the bishops who received him two or three times—I asked him why he placed so much emphasis on minorities, in his speeches and during his travels. He replied: we are moving towards globalization where everyone will be 'mixed together'; people are going to want to go back to their roots. In Brittany, you have these roots, as we do in Poland. Everything that happens on the cultural level that affects this minority seeking to express itself is important and can be a path to faith".[63] The Catholic Church's long-held position on territorialization and becoming rooted locally is now under threat from globalization.

However, pro-patois Catholics should not be placed in opposition to erudite Protestants. The Catholic Counter-Reformation reconquest drew on high culture and not on popular cultures.[64] The Church simply decided not to leave a single cultural niche unoccupied.

And so the entire cultural sphere has found itself caught up in the rivalry between Catholicism and Protestantism.

Whereas the "sacred" language can be reserved for "sacred" use (liturgical but also political), the lay language, standardized and set down in written form and using the alphabet of the sacred language if need be (Yiddish, Persian, Urdu, Osmanli), serves as a medium for lay literature, particularly since the sacred language is reserved for the production of religious works, leaving the profane space open. That is how Yiddish spread initially as a written language because it peddled a lay literature (tales of chivalry) from the outside, aimed at a new readership that had no access to Hebrew, the only written language of letters.[65] Meanwhile, Persian spread in the field of poetry (Rudaki, Ferdowsi) because for a long time educated Persian speakers and religious thinkers including Avicenna wrote their philosophical and theological works in Arabic. But in becoming autonomous, this lay literature helped divide the religious marker from the cultural marker, and there comes a point where the religion no longer recognizes itself in the culture it has spawned.

In the Muslim sphere, neither the ruling powers nor the religious authorities had a language policy. The prestige of Arabic was such that it modified the existing languages, imposed its alphabet and infused its vocabulary without the need to legislate or issue decrees. Turkish, Persian and Hindi have become Arabized and Islamized at the same time, thus helping to give a strong cultural coherence to a Muslim world which extends from Morocco to India and Central Asia. Populations which have never been under Arab political control have adopted the Arabic alphabet and incorporated a considerable number of Arabic words into their vocabulary, going well beyond the purely religious or administrative fields (this applies to the Uighurs and the Kazakhs for example, even if the influence of Arabic is exerted through Persian). The use of a common terminology and alphabet truly has created a common cultural sphere.

These days, when there is more talk than ever of a Muslim civilization and a Muslim world, this common universe of meaning has been linguistically destroyed by state secularization policies carried out since 1920, dressed up in various ideological justifications. Post-1918, radically different regimes—the Soviet Union, Kemalist Turkey, imperial Iran—all implemented a similar language policy, based on the double imperative of "de-Arabizing" and "de-Islamizing". In several cases, a new alphabet was introduced (USSR, Turkey, Xinjiang in China), archaic words were reinstated (Iran, Turkey), loan translations and neologisms were incorporated, there were borrowings from Western languages (Russian for the USSR). And it was not just a question of religion: in the 1930s, the Arabic word for aeroplane *(tayyara)*, initially common to the entire Muslim sphere, became respectively *havap-eyma*, *uçak* and *samoliot* in Iranian Persian, Turkish and the Soviet languages of Central Asia. In the 1980s, The Turkish embassy in Paris intervened remorselessly in order to persuade INALCO (the Institute for Oriental Languages and Civilizations) to stop teaching Turkish within the same department as Arabic, which presupposed a common core Islamology syllabus. Nowadays, students of Turkish have no compulsory courses on Islamology or Middle Eastern culture. There is definitely a performative dimension to these policies: they represent a departure from the past and although those responsible for this decision claim only to be observing developments, the result is a severance.

The elimination of religious markers in Oriental languages, apart from Arabic, was a relative success, recently resulting in a voluntarist return of this marker among religious activist speakers of those languages. Religious markers, formerly embedded in the language, became floating once more. Speakers of the language used them as explicit elements of religious identification as opposed to them simply being part of communication, as with the greeting *salaam-u-alaikum*, for example.

Two languages in particular encountered a problem with their own secularization: Arabic and Hebrew. Considering Arabic as the language of the Qur'an poses the problem of the sacredness of language: if the Qur'an is "uncreated"—i.e. it existed before being revealed—then the Arabic in which it is written is also a sacrosanct, untouchable language. The book by Taha Hussein, *Pre-Islamic Poetry*, was censored in 1926 by the University of Al Azhar precisely because it posited the profane autonomy of the Arabic language. Christian Arabic writers' attempts to develop a "literary" and no longer "literal" Arabic were greeted with suspicion by Muslim religious authorities who, in Sheikh Tantawy's words, rejected the "Christianization of Islam"—which is tantamount to qualifying, in religious terms, what is nothing other than the shifting of Arabic towards the lay.[66] In 1981, again in Egypt, the book by Fikri Al Aqad, *History of the Arabic Language*, was banned. The effect of today's hardline attitude towards the uncreated nature of the Qur'an, linked to the growth of Salafism, has been to sacralize Arabic even more and to interpret any over-profane use as a sort of blasphemy. Censorship, official or otherwise, of novels and short stories written in Arabic has increased, particularly in Egypt: the Egyptian author Farag Foda was assassinated in 1992, after being declared an apostate by Al Azhar; in 2000, the Syrian writer Haydar Haydar saw his book *A Banquet for Seaweed* banned in Egypt. Of course, the threats are also aimed at authors who do not write in Arabic, as the Salman Rushdie affair shows, or that of exiled Bangladeshi feminist writer Taslima Nasreen, but these international cases with a high media profile mask the reality of a much wider censorship of books published in Arabic. There was no campaign against the translations into foreign languages of the *Thousand and One Nights*, but the Arabic edition was banned in 1985 in Cairo by the official authorities, as if, fundamentally, the fact of writing "lay literature" in Arabic was an aggravation.

An astounding number of Arabic authors write today in other languages—in English, like Ahdaf Soueif, Laila Lalami *(Other Dangerous Pursuits)*, Hisham Matar *(In the Country of Men)*; in French, including Driss Chraïbi, Tahar Ben Jelloun, Fouad Laroui, Rachid Mimouni, Amin Maalouf; and in Dutch, for example Hafid Bouazza, Abdelkader Benali, Mustapha Stitou; Sayed Kashua writes in Hebrew *(Dancing Arabs)* and has never been translated into Arabic. For many of these authors, one of the reasons for their choice of language is the discrepancy between classical and spoken Arabic, as described by Kashua.[67] However, it is a subject that is politically taboo: Arab States refuse, for political reasons, to take spoken Arabic into account. Drawing their legitimacy either from pan-Arabism, or, nowadays, increasingly from the prevailing Islamo-nationalism, they need to uphold the myth of the "Arab nation" by referring to the sacred character of the language and not to its diversity.

Suddenly, the "profane" is expressed in dialect or in other languages. Authors who claim a non-religious Arabness have difficulty in becoming established. This perhaps explains the appearance of the concept of "Muslim atheist" promoted by the Tunisian-born French writer Abdelwahhab Meddeb to take into account the pervasiveness of the religious reference in modern Arab literary culture.[68] But ultimately, in turning it on its head, is he not echoing the religious question: can there not be any form of Arabness except through Islam?

After the publication of a report by the United Nations Development Programme (UNDP) in 2002, there was a sudden awareness that there was a crisis in Arab literary culture in the second half of the twentieth century.[69] The fact that the entire Arab world translated only 20 per cent of the books that Greece alone translated in a year is not attributable to Islam, since both Turkey and Islamic Iran are much more active when it comes to translations. Furthermore, it is sufficient to look at the list of teaching staff in American and British universities to see the number of people of Arab origin who are present in the intellectual and cultural spheres. The awareness is also illustrated by the sudden appearance, after 2001 (for there is an established link between radicalization and cultural crisis), of foundations to promote secular Arab culture, a departure from all the efforts of the institutes supported by the Saudis to promote the concepts of "Islamic sciences", "Islamic finance" or "Islamic culture".

After the huge wave of re-Islamization both top-down and bottom-up, it would seem that after 11 September 2001 we witnessed the beginnings of a voluntarist secularization process spearheaded by some governments and institutions. An observation I made in the past seems to be increasingly accepted nowadays: it is not the clash of cultures but the deculturation of religion which is the source of violence.[70] In January 2007, the ruler of Dubai, Sheikh Mohammed bin Rashid al-Maktoum, announced that he was establishing a 10 billion dollar fund to promote the development of culture and "knowledge". He spoke of the development of a "knowledge society". But nothing was said on the issue of language. It was chiefly a matter of information technology, Internet and technology. Now the language for the advance of these fields is English. At the same time, the Emirates are pursuing an arts development policy by financing museums such as the Abu Dhabi Louvre. The aim is to encourage the fine arts in the Arab world by departing from the "Islamic arts" / "popular folklore" dichotomy found in local museums until now. But the development of the fine arts also supposes a degree of democratization and the removal of religious censorship, which still remains something of a challenge. Lastly, the language question remains open: since 2002, the Emirates have launched initiatives to support fiction writing in Arabic (establishment of the International Prize for Arabic Fiction and the Sheikh Zayed Prize, while a wealthy Egyptian entrepreneur, Karim Nagy has launched the Kalima project to translate international works into Arabic).

Cultural secularization involves the autonomization of a vernacular language which, until now, had remained incomplete for Arabic. But neo-fundamentalism also needs this autonomization in order to prosper, since it is both an agent and product of deculturation. That is why Islamic neo-fundamentalism had no difficulty in adapting to foreign languages; it uses Arabic as a sort of religious marker that serves to give emphasis to a speech in English or French by peppering it with incantations or non-translated expressions. As a result of globalization, in Islam more perhaps than in other religions, the dissolution of the very close link between language and the sacred results in a greater symbolic violence, due to the lay language not having sufficient autonomy. Salafism then becomes a very powerful instrument of deculturation. And that is the paradox of the Arab world: whereas this very close link between language and religion should have led to a strong reaffirmation of cultural identity, the crisis of culture automatically results in a crisis of religion, which then transposes itself not into a new culture but into a violent form (in any case symbolically) of deculturation, embodied by Salafism. That is why the reculturation of Arabic through the development of a lay (but not necessarily anti-religious) literature is certainly one element of a deradicalization policy. It remains to be seen whether this development can take place from the top down and as a result of financial incentives. For literature is not a technical subject: it is the expression of real-life individuals.

This same tension is found in Judaism, but it is resolved differently. When Hebrew and then Aramaic ceased to be spoken languages, they became sacred languages, monopolized by the religious sphere and were therefore not a suitable medium for a lay literature. Of course, the Jews adopted profane vernacular languages which could act as a vehicle for popular literature. But among these languages, Yiddish had a particular destiny.[71] It became independent of German because it became the language of the Jews in a non-Germanic context (Baltic, Slav or Romanian); and it was written in the Hebrew alphabet and then became the medium for a lay literature. Initially, the religious authorities objected to it, even if they then used it for educational purposes to reach those who did not have access to Hebrew (women especially). Up to this point, the scenario is shared by Ladino, the language of the Jews expelled from Spain who settled in the Ottoman Empire.

But with the phenomenon of the *Haskala* (Enlightenment) and leaving the ghetto, the choice was between adopting the language of the country ("real" German, Russian, Polish, etc.), at the expense of Yiddish, and confining Hebrew to the sacred, or making Yiddish an ethnic language, the language of the Jews, by placing it on the same level not as Hebrew but as German or Russian. Beyond the controversy which divided the elites, Yiddish effectively became not only the vehicle for a rich lay culture, by becoming divorced from the sacred Hebrew language, which was reserved for study and the liturgy, but also by rejecting the assimilation that adopting the major European languages would entail.

However, the paradox of Yiddish is that the autonomization of a lay language was spurred by two diametrically opposed movements, even if they both originated in the ultra-orthodox Jewish communities of Central and Eastern Europe.

On the one hand, Yiddish was promoted by nationalist secular Jewish intellectuals, typified by the Bund movement. They were ethnic anti-Zionist nationalists, and generally socialists. For them, Europe was the home of the Jewish nation as a non-territorial community group, with its language, culture and institutions (it was half-way between the secularized model of the Ottoman *millet* and British, or rather Canadian-style multiculturalism). The transition from religion to culture happened in Yiddish.

On the other hand, Yiddish was also promoted by the ultra-orthodox Haredim and Hasidim, who refused assimilation, just like the ethnic nationalists, but who considered that religion is central to Jewish identity. Simply, for them, the fact that Hebrew was the sacred language prohibited its lay use, which would sully it (this position still has its adherents today), and therefore the purpose of Yiddish was to be a lay language so as to preserve the sacred language instead of vying with it.[72]

A third group, that of the Zionists, initially hostile to the revival of Hebrew as a spoken language (Herzl was for a multilingual Israel on the model of Switzerland, where the Jews would speak their various European languages), quickly came round to the solution of modern Hebrew, the national language no longer of the "Jewish people" but of the State of Israel, defined as ethnically Jewish and religiously secular. The Hebrew language was therefore secularized by Zionism, before becoming the medium for a rich lay literature. Yiddish as the language of a lay literature (which was prolific) did not survive the Holocaust. But it survived as a vernacular language in the case of the Haredi Jewish communities who have maintained it as a lay language, so as not to de-sacralize Hebrew through day-to-day use: it is therefore defined as profane by an attitude that is first and foremost religious, and that is precisely what prevents it from being the vehicle of an autonomous literature. It is out of the question for the Haredim to produce culture outside religious didacticism; for these same communities are opposed to everything that would constitute a secular cultural output: novels, plays, poetry, television, cinema. Therefore, all that remains is educational literature (God-fearing novels).

Religions thus create profane culture, since they build tools which then function outside the religious framework. But it is this link which modern-day religious revivalism is calling into question. It remains to be seen how and why.

4

CULTURE AND RELIGION

THE DIVIDE

When Believers and Non-Believers Share the Same Culture

a) The Impossibility of a "Religious Society"

Religion creates culture, most of the time implicitly, because religion is also lived as a culture. It is inevitable that religion has a cultural "spin-off", for no society can maintain itself solely on the basis of an explicit belief. Governance can function only if the prevailing religion develops as a culture—in other words as a symbolic, imaginary system that legitimates the social and political order but does not make faith a condition of communal life. It is conformity, not faith, that forms the basis of a society; that is the difference between a community and a society.

But contrary to beliefs about religious ideologies, a faith community never is and never can be a true society, for such a community presupposes either that the citizen is profoundly and always religious (which cannot be maintained by coercion and therefore relies on the individual, in other words the political, and not on God's transcendence), or that religion is divested of its entire religious dimension in favour of external norms. That is what I set out to demonstrate with regard to Islam in *The Failure of Political Islam*.[1] In the Prophet's era, the community, which serves as a nostalgic paradigm for the advocates of an "Islamic state", had no option but to transform itself into a "real" society in order to survive: what is described as a fall or decline is the inevitable consequence of political success. That is why there is never any real competition between religious loyalty (ultramontanism towards the Vatican, the Islamic *ummah*, Jews and Israel) and national loyalty. A community is no more a society than a society is a community (even if it likes to think of itself as one), as Max Weber pointed out by making a distinction between *Gesellschaft* and *Gemeinschaft*, and as the anthropologist Maurice Godelier demonstrates:[2] what is true of anthropological communities (based on relations of kinship), is also true of religious communities. This also applies to Calvinist Protestant communities that were unable to transform themselves into proper states, despite having controlled towns such as Geneva or Boston.[3] A society is based on sovereignty, starting with the appropriation of a territory. A society is first of all political, never religious, even if it calls on religion to legitimize power relations. And that is why the appearance of religion in the political sphere creates so much tension: because it cannot succeed. Religion's slide towards culture is therefore a form of domestication and instrumentalization: this explains the apparently paradoxical position of non-believers or agnostics who praise religion, from the anti-Dreyfusard journalist Charles Maurras to Nicolas Sarkozy.

The failure of politico-religious societies (American Puritans, Iran's Islamic Revolution) derives from the fact that they are officially unaware of their true means of operation (along political lines) in favour of a discourse on the leaders' and the citizens' virtue, and therefore the presumed non-virtue of any opponents, who are dismissed as unbelievers. This phenomenon of exclusion of the other in the name of purity also occurs in revolutionary ideologies: purity of class or purity of race. These are untenable systems, from Savonarola's Florence to the Khomeinist Revolution, including Calvin's Geneva; and this effective reduction to the temporal ultimately produces secularizations.[4] The tension between politics and religion cannot be resolved by establishing a "religious" political system.

In order to endure, a society cannot rely solely on the explicit, but must build itself on the implicit and the unspoken, even if there is a consensus on the core values (which is not always the case). It must accept and not diminish its marginal elements, deviances and othernesses—from the brothel to carnival, from homosexuality to drug or alcohol use. This was often the role fulfilled by "popular culture", which also functioned as a regulatory system as it provided an outlet and the opportunity for mockery without challenging the established order. In modern consumer societies, "diversionary" practices also serve to subvert the ruling order.[5] The problem is managing, not restricting, the marginal elements: places of transgression (red-light districts), moments of transgression (holidays, carnivals), marginal elements, as well as private life and political opposition. There is no culture unless such spaces exist.

Societies that claim to be religious above all suppress these marginal elements and deviations, and are therefore condemned to permanent instability, as the demand for purity puts each person in a precarious and untenable position. These are societies rife with doubt and suspicion, and therefore fear (as in the Stalinist Communist systems where any hero can become a traitor). After the Wars of Religion in Europe, the idea that to be loyal, the subject must share the sovereign's religion (one law, one faith, one king), persisted for a long time, an idea confirmed both by the Edict of Nantes and its revocation, but here this religious affiliation is purely nominal, it does not imply piety.

The conviction that all members of a society must explicitly share one belief system is absurd and can only result in permanent coercion. While lamenting the lack of faith, traditional (non fundamentalist) religion is more realistic in substituting conformity for conviction, and organizing this in its own way. This is what the whole debate around *takfir* (declaring apostate a Muslim whose acts are in violation of the faith) in Islam, and confession in Christianity is about. Depending on whether it is upheld in private (Catholicism) or the subject of a public avowal (early Protestantism), the relationship between personal faith and the public person is totally different (and this legacy is apparent in the American taste for public confession, now televised). In the early days of Christianity, penitence was public and forgiveness was granted only once; this stopped when Christianity became a mass religion. Private confession (in the ear of the priest) represents a relaxing of discipline, and was introduced when "Christianity" was at its peak (in the twelfth and thirteenth centuries), i.e. when everyone was "assumed" to be Christian. Henceforth, in Catholicism, there was a complex "management" of transgression: description, categorization (list of sins), grading, confessional techniques (confessor's manuals), atonements, indulgences, forgiveness, repentance, etc. It was a question of avoiding the all-or-nothing approach, which is precisely what Calvin was to advocate. Protestantism's desired utopian return to the source also implied a return to discipline.

The same applies to *takfir* in Islam, which makes simple social conformism impossible since it demands from all a manifest faith and practice. Terrorist movements are quite naturally "takfirist", whereas *takfir* is banned in Islamic Iran precisely for reasons of governance. In Judaism, the question of an outward display of explicit faith occurs regularly in Israel insofar as conversion, which guarantees access to citizenship, is entrusted to orthodox rabbis. In May 2008, the Ashdod Rabbinical Court decided to nullify the conversions carried out by Rabbi Haim Druckman, because the outward behaviour of one of the converted women was not in keeping with her purported religious convictions.[6] Such a decision suddenly makes the concept of citizenship more fragile: the Great Rabbinate therefore endeavoured to revoke it, more out of concern to maintain public order than because of the fundamental issue at stake.

If traditional religious societies are only held together by formal adhesion which is often simply conformism (and the other side of the coin, hypocrisy), it is also because they see real transgression only in the exception, i.e. scandal and therefore spectacular punishment, which then becomes another form of exceptionality. It would be mistaken to think that, in a society steeped in the cultural manifestations of religion, everything is religious. In a way, it could even be said that the profane and/or secular sphere is more developed in such a society, since the question of frontiers does not arise except in the scandal of the exceptional transgression. There is no paradox in seeing extreme punishment going hand in hand with a demand for extreme proof in many religions, which makes the application of penalties (outside a specific political context) almost impossible: the *hudud* laws in Islam, which entail the death sentence and amputation, are very difficult to apply, or they fulfil the desire to set an example in a context that is primarily political. The courts of the Catholic Inquisition adhered strictly to procedure. The Inquisition was a demand for conformity (but also for the eradication of the enemy within), which targeted specific categories of people (in general the *conversos*). The most shocking aspect of the execution of the Chevalier de la Barre, who was tortured and put to death in 1766, in Paris, for not having removed his hat during a procession of the Blessed Sacrament, was the discrepancy between the offence and the punishment. This discrepancy is explained by the fact that the sentence was not due to a sincere indignation at the religious transgression, but to the political will of a Gallican Paris Parliament that wanted to demonstrate that it was better equipped than the Church to defend the symbols of Christianity.

Religion's extension or dilution (depending on one's point of view) within culture makes all the more sense in that religion itself creates the instruments for its transformation into culture, even if it uses existing operators (what I referred to earlier as formatting). Secularization in the strict sense in no way implies a conflict or a brutal separation from religion, as can be seen from the examples of Northern Europe, the USA, Great Britain, and even Thailand and Japan. Nor is the separation between Church and state necessarily a conflict between culture and religion conceived as two different belief systems, secularized or religious, as is also evidenced by the case of the USA. Moreover, numerous Gallicans were and are devout believers (General de Gaulle could doubtless be placed in this category).

b) Orthopraxy: When Secular and Religious Parties Agree on what is Good

Secularization does not necessarily imply a conflict, or even a breakaway from religion. A secularized society can remain in step with religious culture and values. Secularization affects faith, but not necessarily values, and when it is political (separation of religion and state), it does not automatically involve a debate on moral values: supporters of the clergy and anticlericals can share the same conception of morality, and changes in practice do not automatically result in a conflict between religion and culture.

The words "divorce" and "split" apply when believers and non-believers no longer find themselves with a shared "orthopraxy", even if for different reasons. Likewise, to use the word coined by Danièle Hervieu-Léger, we speak of "exculturation" when believers no longer identify with the surrounding culture, and when this culture no longer accepts religion.[7]

In many secularized societies, including republican France of the nineteenth and the first half of the twentieth century, the opposition between believers and atheists did not necessarily hinge on the issue of values, since they shared the same orthopraxy. The non-believer did not assert different values, but on the contrary claimed to be as "moral" (if not more so than) the man of religion, suspected of hypocrisy. The morality (the "morality of our fathers"), which Jules Ferry, France's

Minister of Education, included in the curriculum of the secular educational system he made compulsory in 1881, was not so far removed from Christian morality; as a matter of fact, it is a fundamental principle of this secular morality to be consensual and not to promote values that are antagonistic to religious values. Already the Napoleonic Code had a Christian vision of the family (on adultery, marital sin), which lasted until the end of the twentieth century, i.e. well after secularism had been enshrined as a constitutional principle. A woman was deemed "loose" irrespective of religious beliefs: the concept of "moral standards" was laid down in the law of the secular republic and in the administrative circulars of Republican France. In the 1920s, the vote for an anti-abortion law in France met with a certain consensus and certainly did not set believers against secular voters: there was strong pro-life support on the left (in the 1960s Jeannette Vermersch, partner of Maurice Thorez, first secretary of the Communist Party, took a stance against the liberalization of contraception). The idea that women were different from men and found fulfilment in motherhood prevailed in mainstream culture in the France of the Third Republic.

In many of today's Muslim societies, there is a similar consensus on values and norms—a consensus that owes little to explicit reference to *sharia* law.[8] Orthopraxy here derives not from a religious practice or from an ideological demand, but from a consensus on what constitutes a shared horizon of intelligibility, which largely explains why the incantatory reference to *sharia* law generally goes alongside an indifference towards its actual implementation. Hence *sharia* is never (and never has been) fully applied, for the reasons we have continually underlined: the community of the Prophet's era was a religious community and, when it later became a political society, this was part of a political process which meant that no ruler could accept the complete autonomy of *sharia*. The ruler therefore sought to curtail it in two ways: by restricting its sphere of application (in general to personal status, family law, and possibly some penal regulations), or by codifying it along the lines of Western positive law, so as to include it in the field of state law (the Ottoman *mecele* or *mejele* Code, which remains in evidence to some degree in the legal systems of the various Arab countries). Any demand for the application of *sharia* in its entirety means an end to the political authority's autonomy, which is the aporia or insoluble contradiction inherent in the concept of the "Islamic state".

So where does the "demand for *sharia*" come from? From two very different places: firstly, from a fundamentalist impetus that is tantamount to refusing all references to history and culture, and therefore reduces social life entirely to a system of explicit norms; and secondly, by contrast, from a cultural orthopraxy, for which *sharia* is a virtual horizon of intelligibility and no longer a specific code. Beaudouin Dupret and Jean-Noël Ferrié's research shows that the Egyptians invoke *sharia*[9] but practise it very little (no stoning, for example); it is a (very) pious hope, which is associated with the definition of a concept of "civility" (Ferrié) and not with a legal code.

If the reference to shared values is understood as a horizon of intelligibility and not as a set of explicit norms to be implemented by all possible means (legal and political), then conflicts of norms are manageable, whether they concern the question of brothels in a traditional Catholic society (where their acceptance has nothing to do with a relaxation of morals), or the contradiction between the Pashtun tribal code *(pashtunwali)* and *sharia*. The discrepancy between the norm and practice is experienced in a horizon of intelligibility which goes beyond it: I am a practising Catholic, but I can sin; I am Muslim, but I can be a bad Muslim. There is nothing schizophrenic about it. Conversely, with the arrival of the Taliban or of a Savonarola, condemned to death in 1498 for defying papal authority, everything changes: the norm is explicit and must be universally applied.

The problem comes from the break with orthopraxy and the weakening of the horizon of intelligibility. That is when the ties between religion and culture are severed: in the eyes of religion, culture ceases to be profane and becomes pagan.

The exculturation of religion is a key development in the present-day evolution of religion. It is both a consequence and an instrument of globalization and it largely explains the success of fundamentalist forms of religion. It has nothing to do with acculturation: this is not the clash between different cultures, it is a separation of culture and religion.

Divorce: Culture as Neo-Paganism

The exculturation of religion occurs when the religious norm breaks away from culture.[10] For religion, culture suddenly appears as paganism and no longer merely as a profane or secular reality, borne by religion like the shadow of itself.

This happens in societies which have undergone a process of secularization. But there is no automatic link between exculturation and secularization. A secularized society can remain culturally religious, and exculturation can occur in societies which claim still to be profoundly religious but which no longer place this religion within the framework of a complex traditional culture, as is the case in the countries of Muslim culture. The divorce between religion and culture can therefore occur outside the classic secularization process.

In November 2007, the Moroccan press reported on a video circulating on the Internet, showing a "homosexual marriage" in the town of Ksar el Kebir: a man dressed as a woman is dancing surrounded by guests. There was a huge scandal. However it was more likely that the video showed a traditional exorcism ceremony during the festival of the local "saint" Sidi Madloume. We are therefore on the hitherto acceptable margins of a tradition that is supposed to be religious, perhaps also linked to *gnawi* music (practised for a very long time by the descendents of the Guinean slaves whose lineage lives on today). Suddenly, something that was both marginal and accepted becomes the subject of scandal and is no longer understood as the expression of a popular culture on the margins (margins in every sense of the word: social, as it is associated with bad boys and the socially relegated; psychiatric, as it is linked to healing; and lastly religious as it is connected to "the worship of a saint" which the dominant Salafism condemns). First of all, marginality no longer exists, because the ceremony filmed by a participant was immediately put on YouTube and widely broadcast: through technology, the incident was decontextualized and globalized. It was then interpreted through explicit norms, both neo-fundamentalist and Western—the condemnation of homosexuality, but homosexuality as defined by the West (referring not to the act but to the nature of the persons committing it). It is only in recent years that the debate on the legalization of "homosexual marriage" has gripped Western countries and become an election issue: but it has immediately spread around the entire world as a universal paradigm, devoid of any religious, cultural or simply legal context.

What is the legal definition of marriage? Marriage, in Islamic law, is a simple contract which is closer to the French PACS (civil contract between two partners, though irrespective of gender in the latter case) than to the secularized form of Christian marriage, which remains rooted in Napoleonic-type law. However, this "Western" marriage symbolism suddenly becomes a universal form which stifles both Islamic law and the local cultural imagination. Simultaneously, the explicit Islamic religious norm, Salafist in this case, effects the same operation: erasing the local cultural imagination and espousing this legal concept of Western marriage. The imagination vanishes behind the reality of a symbolic system. The implicit is commanded to be explicit: for many Moroccans, if what they see on the video seems to them to be contrary both to their religion and their culture, it is precisely because the religious norm has erased the cultural imagination. The Internet creates a uniform, undifferentiated space, open to the gaze of everyone. There is no longer a centre or margins, no more gradation or variation of the norm on the one hand, or, more importantly, on the other, the norm is defined as a religious and universal norm based on a paradigm ("homosexual marriage") borrowed from the modern-day West.

So it is not a secularization process that makes such a ceremony seem strange in the eyes of Moroccan public opinion, but a neo-fundamentalist process, in other words one of asserting universal and abstract religious norms, divorced from any cultural context. The knowledge of a popular culture has suddenly disappeared. But these norms are also summary, very poor reconstructions, where religion is no longer founded on knowledge but on a mere normative code (do/ don't do, *halal/haram*). We are aware of the extent to which fundamentalism of any kind ultimately rejects the complexity of all religious learning. Holy indignation is indeed holy ignorance.

This phenomenon of exculturation is even stronger in secularized societies, since the profane has lost its religious associations. Religion then has difficulty in reconnecting with a society now posited as an otherness. The cultural and the religious markers are disconnected. The need to rebuild itself within the purity of faith alone spurs the religious community voluntarily to sever the religious markers from a culture deemed pagan, and to then attempt to monopolize them. The community lives as a minority, even if the religion it claims is sociologically dominant—which is the case of Protestantism in the United States and Islam in the Middle East.

In June 1997, the Catholic patriarch of Venice, Bishop Scola, demanded the withdrawal of the dance performance *Messiah Games* by Felix Ruckert from the Venice Biennale, for in his view it was a sado-masochist interpretation of *The Passion of Christ*. In February 2005, an association close to the French episcopate, *Croyances et Libertés*

(Beliefs and Freedom), succeeding in persuading the courts to ban an ad by the fashion designers Marithé and François Girbaud, which featured Leonardo da Vinci's *The Last Supper*, replacing the apostles with scantily clad young women. The court acknowledged the damage suffered by a community of people whose feelings might be wounded: the argument was not that of blasphemy (which does not exist in French law), but of *pretium doloris* (tort) and of anti-racism, in other words of the defence of a group defined by race, religion or sexual orientation. This ruling was quashed at appeal. It is interesting because it disconnects the cultural marker from the religious marker. The community of believers sees itself as having a sort of copyright on the religious marker, in this instance the *mise en scène* of a sacred text, whereas Leonardo da Vinci's painting supposedly belongs to a shared artistic heritage.

This is a problem, since either these religious symbols (*The Last Supper*) are universal and belong to Western culture, or they are specific to the community of believers, represented by an institution, the Catholic Church. But in a society like that of Europe, where art and religion have been profoundly interconnected, religious symbols belong to believers and non-believers alike. A living culture is constantly the subject of subversions, reversals and re-interpretations, even in its most trivial aspects (such as Quebecois swear words).

However, in recent years, the Vatican has systematically been reminding us of Europe's Christian origins, and Christian Democrat MEPs demanded that these Christian roots be mentioned in the preamble to the future European Constitution. But to say that there is a shared heritage is to permit anybody and everybody to appropriate it, including for the purposes of mockery, or regrettably for commercial reasons. The protest against commercialization extends beyond Catholic activist groups. If the advertising world seized on *The Last Supper*, it is because *The Last Supper* resonates with us. This subversion is a homage to the familiarity of religious references (an ad of this kind would make no sense in Yemen, for example). Banning the ironic or even blasphemous use of a religious paradigm amounts to excluding it from the cultural arena to locate it solely in that of the sacred. It then becomes the exclusive property of the community of believers, which demands to be recognized as such. It is no longer culture that forms the basis of identity, it is faith alone. The "pure" religion is the one that breaks away from all cultural references. In appropriating the management of religious symbols, the Church asserts the opposite of what it intended to say in insisting on the importance of Christian culture in Europe. It is no longer defending a universality (even if it does think that its particularism has a universal value), but an inward-looking minority community, and it has to ask the law to protect the sensibilities of its members. This communitarian mindset is similar to that of those seeking to defend gay rights or ban sexist jokes. Its action is consistent with what has been observed in the religious arena, starting with Islam: religious revivalism flourishes by separating religion and culture, isolating religious markers from any social context and establishing a definitive division between believers and non-believers, apostates and sceptics. But the Christian culture, to which Europe can justifiably lay claim, has little in common with a faith that is pure and therefore very fragile and comes begging for the protection of the courts. Religion has just broken away from culture: the Church has become an agent of secularization.

Examples can also be found in the Muslim world. One of the strangest of these is the prohibition of Christians using the word "Allah" for "God" by the Malaysian Interior Minister. The word is reserved for the Muslims' God. But in Arabic, Allah means God in general, as is clear from the use of the word by Arab Christians. Here too the religious marker is severed from its cultural usage (in this case linguistic) and seized upon by a religion seeking to affirm its identity.

Thus the ambient culture is perceived by believers as a threat to religion; a permanent blasphemy. This exculturation of religion is a two-way process: religion loses its cultural foothold, and culture forgets its religious sources and all lay religious knowledge. Whereas in today's Muslim world it is frequent to meet secular intellectuals, even publicly declared atheists such as Abdelwahhab Meddeb, one of France's most respected Muslim writers, have been imbued with a solid religious culture—this is hardly the case any longer in the ex-Christian West. The anti-clericalists of the nineteenth century had a religious culture, often because they themselves came from religious backgrounds (Catholic secondary schools, schools run by educational religious congregations including the Jesuits); on the other hand, the late twentieth-century agnostics are often more indulgent towards a religion which they see as incongruous, strange, exotic or excessive rather than threatening—as attested by the popularity of John Paul II—since it is alien to them. It is no coincidence that since the end of the twentieth century there has been a debate in France as to whether religion can be taught from a profane or secular standpoint, since effectively there is no longer a lay knowledge of religion. There is a paradox: those who return to religion, as converts or as born-agains, do so without religious knowledge, which they may or may not subsequently acquire, but it will be a knowledge divorced from any cultural context. The erosion of religious knowledge in fundamentalist circles is particularly striking.

Culture That Has Forgotten its Religious Roots

A common drawback today is that lay culture has forgotten its religious roots. This is not as a result of anti-clericalism or a militant anti-religious stance: it is ignorance. People no longer know what religion is, even if they continue to use the label. In France, in 2006, a survey was carried out among people who had explicitly replied *yes* to the question: "Are you a Catholic?"[11] In answer to the following question: "What is the main reason for defining yourself as a Catholic?", 55 per cent replied that it was because they were born into a Catholic family, and only 21 per cent because they believed in the Catholic faith. The survey also revealed that only 26 per cent of people who call themselves Catholics in France are convinced of God's existence. In 2007, the Archbishop of Paris, André Vingt-Trois, made the following observation: "As a result of the huge decline in religious teaching, many adults are no longer able to decide where they stand in relation to the Christian faith, for they are completely ignorant. For them, its symbols, its references, have become foreign or exotic. Furthermore, a certain number of Catholics have not yet realized the extent of the social consequences of this transformation. So in today's society, values are no longer based on the belief in God, the love of one's neighbour, the importance of sharing or the willingness to help others".[12] On the subject of religious instruction, he adds that "it is less a matter of consolidating or transmitting the faith but of introducing it, in a context where, of the 70 per cent of French people who call themselves Catholics, only 5 per cent are actually practising".[13]

Commenting on this survey, Father Madelin says:

Can we speak of a minority culture? Indeed we can, if we consider the number of Catholics who practise their faith. But for me, living in Brussels, this is not specific to the French. A Belgian bishop recently stated that his Church would soon find itself a minority like the Church in Turkey, in a configuration where the influence is no longer that of the primordial matrix. [...] The number of children attending religion classes has plummeted in France. This point, which was not included in the survey and over which the Church draws a coy veil, is however crucial. It explains why, in this age of the second generation that has not received a Catholic education, French Catholics do not follow the dogma. They simply no longer know it![14]

This ignorance is a source of concern even in lay circles: in France, the European Institute of Religious Sciences was opened in 2006, in Paris, in response to the demand for lay knowledge of religion. But how do you teach religion without mentioning faith?

All religions share the same grievance.[15] Even mainstream religions are setting about reconverting people who nominally claim to be of that faith but have lost all religious knowledge: this is the goal of movements such as the Tablighi in Islam or the Lubavitch in Judaism.[16] For them, it is a matter of reconnecting a nominal affiliation with actual practice.

In spring 2006, Quebec's motorways saw the burgeoning of an unusual advertising campaign: typical Quebecois swear words such as *tabernacle* and *calice* appeared in large letters, followed by their definitions, in small type, which are religious. The campaign was spearheaded by the Bishop of Montreal with the aim of showing that these swear words had Christian origins. People only swear by the sacred, in both senses of the word "swear".[17] But, when people continue to swear without knowing by whom or on what they are swearing, it means that mainstream culture has lost all its religious moorings. The Church has found no better solution than to use this profane ignorance to transmit religious knowledge, or simply to remind people of its existence.[18]

There is a new controversy in the Christian world, this time over religious festivals. The arrival of Halloween in France in the late 1990s angered some bishops, who condemned it as a "pagan" festival—which it is—reinforcing the slide from profane to pagan, which isolates religion from culture even more. The de-Christianization of Christmas is blatant: few people attend midnight mass these days, and Father Christmas/Santa Claus is more important than Jesus. But this de-Christianization becomes explicit in a "multiculturalist" framework, where a number of voices are clamouring for all Christian references to disappear in favour of a religious neutrality: the word "Christmas" is often evaded in the United States in favour of "Holiday" or "*Yule*" (a Germanic word for the December equinox); American department stores have systematically begun replacing their *Merry Christmas* banners with the religiously neutral *Season's greetings*, much to the displeasure of many Christians.[19]

Confronted with this disconnect between lay culture and religion, two contrasting attitudes are emerging among the Christian authorities. On the one hand are those who are fighting to re-Christianize Christmas by preserving the word "Christmas" and thus reinstating the connection between the religious and cultural markers (see the declaration of Pope Benedict XVI of 9 December 2006, requesting that ostensible Christian symbols such as the crucifix continue to be displayed in classrooms and court rooms). On the other hand are those who, in line with fundamentalist Protestant tradition, want to separate the religious sphere completely from a lay culture seen as structurally pagan; the model for this tendency is the expulsion of the merchants from the Temple, a recurrent theme in the writings of theologian Karl Barth. In actual fact, the Protestants' desire to separate state and religion has nothing to do with liberalism—quite the opposite—it is a form of fundamentalism (similar to that of Shia Islam). The American Puritans did not celebrate Christmas, since for the strict Protestants there was no Biblical foundation for this celebration, and in the early nineteenth century Congress used to sit on Christmas Day. Modern-day Christmas, a family festival celebrated by the fireside, with a Christmas tree and presents, is a first step towards the de-Christianization of the birth of Christ, for it started in Victorian England following the publication of Charles Dickens' novel *A Christmas Carol*. This was a departure from the Christian celebration of the period, when people left the warmth of their homes to walk through the cold night to Church. Once again, a "Christian tradition" turns out to be a cultural construct.

This "paganization" of religious festivals can be found in Judaism and Islam too: the number of *halal* turkeys sold in the United States for Thanksgiving has soared since 2001 (here *halal*, a Muslim religious marker, is placed over an American cultural marker, paying no heed to the festival's religious significance), and Jewish festivals are often combined with Christian ones, especially when the calendars coincide, which means that the religious markers on both sides are treated as cultural markers.[20]

By extension, the disconnect between religion and culture leads to the loss of the world in-between, of nuance. The sphere of religious culture comprised the transitional space between non-belief and the faith community. It was constructed in the mid-twentieth century as a sociological object, when believers were classified according to their degree of practice. Gabriel Le Bras had introduced quantitative methods in 1931, and Canon Boulard, a priest, mapped religious practice in France in 1947, which resulted in adaptations of pastorals and the involvement of priests in lay activities, culminating in the worker-priest social experiment. The Second Vatican Council endorsed *post hoc* this "embodiment of Christianity" in social activity. But the advent of Pope John Paul II in 1978 witnessed a return to the "faith community" where the "people of God" were paraded before the media; there was no room for nuance which was increasingly being replaced by the principle: "you're either one of us or you're not". By making the criteria of belonging more stringent,[21] religions contribute to this growing dichotomy and to the erosion of a profane religious culture. Religion is thought of in terms of "full versus empty", of belonging, commitment and identity, and no longer of presence in the world. The "world", i.e. the surrounding society, becomes suspect, threatening, contaminating, for it is hostile, materialistic and impure—in a word: pagan.

Pagan Modernity: the Atheist's New Gods

Religions see culture's breakaway as a betrayal by culture and not as religion turning in on itself ("France, eldest daughter of the Church, are you still true to the promises made at your baptism?" exclaimed John Paul II on his first visit to Paris in 1981), or as a "cultural invasion" (*tajavoz e farhangi* in Iran).

When culture abandons religion, the result is not only the end of orthopraxy and a shared horizon of religious culture, it also promotes new values and references which are antagonistic to those of religion. Nowadays, religion condemns cultural neo-paganism. These values and references do not develop as a coherent system aiming to replace religion—which the major ideologies like communism did. In the conflict between Christianity and Marxism, there was symmetry, very often recognized by the stakeholders on both sides: there were two visions of the world which ultimately claimed to answer the same questions. However, today's neo-pagan culture does not offer a coherent system of values or references.

What are these new paradigms? Their central themes are sexuality, women and reproduction, and the place of the individual, and therefore of freedom, and wariness of any transcendental order. These are of course closely interlinked: the human being has replaced God. The rise of feminism with its demand for equality goes hand in hand with the idea that individual freedom should take precedence over nature. That is the crux of the abortion debate, which was probably the major debate of the second half of the twentieth century, since it embodies all the paradigm changes. Biological sex no longer determines gender; procreation is not only a choice but has become increasingly artificial; the family is no longer necessarily the framework for having children; the individual demands the right to self-determination, in terms of appearance (plastic surgery), affiliation and reproduction. Not only are values disconnected from nature and all transcendence denied, but the very notions of value, norms and ethics are being questioned, even though there has never been so much talk of universal norms (legal and political, such as democratization and human rights) as during this period. So it is not a question of a clash between a secular, libertarian world without norms and a religious world governed by a transcendental order, but of two fundamentally different definitions of human nature. Although the notion of individual and personal freedom (i.e. of human rights) stems from a common matrix with the Christian West, it finds itself in conflict with the Catholic world view that human rights are secondary to duty and to nature.

It was not the introduction of these new paradigms however which severed religion from culture, since all religions have undergone adaptation. Religion is also subject to changing cultural paradigms. As the historian Von Greyerz wrote regarding the period of the Reformation in Europe, culture does indeed have an autonomy from religion: the changes in religiosity, in attitudes toward religion, precede religious changes themselves. There was a pre-Reformation in Europe, that is, changes which were not a consequence of the Reformation but rather determining factors for the Reformation. Furthermore, it has been observed that there were parallel developments in the Catholic and Protestant worlds during the sixteenth and seventeenth centuries (an interest in education, for example). In short, certain things that were seen as consequences of changes within religion were actually the triggers for these changes.

During the twentieth century, the major religions encountered two contradictory movements: one was the accommodation of and even adaptation to cultural changes; the other was the acknowledgement of a breakaway and the condemnation of cultural paradigms as neo-pagan. For example, the pro-life versus pro-choice debate is much more than the extension of the "secular" versus "religion" conflict since it does not reflect a power struggle but a conflict between fundamental values. This is way beyond a corporatist defence by a patriarchal religious institution allied with the conservative right. And yet, the Catholic Church—militantly anti-abortion since Pope Paul Vi's 1968 *Humanæ Vitæ* encyclical and vociferous in affirming the pre-eminence of life in all its forms—did not align itself with the conservative or neo-conservative right (except in precise, one-off instances: the Christian American right and President G. W. Bush, the Spanish episcopate and José Maria Aznar's Popular Party). On immigration, the environment, and social relations for example, the Catholic Church takes a more progressive stance than the conservative camp.

a) The New Paradigms: Sexuality, Women and Homosexuality

The relative consensus and prevailing orthopraxy with regard to these three issues was overturned at the end of the twentieth century.

For example, priests' chastity has become a central issue for the modern-day Catholic Church because it seems incongruous in today's Western world (and always has been in Islam). However, this was not an issue of great importance in the Middle Ages; independently of the actual practices of those concerned, chastity was culturally positive in Christianity, and therefore transgression was experienced as a marginal problem, which did not challenge the core values because it was not proclaimed. For the priests, transgression was managed on the fringes—a social space including prostitution, a personal conscience space that went with the concept of "weakness of the flesh", a ritual space within the framework of confession. But the teachings of the Churches on chastity have nowadays become inaudible, because sexuality has become a value in itself: priests' celibacy for Catholics, abstinence as a means of contraception or of combating AIDs, virginity until marriage, evangelical and Catholic opposition to divorce—all seem incongruous today. What used to take place on the margins (abortion, homosexuality, drug use, prostitution) now happens in public, either through those who "come out" and form pressure groups (abortion rights, recognition of gay marriage), or through the shrinking of the private sphere thanks to communications technology (Internet, social networking sites such as Facebook), controls (police records) and an increase in the types of social relations being governed by law (for example, the extension of the definition of rape, child abuse, violence—and the concept of harassment). This means that entire swathes of private life have come into the public domain, as a result of a desire for expression, an affirmation of "identity", or of denunciation. Nowadays, the reduced space on the fringes or simply twilight zones, the exposure of private lives, the demand for transparency, authenticity and truth plus religion's repositioning of itself have resulted in a number of prime movers resisting sexuality being treated as a "weakness", since for them it is now a dimension of human authenticity (take for example the cases of priests' partners demanding recognition as such, or, in the case of Anglicanism, of gays coming out and demanding to be ordained). Nowadays "scandal" is permanent. Religion blames the new paradigms on materialism, pornography and selfish pleasure, seeing them as embodying the new idols of a society that has reverted to paganism (sometimes literally, with the development of movements that declare themselves as pagan, such as the Wicca).

The importance of the challenge to priests' celibacy is part of the fallout from religion's split from mainstream culture on the issue of morals. But the new paradigms also affect part of the Christian community, so that religious markers no longer even appear as a reference to a past culture, but very much as simple diktats from a hierarchy that is increasingly devoid of pedagogy. In 2005, two French Catholic priests, Bernard C., aged fifty-eight, priest of the parish of Villeneuve-sur-Lot, and Pierre B., aged sixty, of Port-Sainte-Marie (Lot-et-Garonne), were forced to leave the priesthood because the existence of their partners and children was made public.[22] But local villagers, who were perfectly aware of their situations, signed a petition in their support: they did not see why there was any incompatibility, since their culture is that of the new paradigms (individual freedom, right to sexuality). On the other hand, public opinion suddenly found paedophilia, which has probably always existed in the Church, unacceptable, catching the Catholic hierarchy unaware in its inability to get to grips with the issue; its prime concern, without necessarily being over-lenient, was to avoid scandal.[23] Likewise, in the United States, the attempt by the evangelical Churches to promote the wearing of a chastity ring indicating that the wearer is against pre-marital sex does not appear to have reduced the number of people having premarital sexual relations, which is reflected in the attempts to promote a declaration of "second virginity" ("I've done it but I won't do it again"). According to sociological studies, the concept of chastity itself is being challenged by the extreme banalization of sex. Certain acts like fellatio are no longer considered sexual, as President Clinton claimed in his famous defence which came across as the ultimate hypocrisy to people of his generation, but apparently young people did not see it that way.[24]

When it comes to homosexuality, the gulf between religion and the prevailing paradigm is even more blatant. Criminalized until the 1960s in most Western legal systems, homosexuality is not only tolerated, but has now become recognized and protected by a whole series of laws which treat homophobia as racism. It is unheard-of for a paradigm to change so fast within a culture without external pressure.

Suddenly, the homophobic campaigns, based on prejudices which were once rife throughout Western culture, appear today as hate campaigns spearheaded by religious fanatics. The campaigns led by Protestant fundamentalist groups are often considered by the authorities as racist-type discrimination (in Sweden or California, for example). In 2003, the Swedish Pentecostalist minister, Ake Green, was prosecuted for having described homosexuality as a "social cancer"; sentenced initially, he was acquitted by the Supreme Court in the name of freedom of expression and of religion. He was therefore prosecuted for denigrating a community, but acquitted by virtue of the same arguments: he belongs to a community which has the right to express itself. The acquittal in no way endorses his statements, but on the contrary places him within a community among others. The disconnect between religion and culture is total. In contrast, religions, particularly Christianity, view their battle against homosexuality explicitly as the affirmation of the superiority of the Word of God over culture: "The Gospel must take precedence over culture", declared Bishop Drexel Gomez of the West Indies during a meeting of Anglican opponents of ordaining gay priests.[25] Since then the Anglican Church has been on the brink of a schism over the issue.

We note in passing that the powerful Dutch populist orator Pym Fortuyn started campaigning against Islam after hearing the Imam of Rotterdam, Khalil el-Moumni, state on television, in May 2001, that homosexuality was a disease threatening society; this opinion is shared in conservative Christian circles, but on this occasion it was made an Islamic specificity. In fact this is a good example of the horizontal recasting of different religions around autonomous religious markers (condemnation of homosexuality) taken up outside any cultural context. The Dutch courts acquitted el-Moumni of incitement to hatred for the same reasons as the Swedish minister had been cleared.

In 2008, in Sacramento, capital of California, tensions erupted between the gay community and an evangelical Russian immigrant community (a young homosexual was killed in a brawl).[26] Here too the conflict was treated by the press as a conflict between two "communities", one of which (the evangelicals) was seen negatively as encroaching on the rights of the other; but the incident was not analysed as a social problem. The ethnico-religious character of the evangelical community was systematically emphasized by the press. Religious communities, far from expressing a cultural consensus in their homophobic crusade, appear as intolerant minority groups.

On the other hand, in Muslim countries and in many parts of Africa, the rejection of homosexuality is still part of an orthopraxy, and its existence is frequently denied. During a press conference in New York in 2007, President Ahmadinejad of Iran stated that there were no homosexuals in Iran, while at the same time in Egypt several trials and anti-gay press campaigns defined it as the result of foreign influence. While Islam has never demonized the practice of sexuality in itself, and has even always recognized the legitimacy of pleasure, it remains intransigent on the issue of homosexuality, not necessarily as an incidental practice, but as the definition of a legitimate category, in common with the conservative Christian and Jewish stance.

Feminism also marks the establishment of a new cultural paradigm which poses a problem for religion. There was nothing specifically religious about gender inequality, which varies from one faith to another but is always a factor in religion, while being part of the general culture. Here again there was an orthopraxy upheld both by the law and by common morality (gender inequality within the couple in the eyes of the law persisted in France until the 1970s; a certain number of professions were exclusively male preserves, either officially or unofficially, and the constant discourse on the biological differences between men and women was not confined to Christian fundamentalists). Sexist jokes were not specifically limited to religious groups. As long as the restrictions on the role of women were part of wider culture, the teachings of the Church did not pose a problem. "Equal in dignity and unequal in social status" was a shared slogan. And yet feminism was very quickly embraced by the establishment, at least in theory, as being integral to Western values. It is put forward today as a characteristic of the West compared with Islam.

Today, the West's major criticism of Islam effectively concerns the status of women (the campaign in Ontario around 2004 against the establishment of a *sharia* court on the model of the existing rabbinical courts hinged not on the principle of secularism, but on the different status of men and women in Islam), but this is a very recent phenomenon: the issue does not feature in the religious polemics of the Middle Ages or even of modern times. When Christian authors condemned polygamy in Islam, it was to censure the supposedly unbridled libido of Muslim men, not to defend women's rights. The emancipation of the Muslim woman became a central issue much later, as part of the strategies of the colonial and even postcolonial West. In the 1930s, the Soviet Union made women's emancipation the core issue of its Sovietization policy in Central Asia,[27] as did France in the Algerian War (but not during its previous colonization); and it has remained a central issue ever since, from the *Ni putes ni soumises* (neither whores nor slaves) movement in France to the support for Somali-born former Dutch MP Ayaan Hirsi Ali, known for her outspoken criticism of conservative Islam and the campaign against the Afghan Taliban championed by *Elle* magazine in 2000 and 2001.

Women's and gay rights therefore played a key part in the redefinition of religious markers in the second half of the twentieth century. The split is between those who embrace the new cultural paradigms, even reluctantly, and those who redefine religion by focusing on religious markers that are explicitly at odds with a culture now considered pagan. This process is clearly lengthy and complex. Globally, the issue of women's ordination led to an initial division between the various liberal Protestant Churches and Reform Judaism which accepted it. However, the Catholic Church, orthodox Christians, orthodox Jews and the majority of the evangelicals rejected it. Islam is experiencing the conflict less brutally, given the hazy definition of an imam. The first female imam (Amina Wudud) has opened her mosque in Washington, and for the first time, there have been applications from women for the position of Muslim chaplain in the American armed forces.[28] Meanwhile, mixed mosques are becoming widespread in the West.[29]

Liberal Protestantism and Reform Judaism were the pioneers of the ordination of women. The first woman rabbi was appointed in the 1930s in Berlin, and the first woman minister of the Protestant Church of France, Élisabeth Schmidt, in 1949 (but on condition that she did not marry); it was only in 1966, at the Synod of Clermont-Ferrand, that the principle of the unconditional ordination of women ministers was adopted. In November 2006, Jefferts Schori, a woman who was already a bishop, became primate of the American Episcopal Church at the age of fifty-two. The debate also embraces the theological aspect, a number of feminists argue for the divine being to be gender neutral, which reinforces the conservatives' view that the ordination of women is only the preface to a questioning of the very notion of God the Father.[30]

Even religions that want to confine women to the role of wife and mother have to take into account the new paradigms and adapt, without going beyond the boundaries, particularly as they are all aware of the phenomenon of sexual dimorphism. In other words, the more general religious practice decreases, the greater the role played by women in religious life, even in the organization of the community itself. Today, in France, religious education and parish life are mainly taken care of by women. Islam is experiencing the same phenomenon of the strengthening of the role of practising women in a context where Muslims are a minority: the headscarf issue is the proof of women's increased contribution to the visibility and the management of the religious community. The attendance, even sporadic, at religious events organized by major Islamic bodies, like the Le Bourget festival of the Union of Islamic Organizations of France (UIOF), shows the extent to which women play a key role in organization, management and public relations. Even Orthodox Judaism is affected.[31] For Salafism and for the orthodox Jewish movements alike, the need to rethink women's roles has also come about as a result of women's entry into the job market, which is unavoidable, even though it is often discouraged. And so the Israeli Labour Minister set up a job centre for Haredim women to counter the risk of poverty among the Orthodox community.

As regards homosexuality, there are two stages. First of all, groups campaign simply for gay believers to be considered as normal believers ("David and Jonathan" for the Catholics, Keshet for the Jews of Boston,[32] Salaam, the Queer Muslim community of Toronto, more akin to the former); in general they lead to a change in tone on the part of the religious authorities (where they adopt a line that is more medical than theological), but not in fundamental attitude. However, since

2000, the real conflict has centred on the issue of gay marriage and the acceptance of openly gay ministers. And here the debate is bitter and the rift profound, particularly in the Protestant Churches.[33]

And finally, the debate on artificial reproduction has also further isolated the Catholic Church, whereas most of the other religions are more open (including orthodox Judaism).

b) Neo-Paganism

Believers are alarmed not only by the changing paradigms relating to sexual behaviour but by the more serious disappearance of God altogether and the fact that the individual is the point of reference for all norms; the quest for spirituality no longer looks to God, but to postmodern religions. Both the disappearance of God and the search for substitutes display evidence of paganism.

Bishop Roland Minnerath, at the time professor of theology at the University of Strasbourg, writes: "Modernity reveals that entire swathes of Christianity are in the process of *pseudomorphosis*, a term taken from mineralogy, used by H. I. Marrou to describe the mutation of pagan religiosity in the second century. Nowadays, this concept is applicable to Christianity: within the unchanged outer casing of Christian words, rites and symbols, the content has changed and is changing and has become imbued with a new purely secular meaning, within a perspective from which the mystery of God is absent"; we are therefore witnessing a reversal of the processes which made the transition from paganism to Christianity possible. He adds: "Postmodernity paves the way for the irrational, gnoses and sects, with the New Age promising the fragmented individual a cosmic communion at a time when social or simply family communion has become impossible. Postmodernity is not conducive to a return to Christianity. It shows no interest in knowing the God who is transcendent and incarnate, creator and redeemer of the world and of humanity".[34] The divorce between culture and religion could not be more pronounced. This is particularly true of Spain, where, during the 2004 elections, the Catholic Church suddenly noticed it was culturally, and not only politically, a minority: the Archbishop of Madrid, Cardinal Rouco Varela then condemned "the culture of secularism" as a fraud.[35]

The values of freedom take precedence over those of the Church, which attempts to link the two, but its message goes unheard, as Pope

Benedict XVI acknowledged during his visit to the United States in April 2008, when he declared in New York: "'Authority'. 'Obedience'. To be frank, these are not easy words to speak nowadays. Words like these represent a stumbling-stone for many of our contemporaries".[36] Religions find the issues which are at the core of contemporary values—freedom, democracy and human rights—problematic. The fundamentalists reject them outright while the more moderate conservatives try to give them new meaning. But what is to be done when the religious establishment accepts the framework of democracy and institutions (and this is equally true of the Catholic Church, the Protestants, the conservative Jews and an increasing number of Islamists), but at the same time claims there are non-negotiable values ("life" for Christians who are anti-abortion, *sharia* law for the conservative Islamists). The dichotomy does not necessarily involve a conflict, but it places religion in a position of exteriority.

The new idols and beliefs, from Madonna to Harry Potter, Halloween and Dan Brown's *The Da Vinci Code* are another target. Not that these are new religions, but because thanks to them neo-pagan beliefs form the backdrop for contemporary culture, thus demeaning the major religions which have become mere avatars of the new beliefs. The success of *The Da Vinci Code* surprised the Catholic Church as not only does the novel destroy Christian theology from within, but it turns present-day Christianity into a sect, a plot, a successful heresy even: in fact it overturns the relationship between majority and minority, sect and Church. What doubtless shocked the Church above all is that this theory managed to sound plausible, if not true. This same battle is also to be found in Islam, but on two fronts. The first, Salafism, fears above all the Christianization of Islam and sees the cultural invasion as a form of Westernization. But there is another tendency which advocates an alliance between the major "religions" against the "pagans" and seeks common ground. Likewise the Catholic Church is also looking for allies in secular circles to combat Halloween, this time presented as a form of Americanization. There is a constant ambivalence in the battle against paganism, which zigzags between arguing that it is eroding religion and resisting imported foreign cultures, namely Western culture in the Orient, and American culture in Europe. That is why there is such a strong shared anti-American feeling, as the USA can be held responsible both for neo-paganism and Christian evangelicalism.

Refusing to legitimize homosexuality plays a major role in this endeavour to create a united religious front against materialism and neo-paganism. This is illustrated by the opposition to Gay Pride in Jerusalem in 2007 and 2008, to gay marriage in California in 2008 with support for the reinstatement of Proposal 8 banning same-sex marriages, and the joint communiqué issued by four religious leaders of the French city of Lyon, in 2007 opposing the legalization of gay marriage (the bishop, the rabbi, the imam and the evangelical Christian minister—the Reformed Protestant minister did not sign).

And now a new controversy has emerged: the evolution debate. Confined since the end of the nineteenth century to an American fundamentalist Protestant fringe, it has gained a new momentum in the United States with the intelligent design theory, which makes it possible to reintroduce the idea of a grand evolutionary design without appearing to promote a literalist interpretation of the Bible. Thus it is possible to rally a broader front in order to ensure the inclusion of intelligent design in the school curriculum; it also makes it possible to rally Muslims, as it is no longer the Bible as such that is being promoted. Around 2000, the storm suddenly crossed over to Europe both with the dissemination in European languages of works by the Muslim writer Harun Yahya (*The Atlas of Creation*), who echoes the arguments of the Protestant fundamentalists (another instance of a typically Christian debate imported into Islam by fundamentalists, who unwittingly become the agents of Islam's Christianization), and with disparate comments by Catholic dignitaries distancing their religion from Darwinism (for example the Bishop of Vienna, Cristoph von Schönborn, writing in the *New York Times* of 7 July 2005). The notion of intelligent design is gaining currency in Christian and Muslim circles, and this represents a definite rift between culture and religion, since, like Galileo's theory that the earth moves around the sun, evolutionism had become an integral part of shared culture, outside strictly scientific debate. Furthermore, the evolution debate underscores another crucial division: that between religion and science; it is not that religions have suddenly become obscurantist, but quite simply because religion no longer sees the affirmations of science as objective and neutral. The split goes beyond culture: it impacts on the relationship between science and faith.

A recurrent issue in the Muslim world is the condemnation of *kufr* (disbelief) which supposedly lies at the heart of Muslim society and of culture. The loss of religious certainty means that at any moment the legitimacy of a particular practice can be called into question, from credit cards to shaking hands. Not that this is a return to an archaic traditional vision which did not have these problems. The question arises from the fact that current cultural and social practices, in the Muslim world too, do not derive from a traditional Muslim culture. Nothing is clear: religious practices are no longer embedded in the surrounding culture, they have to be reformulated, imposed (note for example the role of religious police in Saudi Arabia) and explained. *Kufr* is at the very heart of society because it is not recognized as such: it has acquired the social visibility that religion no longer has.

The *ulemas* associate neo-paganism in Islam with Western influence, which suddenly allows deviances to be externalized by labelling them a foreign import, as is exemplified by the trial of gays in Cairo (2001), Ahmadinejad's declarations that there are no homosexuals in Iran, or the repeated condemnation of Satanism in the Arab press. Here, as with sexuality, the prevailing orthopraxy means that there is a relative consensus on these matters and that there is no distinction between the religious stance and the secular. But, as in the case of the "homosexual marriage" in Ksar el Kebir, this is in fact a process of exculturation: everything that does not come within the explicit religious norm is considered as not conforming to the "authentic" culture. The crisis of faith is associated with growing Western influence. Thus, the defence of religion is recast as the defence of a cultural identity, of an "authenticity", which itself is cut off from the complexity of the real culture. The word "culture", as is often the case in contemporary Islam, does not designate otherness in relation to religion, but the reformulation of this religion into a number of norms in isolation from any real cultural context, and in particular from popular cultures. For many Muslim community leaders in the West, as well as for politicians from the Muslim world, to speak of "Muslim culture" is a way of expressing an abstract conception of religion in the idiom of multiculturalism, a concept promoted in numerous quarters in the West. Paradoxically, multiculturalism is used in a way to deculturalize traditional Islam(s) in favour of a global and homogeneous set of abstract religious norms (single sex education, the headscarf, *halal* etc.), while using the West's own lexicon. It is in the Muslim countries that the issue of defending cultural identity has been the strongest: to give way over cultural values is to give way over faith and religious identity, and vice-versa. But at the same time, profane culture in the Arab world is fast disappearing under the dual pressure of Salafism and Westernization. The paradox is therefore that the promotion of a normative Islamic culture is detrimental to classic, popular cultures, and not to Westernization.

c) The Severing of Ties

Despite nostalgia for the good old days, when religion was embedded in culture and culture imbued with religion, the severing of these ties has been observed almost everywhere, including in societies where there is a majority religion. But often the first symptom of the disconnect between religion and culture is an internal division within the religious community, in the form of a schism or of a waning interest. The severing of ties became increasingly frequent from the 1960s, reflecting diverse responses to exculturation. In Catholicism, the driving force behind the split was Bishop Lefebvre who founded the Saint Pius X Fraternity in 1970 and broke with Rome in 1975. At the other end of the opinion spectrum was the departure of large numbers of priests and followers who tiptoed off without actually breaking away.[37] During this same period, inspired by the thinking of Sayyid Qutb, radical Muslim groups broke away from mainstream Islam, denouncing as apostates any Muslim leaders who refused to break off relations with the West and existing regimes: there was a spate of assassinations of Muslim religious dignitaries in Egypt (the Minister for Waqfs, Sheikh al-Dhahabi, in Cairo in 1977) by Shukri Mustafa's *Al-Takfir wal Hijra* (Excommunication and Exodus) group, as well as the storming of the great Mecca mosque by Juhayman al Utaybi in 1979.

In Protestantism, the many different Churches offered an array of choices so changes took the form of moving from one "denomination" to another, and thus from established Churches (Anglicanism, Lutherism, Episcopalism, Methodism) to Pentecostalism and evangelicalism, which went hand in hand with exculturation and deterritorialization (people left their parish and local social networks to attend often distant places of mass worship). However at the beginning of the twenty-first century, internal splits on the question of homosexuality emerged, particularly in the Anglican movement, where a schism has been brewing between a faction that refused to legitimize homosexuality (comprising the African Churches joined by white American parishes and a handful of English bishops), and the Anglo-Saxon majority, since the American Episcopal Church appointed the first openly homosexual bishop in 2003. In Judaism, the division between Reform, conservatives, orthodox and ultra-orthodox goes back to the nineteenth century when it was sparked off by the issue of incorporating and accepting secular values. This division was deepened by the creation of the State of Israel, where the orthodox have the monopoly on public religious practice and the rabbinical courts, which puts them on a collision course both with the secular community and also with the majority of American rabbis.

Breaking away also presupposes established procedures for entering (and being expelled from) the community, since the "sociological believer" (one who is born into a religion as opposed to choosing it) is no longer recognized. For the Protestants, it was the requirement to be born again by explicitly requesting baptism. Since the Second Vatican Council, the Catholic Church has been running educational courses for those wanting to be baptized: it is not enough just to request baptism, and sometimes it is not sufficient to have been baptized as a child if people have subsequently stopped practising. For marriage too, non-regular churchgoers are now asked to attend classes. Everywhere, in Judaism and Islam alike, conversions of convenience (for marriage purposes, for example), which were relatively easy until the 1960s (it was just a matter of finding the right rabbi), were called into question, and prospective converts now have to go through a proper process which takes a certain amount of time. Conservative rabbis campaigned against mixed marriages, for they now refuse conversions of convenience, and are moreover highly sceptical of genuine conversions: they therefore advocate endogamy. I am not aware of any studies on conversions of convenience in Islam, but my experience in my professional milieu (where by definition there have been a lot of mixed marriages) is that thirty years ago it was sufficient to say the *shahada* and the matter was settled, whereas today countries like Tunisia (even though purportedly secular) and Morocco insist on applicants undergoing proper training and being tested by imams.

d) Religious Purity

Once the split between religion and ambient neo-paganism has been internalized, there are two ways for religion to go: turning inwards or reconquest (which does not preclude reconquest after turning inwards). Turning inwards occurs on the affirmation of a clear separation between the community of believers and the rest of the world: the shades of grey, nuance and ambiguity disappear; in other words, the cultural sphere. The main issue becomes "them and us": the discriminating factor being active faith, not just mere belonging. The new Protestant groups are "confessing"; in other words, to be counted as a member of the community adults must make a personal commitment, by being baptized anew, for example: there are no half-measures, no "sociological Christians". Personal faith must be declared and worn as a badge. So there is an emphasis on being born-again, being reborn into the faith as an adult. Even in religions that do not make it a theological principle, this return of the believer to a manifest faith is valued: this applies to the Muslim Tablighis as well as to the Catholic Charismatics. Orthodox Jewish groups, like the Lubavich, encourage those they call the *Baal Teshuva* (returnees) to revert to strict practice, renouncing a life that is not entirely governed by religious norms and markers.

As the philosopher Jean-Luc Marion says: "Christians should first of all be concerned with Christ, since non-Christians are concerned chiefly with the Church. For the rejection or acceptance of the Church does not derive from an ideological or even spiritual choice, but from a choice by God in Christ. The Christian or the non-Christian materializes by replying yes or no to this choice".[38] It is all or nothing. The strongly Calvinist notion of the chosen is very much back on the agenda, including in Catholicism; in the novel *Left Behind*, by the American evangelicals Tim La Haye and Jerry Jenkins, the chosen are suddenly called to God, leaving the profane world in a state of crisis and war.

Whereas Catholics generally seek to remain connected to culture and to keep it within the religious sphere, evangelicals and Salafis find the concept of culture itself problematic. They want to be rid of mainstream culture. Ignoring this pagan culture is a way of salvaging the purity of their faith. It is holy ignorance. What David Martin says of the rules established by the Pentecostalists in Latin America eloquently defines the relationship of the new religious movements to culture:

These rules are rigid and puritanical, particularly the total ban on alcohol, tobacco and drugs, the tight controls on sexual behaviour and the hedges erected between believers and worldly temptations—cinema, dancing, football (because of its association with drunkenness and bad language), theatre, secular literature, and the entertainment of the mass media are all forbidden.[39]

In this second quotation from an American theologian, it is clear that there is not an opposition between "good" and bad culture, but quite simply between faith and culture: "In order to live lovingly, we must somehow refuse to live in fear in a culture that constantly confronts us with well-publicized dangers... I suggest that the rhetoric of romantic love in our entertainment culture effectively functions as ·'misdirection'".[40]

The "early years" paradigms therefore serve to bypass culture, which is seen as a product of historic contingencies, as an accretion which is at best useless, at worst, damaging. For Protestants, these "early years" are the time of Jesus and more specifically of the apostles. It is a matter of living one's faith as the early Christians did.[41] The Biblical texts are followed to the letter, ignoring the literary and historical dimension of these scriptures; for example, the fact that the *Book of Acts* is filled with literary references, highly crafted and written in a complex style.[42] On the contrary, it has been taken as the guide for the modern-day itinerant preacher. Ignoring culture does not mean rejecting cultural references or writings, but deliberately neglecting their cultural dimension. This also explains why, for the Protestants, translation does not pose a problem: the well-known disadvantage of any translation (loss of cultural and literary connotations, hence the Italian saying *traduttore, traditore* [translator, traitor]) becomes an advantage, since dodging the text's resonances allows the message to be understood immediately outside any cultural dimension. Translation is a plus, since it makes it possible to extract meaning devoid of context: it is a reversal of the problem of literary translation. The meaning is guaranteed by the presence of the Holy Spirit, not by the clarity of the writing.[43] Historical, linguistic or literary knowledge is unnecessary if one is assisted by the Holy Spirit.

This veneration of the early days to the detriment of history is also found in Islam among those who see the first Muslim community as the paradigm for all Muslim societies, which cannot be superseded, and who consider that the pinnacle of devotion is the emulation of the Prophet (as among the Tablighis and the Salafis), and not theological knowledge.

The new religious movements are therefore reluctant to participate in social movements for they fear the dangers that engagement with the world means for their faith. In her study on the spread of evangelicalism in Latin America, Bernice Martin mentions the minister

Caballo de Pueblo Hundido in Chile, who condemns football not out of opposition to the sport in itself, but because it is associated with cultural behavioural traits that go against religious practice (for example, the use of alcohol), even if he himself has no reticence towards material or professional success. It is not through asceticism that he is opposed to the sport, but because football is associated with an immoral culture.[44]

The Catholic Church, which in Europe opened up and lent churches to other faiths in the 1950s and 1960s, now closes its doors not only to other religions but even to lay activities, such as non-religious cultural events. Parishes in France refused to "lend" their church for Telethon concerts in 2007, bishops even spoke out against taking part in the Telethon, which fundraises for muscular dystrophy research, because such medical research might involve the use of embryos. Everywhere defending the group's identity and values takes precedence over social and pastoral concerns.

In some cases, physical attacks are carried out on the vectors of alien culture: the Taliban, both Afghan and Pakistani, prohibit television and video; the ultra-Orthodox Haredim Jews of Jerusalem rail against the last cinema left in the Mea Shearim neighbourhood, the Edison, whereas others have tried to develop a *kosher* Internet. For the problem is general: how can you use modern technology while separating it from the values it conveys?

In an American evangelical university, the preacher suggested that the students themselves isolate the negative cultural markers by writing them down on scraps of paper which were solemnly (accompanied by a prayer) thrown into the rubbish bin, along with objects symbolising pagan culture, all of which were "cultural garbage". This is the list: "Ryan Seacrest, Louis Vuitton, Gilmore Girls, Days of Our Lives, Iron Maiden, Harry Potter, 'need for a boyfriend' and 'my perfect teeth obsession'". One had written in tiny letters: "fornication". Some teenagers threw away cigarette lighters, brand-name sweatshirts, Mardi Gras beads and CDs—one titled "I'm a Hustla". The second stage consisted of rebranding: in replacing the cultural markers that had just been thrown away with religious markers, but with the same form (especially printed T-shirts); the preacher declared: "I strip off the identity of the world, and this morning I clothe myself with Christ, with his lifestyle. That's what I want to be known for". The journalist adds: "Outside the arena in Amherst, the teenagers at Mr. Luce's

Acquire the Fire extravaganza mobbed the tables hawking T-shirts and CD's stamped: "Branded by God". Mr. Luce's strategy is to replace MTV's wares with those of an alternative Christian culture, so teenagers will link their identity to Christ and not to the latest flesh-baring pop star".[45]

Muslims living in the West are advocating "Muslim outfits", that go against current fashion: from the Salafist *shalwar kamiz* to the *dawawear* of "market Islam" to use the term coined by Patrick Haenni, it is a matter either of ignoring or of "rebranding" clothing fashion (by giving it a religious marker).[46] The prevailing cultural markers are replaced by religious markers, but which are worn exactly as if they were cultural identity markers.

A minority separatist vision is established. This minority discourse is now explicit, including in societies where religion is culturally dominant. We have even witnessed American evangelicals protesting against discrimination against them in schools and public spheres in the United States itself, or filing complaints claiming that competitive university entrance examinations discriminate against them because of their different sensibility; again, in doing so, they are adopting a communitarian attitude ("Don't touch my community!") and not one of evangelization.[47] Richard Turnbull, the principal of Wycliffe Hall, an Anglican theological college in Oxford, which is in no way marginal, states that 95 per cent of the British population will go to hell unless they repent and listen to the Word of God.[48] While there is nothing reprehensible about this theory from the theological point of view, it contrasts sharply with the restraint of the Anglican establishment and clearly shows a challenging of the link between the Anglican Church and British society coming from within.

In Islam, the radical groups of the 1960s and 1970s defined themselves by the names they chose, as small minorities within a world that had become Muslim in name only: the "Saved from Hell" or "Excommunication and Exodus". But, more generally, the Salafis promoted the *hadiths* of the Prophet that emphasize the inevitable division of the community, for example between seventy-two "sects" (*firqa* is the word for sect) of which only one will be saved (this is a very Calvinist theme: another sign of religion's standardization). On the Internet, a Muslim *a capella* (*nashid*) song became very popular in the noughties. It began with a video showing an activist who, having been sentenced to prison in Egypt, hums this song behind bars. It is called *Ghuraba*,

"The Foreigners", but these foreigners are the good Muslims, who are foreigners in this world because they are in a minority, because they are indifferent to mainstream culture even though it claims to be Muslim—"*ghrabaa' hakazhal ahraaru fii dunya-al 'abiid*" (foreigners: this is how they are free in a world of slaves).

In late 2007, a strange correction notice was printed in the Israeli daily *Yated Ne'eman*, published by the ultra-Orthodox Degel Hatorah group:

> Unfortunately, in the Friday edition an ad appeared that has no place in *Yated Ne'eman* (...) The ad was sent by a group that seeks reconciliation between the secular and the religious. We apologize to readers for the mishap. Steps have been taken so it will not recur. We must clarify that any Jew who believes in the 13 Articles of Faith can never enter into a friendship with those who deny faith in the Creator of the world. (...) We can never forget nor can we reconcile with secularism, which moved hundreds of thousands of children from religious education to an education of forced conversion from Judaism through deception and corruption.[49]

Noah Feldman, a brilliant professor at the Harvard Law School and a practising Jew, describes how, after attending the annual meeting for alumni of the *yeshiva* where he had studied, he received the commemorative photo minus the picture of his wife which had been cropped from the group because she is not Jewish.[50] There is nothing new about the rejection of mixed marriages among orthodox Jews, but what is interesting, in the heated debate that followed the publication of this article, is that the question was posed in terms of safeguarding the community from slander rather than of adherence to religious principles.[51] In 2006, the Lubavitch Rabbi Eliezer Shemtov published *Dear Rabbi, Why Can't I Marry Her?*— a little educational book which was translated into several languages. The campaign against mixed marriages was being waged openly, including in perfectly assimilated and politically liberal circles: the famous American lawyer Alan Dershowitz wrote a book refuting the argument of his son, who informed him that he was marrying a non-Jewish woman but wanted to remain Jewish.[52] Assimilation has once more become a thorny issue in religious Jewish circles.[53]

Religion, thought of as a minority category, thus ends up claiming to be one. "Aged between fifteen and twenty-five, they belong to a strange tribe. Journalists and sociologists have given this tribe a name: the John Paul II generation. They believe in God, they're Catholics (they call themselves "cathos"), they love the Pope and are proud of it, and at the same time they are fully of their era, for better or for worse, and perfectly comfortable with themselves: strange animals indeed".[54] Religion then turns inwards towards identity or reconstructs itself as a faith community (people speak of Catholic identity or Muslim identity, which would have made no sense in medieval times). The paradox is that to build a "faith community", groups use the religious marker along the lines of the current cultural markers; they are thus forged in multiculturalism. Instead of encompassing culture, religion becomes a sub-culture, on a par with worker, gay, feminist or black culture etc. Thus it is not unusual to find the gay stand close to the Muslim stand at events bringing together "minorities", from San Francisco to London.

It is in this sense that the word "culture" is very often used by religions, Christian and Muslim alike. For example, the Italian Cardinal Biffi wrote the following on the subject of defining culture:

Whichever meaning we may subsequently wish to attribute to it (at least among those more commonly accepted and used), the existence and semantic—and not only semantic—legitimacy of a 'Catholic culture' is incontrovertible. And it is in carrying out our duty of safeguarding the 'Catholic culture' that we find the answer to the question we are asking. It means that the fundamental identity of a Christian involved in politics is not guaranteed by the fact that he adheres devoutly to the Creed, respects the sacraments, and accepts God's commandments without reservation. He must struggle to remain firmly faithful to that 'culture' which ultimately derives uniformly, through the different forms of the Church, from Christ and his Gospel. In short, he must remain faithful to a Catholic culture. [...] "Is there such a thing as a 'Catholic culture'? Yes, there is because a Catholic people exists and must exist, despite those who think that Christianity is dead and that is a good thing. Today's Christian society may be a social minority, unlike a few centuries ago, but this is no reason why it should be less alive and less clearly identifiable.

The cardinal concludes that political compromise should not be pushed to the detriment of an identity that must never be jeopardized.[55]

All the vocabulary is there: minority, identity and culture as group culture, brought down to the explicit norms of religion and not to the profane development of religious inspiration. Surreptitiously, religion embraces the multiculturalist discourse by positioning itself as a cultural minority, for which the cultural marker is provided by the religious norm freed from any context. The religious marker serves as an identity marker. Once again religion and culture merge, but because it is the explicit religion which provides the cultural norm, it is indeed culture that disappears, drained by the religious norm.

And so it follows on quite naturally to find Christian Pride events conceived on the lines of Gay Pride, as in Paris in May 2008. The minister who organized it referred explicitly to an "evangelical culture", which is more restrictive than Christian culture, and shows that here the word "culture" refers to an identity, and not to a different content of purely religious markers.[56] Identity here is not the usage of a modern concept that helps to understand the past better: it is a "performative" concept which creates the thing it names.

For example, whereas throughout the twentieth century the Catholic Church in France, in its conflict with secularism, had encouraged parishes to become involved in social, cultural and sporting life again and to place the religious marker on these activities (patronage, sports clubs, summer camps), from the moment Cardinal Lustiger was appointed Archbishop of Paris in 1981, the tendency was rather for communities to become inward-looking while displaying the flag (in this case the cross): community radios, spiritual retreats, pilgrimages, etc. In the 1950s, merging with the surrounding secularism was seen as a kind of vocation (ministers wore lay dress, churches with no external signs were built, it was thought that God's grace manifested itself in profane areas, including in politics, in social and national liberation movements, for example); whereas now manifestations of belonging are re-appearing—clothing, architectural and linguistic. This is the opposite of the liberal trend embodied by the Protestants Friedrich Schleiermacher, Dietrich Bonhoeffer and Harvey Cox, for whom secularization was not only inevitable, but positive, to the point where religion should merge with the secular; in a post-religious world, values are no longer conveyed by religion in itself. In this theology of secularization, the religious marker was obliterated. For today's new believers, it is the contrary: there is nothing positive in the profane, and the religious marker must not only be rehabilitated, but brandished.

The isolation of the religious marker is evident in the gradual appearance of a specific religious "labelling": there is talk of *Catholic* writers (which seems to have begun in 1905) in the same way as during the twentieth century people spoke of "black" or "women" writers. At the close of the century it was the "Islamist" writers who emerged, at the same time as a profane religious literature intent on promoting the religious marker once again in a world without religion[57] and always describes the same scenario: a young woman or man is tempted by worldly pleasures but ends up finding happiness in religion and family life.[58] Religious schools (with some exceptions, of course) tend either to become profane (like private Catholic schools in France), or to teach only religious studies, as is increasingly the case in the *madrasa* and the *yeshiva*. Of course, some tendencies encourage the double curriculum (going to university while pursuing religious studies) and others try to reintroduce secular teaching in religious schools. With hindsight, it is clear that nearly everywhere religion has withdrawn into a sort of identity sub-culture, while claiming to be universal.

Suddenly, this withdrawal leads to a double antagonism, externally and internally. Externally, attacks are launched either through the courts, or through the threat of direct action (the famous, and often imaginary *fatwa*). The proceedings instigated in secular courts are generally based on the principle of defamation against a community which demands to be respected (*The Last Supper* trial, the Danish cartoon case, the Rushdie affair). There are a growing number of cases involving anti-semitism, real or imagined, in the West. In countries with a state religion, we are seeing the revival of, or the demand for, blasphemy laws. Even supposedly "liberal" religions like Buddhism are playing this card.[59] Within the community, excommunication procedures such as *takfir* in Islam and *pulsa danura* among the Haredim are being revived.[60] Evangelical Churches are encountering the problem of "cooling off" from those who are not able to sustain the required degree of commitment. The fact that the religious community is no longer based on conformism, territorialization or the surrounding culture means that people join it as a result of a voluntary decision, but they can be expelled from it just as quickly.

e) Holy Ignorance

Taken to extremes, this rejection of profane culture also turns into suspicion of religious knowledge itself, with the notion that, firstly, there is no need for knowledge in order to be saved, and secondly, that knowledge can distract from the true faith. The Word of God can be transmitted directly, without the mediation of knowledge: that is precisely the function of the Holy Spirit for the Protestants. It is not erudition that enables people to discover the truth beneath the Biblical text, it is because this text is God's living word, because it speaks the truth. One must allow oneself to be inhabited by the Word. Taken to its extreme, this vision is embodied by the Pentecostalists' famous "speaking in tongues" (glossolalia): on the model of the apostles at Pentecost (hence the movement's name), believers, visited by the Holy Spirit, begin to utter sounds which each person understands in their own language. For them it is not a question of suddenly being able to speak Chinese, Tagalog or Hebrew, but of being understood directly through a sound medium that is not linguistic. Here there is no question of theological, linguistic, or cultural knowledge; on the contrary, it is that of a presence un-mediated by knowledge. This is the most typical case of the obliteration of the letter to serve a word that enters directly, without the mediation of language. But, by definition, language is both a vehicle for culture, an object of learning and a tool of knowledge. The obliteration of language in favour of the Word is probably the most perfect example of holy ignorance.

But there are other instances of the transmission of the message without transmitting knowledge: all forms of ecstasy, of meditation, of Zen. In Judaism, where knowledge is traditionally greatly valued, Hassidic movements nowadays place the emphasis on other forms of transmission: the Nachman or Na Nach as they are commonly called organize itinerant groups of musicians and dancers so as to "spread joy".[61] Emotion is passed on, the aim is to share one's joyful religious experience with others, but anything resembling discursive knowledge is avoided, since it is a waste of time and risks straying into secular vanity.

Below is a testimony, admittedly individual, to this justification of holy ignorance published on the blog of Nicolas Ciarapica, a former head of an evangelical centre in Jerusalem. The text criticizes the commercial leanings of the evangelicals in Israel and proclaims (the author's capitals):

But that said, is it not more important to be transformed in the same way as JESUS CHRIST than to become "scribes" puffed up with knowledge? Paul the Apostle PAUL said: "knowledge puffs up". And that is still true. I do not need to know the Hebrew language to understand that I must rid myself of my "ego" to allow the HOLY SPIRIT to transform me daily just like CHRIST... but what I absolutely need to do is to "die within myself", to "negate myself daily", to refute my "own will" in order to obey That of my Master in order to achieve His perfect stature to produce His works through the power of the SPIRIT of CHRIST who will then live fully in me! When I think of the words of our Lord and Master which were as follows: "Except ye become as little children, ye shall not enter into the kingdom of heaven", it would seem as if nowadays you need a theology degree to receive the fullness of the SPIRIT! But our Master taught people through the means of simple parables, and, above all, he brought the kingdom of God to earth by delivering the possessed, healing the sick, opening the eyes of the blind, resuscitating the dead, etc. He overturned the knowledge of the "wise men" and the intellectuals of His time, HE of whom the Pharisees and the sacrificers said that He had not studied the Scriptures. (With them in their classrooms). The HOLY SPIRIT could make the distinction! AMEN".[62]

PART 2

GLOBALIZATION AND RELIGION

5

FREE MARKET OR DOMINATION
BY THE MARKET?

The impact of globalization on religiosity and on religion's continual veering between acculturation and deculturation is to systematize, generalize and accelerate these processes.

Currently there are two main theories relating to the globalization of religion, one which posits the process in terms of acculturation and the other, more recent, "market" theory. They do not fall into two clearly defined camps, but rather two extremes with a whole range of more nuanced positions in between.

Acculturation presupposes that religious transformations are the consequence of a dominant model being imposed, which, in the last analysis, echoes political domination. The "defeated" group adopts or adapts to mainstream culture, either as part of an integration strategy, or as a position of rebellion. The outcome is then described as syncretism (like Kimbanguism in Zaire), hybridization (Voodoo), or "re-appropriation" of the Gospel, when a religious movement (African-American Gospel) opposes mainstream culture (white Protestant America) in the name of that culture's religious values. These three categories, initially used with caution by anthropologists, subsequently became the basis for all postcolonial, cultural and subaltern studies. Religious expansion, or rather the spread of some forms of religion, goes hand in hand with increased domination. According to this position there is no demand for religion: there is an offer that is imposed, either by force or, more subtly, through the constraints of deculturation.

It is interesting to note that French nationalists opposed to Europe and globalization, at both ends of the political spectrum, are the first to resist "foreign" religions—generally American Protestantism or Islam. Quite logically, the "new religions" are suspected of being a contributory factor to the strategic re-juggling set in motion by globalization.

First of all let us examine the question of domination before coming back to the market.

Acculturation as Domination

Clearly, there is no denying the violence of imposing a culture and a religion. However, it is clear that globalization today is an extension of colonialism and that the debate about values (human rights, democracy, women's rights) is also a debate about power (illustrated by the "right to intervene" and the development of a forceful humanitarian sector, the worthy successor of the nineteenth-century foreign missions). The impact of globalization, like that of colonialism, goes way beyond issues of power and alienation, and that is what interests us.

The "purest" case of acculturation is that of the Native Americans of Central and South America, precisely because they were the subject of an immediate, intensive and brutal conversion policy.[1] Two structured cultures, with no previous relationship to each other, came into violent military contact over a very short space of time; Native American culture was defeated, but the indigenous peoples were not exterminated; they were forced into acculturation which took the form of adopting the conqueror's religion. But that does not mean that Native American culture was wiped out; rather it recast itself within the framework of the invader's culture and within a relationship of political domination. Another example is that of the enslavement of Africans in the Americas. If all slavery is by definition absolute domination, it happened that masters and slaves lived in a world where two cultures cohabited, even if it was within a confrontational situation, as was the case in the Mediterranean slave world of the fifteenth and eighteenth centuries: it was possible for acculturation not to occur (the Christian slave of a Muslim master was allowed to remain Christian), or it could be a matter of individual choice (conversion to Islam), but all the protagonists' leading religions (Islam and Christianity) remained stable, in a relationship of antagonistic symmetry. On the other hand, the transportation of millions of African slaves across the ocean to America eradicated their original language and culture and posed the problem of the nature of these slaves' belonging to Christianity.[2]

From this perspective, the expansion of new religions like Pentecostalism, or the incursion of indigenous religiosities into established religions (as with so-called "African Christianity" or "indigenous African Churches"),[3] is seen as an agent of acculturation, in the form of syncretism or hybridization.

Acculturation theory presupposes that there is a mainstream culture and that the vanquished culture makes a comeback as a "minority" culture, either as a substratum or via a merger, or by maintaining a religiosity that can be transposed by borrowing the paradigms of the mainstream religion. For example, in the case of Gospel, according to T. H. Smith, the slaves in America apparently reactivated an African religious matrix with new cultural markers, the text of the Gospels.[4] A similar analysis contends that: "By accepting the Christian minister or priest as the functional equivalent of a native shaman and by giving traditional meanings to Christian rites, dogmas, and deities, the Native Americans ensured the survival of native culture by taking on the protective coloration of the invaders' religion".[5] The author concludes very logically that religious affiliation here is superficial. It is another instance of the anthropological tendency to reduce the religious marker to a cultural marker. Within this framework, hybrid or syncretist religions recombine markers from two different universes because there was repression of the former stratum or the brutal imposition of new markers. The juxtaposition always seems artificial, inauthentic and fragile. Journalists and publishers in their quest for striking book covers have a notable taste for what have been called cultural oxymorons[6]—*Mariachis* and psalms, a headscarfed woman with a mobile phone (or Kalashnikov, computer, jogging gear, etc.), McDonald's and *halal*, a Buddhist monk with a briefcase etc. In other words, the link between the two markers seems incongruous because they refer to two different cultures.

So-called "hybrid" religions or forms of religiosity remix the different markers in a new entity, where religion and culture are merged once again. For the outside observer, there is therefore no religious specificity or autonomy: all the cultural registers (music, food, family, social ties) are conceived of within this framework of hybridity. Syncretism appears as a consequence of domination, and the entire school of subaltern studies developed quite logically as a subset of cultural studies.

But this conception is problematic for three reasons: in reducing religion to culture, it ignores religion's specificity and makes religious invention a consequence of the power relationship, seeing the religious protagonist through the perspective of alienation, in other words of the non-conscious subject. What is meant when voodoo or *milonga* (in Brazil) are described as syncretist religions? For their followers, there is no syncretism, they are true religions. Similarly, for the headscarfed woman with a mobile phone or the manager of a *halal* fast-food outlet, there is no cultural oxymoron, there is no paradox, no contradiction, nothing odd: it is their experience that gives this new combination its unity. Talking of syncretism presupposes a theory of false consciousness and alienation: the subject is unaware of what s/he is doing, her/ his truth is in the external gaze of the observer, placed under the auspices of an impossible neutrality in relation to determinisms.[7]

But it also means that an implicit distinction has been made between "noble" (non-syncretist) religions and mixed religions, which goes back to the differentiation between sect and religion, between "high culture" and "popular culture". Unless, of course, all religions are considered a form of syncretism (Christianity as a mixture of Judaism and new theories of salvation). But in this case the concept of "syncretist religion" is redundant. In a nutshell, the theory of acculturation-domination ignores the autonomization processes, precisely because it reduces religion to culture, a framework within which the autonomization of religion becomes incomprehensible. How can a religious marker function outside the cultural marker? How can religion be exported? Globalization has shattered the link between religious and cultural markers (a link that was already impermanent).

A distinction must therefore be made between (real) domination, alienation, formatting and conversion. Alienation presupposes that the subject is not free and assumes an identity imposed from the outside, aimed to ensure submission. This is the big debate about the headscarf in France: how can a free woman voluntarily choose a symbol of submission? The schoolgirls who triggered the various headscarf cases did not do so under pressure from their parents or brothers. But it is this purported pressure that was transformed into a general explanatory principle, which is what makes it possible to turn this "free" choice into alienation and, moreover, a "cultural" alienation. That is why the media concentrate on the oppression of girls in the *banlieues* by their male peers (and fathers) hence the focus on the *Ni putes ni soumises* (neither whores nor slaves) association, which fights to free young French Muslim girls from their brothers' machismo, and the scandal, among the secular left, when its head, Fadela Amara, became Secretary of State under a practising Catholic minister, Christine Boutin, who believes there is a biological explanation for the social differences between the sexes. At the time of the French Revolution, a similar line of reasoning prompted the constitutive Assembly to ban monastic vows in February 1790: a monk, in taking definitive vows of obedience, voluntarily relinquished his freedom—which was incompatible with his status as a citizen. Alienation, following Marx and Feuerbach's analyses, tended to become the category used by secular thinkers to diminish religion (the other technique being that of reducing it to culture).

The acculturation theory remains highly reliant on domination theories. But the mainstream culture is not necessarily that of the political rulers. For example, in India, Islam, Judaism and Christianity became "Hinduized", in moulding themselves within the caste system, whereas political power resided with a succession of Muslim dynasties most notably the Mughals.[8]

On the other hand, acculturation can work against the ruling powers. Catholicism became established in the colonies as part of a political domination, and yet it helped forge the elites of the newly independent nations. The concepts of "religion", "nation" and people were taken up by the liberation movements. Neo-Hinduism is a reconstruction of complex religious practices and references within the framework of a modern territorial nationalism, and its language is English. The formatting of Hinduism according to the Western category of "religion" is now a factor for reconstituting an Indian identity in Hindu emigration and nationalism.[9] "Western" categories are also subverted in the process. There is mention of hybridization, mixing, but reference should also be made to *strategic mimetism*,[10] in other words borrowing from mainstream categories to reinforce the political vitality of the movement.

In Latin America, the transformation of Catholicism is evident: initially an instrument of Hispanic rule, during the twentieth century Catholicism gradually transformed into liberation theology, challenging the political order and combating American influence. A second wave of Christianization then emerged: Protestant evangelicalism, which explicitly rejected liberation theology and positioned itself on the right of the political spectrum. In Guatemala, in the 1970s, General Rios Montt, who had become a member of the American Church, The Pentecostal Church of the Word, led the country for two years, following a *coup d'état* (1982–1983); he then gave opponents of liberation theology a Christian rationale.

Matters can be even more complicated. The Indians of Chiapas, led by Subcomandante Marcos in their revolt against the Mexican establishment, are traditionally Catholics, but in the 1990s there were two waves of conversions: the first was Protestant evangelicalism which withdrew from political protest, and the second was Islam; and it would seem that Muslim converts had first converted to Protestantism.[11] But the missionary who created this second wave was a white Spaniard, Aurelino Perez, a convert to Islam under the name of Mohammed Nafia and a member of the Spanish group of Murabituns, made up exclusively of converts. Here is a case of a monotheistic religion brought over once again by a descendant of the Conquistadors, as if any good religion had to come from the Conquistadors and the *gringos*, but this time it was a religion that ostensibly adopted a third-worldist and anti-imperialist position. The president of the Murabituns in Spain, Mansour Escudero, demanded the right to hold Muslim prayers in Cordoba Cathedral, a former great mosque, and was expelled from it by the police at the bishop's request; he was then publicly supported by the General Secretary of the Arab League, Amr Musa.[12] The tactics of reason are sometimes unfathomable, especially given that hundreds of thousands of Amerindians recently arrived in Spain as immigrant workers converted to Protestant evangelicalism under the influence of Spanish-speaking ministers trained in the United States.

The growth of Pentecostalism in the indigenous societies of the former colonized countries is regularly defined either as the expression of American cultural domination (in the case of Guatemala), or as a new hybridization. An intriguing case is that of Pentecostalism in Tahiti.[13] Pentecostalism has been spread there by American churches which play on both Christian universalism and indigenism to signal their break with colonialism (making the Pentecostalist Church look "indigenous" and universal, as opposed to French colonialism). Some ministers allow "traditional" dances (but curiously they import the dances of Hawaii, an American state, to Tahiti) and have created a demon theory that picks up on a local tradition. But where is the syncretism? The cultural marker (dance) is artificial, and controversial, and the demon theory is very powerful in Pentecostalism: the closer the Kingdom of God, the more the demons are on the offensive. So here we have a religious paradigm that is independent from a local culture, even if it has helped the religion to become more firmly established.

Going further, there is also evidence that the re-appropriation of a religion by a local group can take the form of ultra-orthodoxy or fundamentalism—in other words the very negation of cultural difference. There is nothing new in that: the Berbers of the High Atlas seized on the fundamentalist version of Islam when they founded the great Almoravid and Almohad dynasties in Spain. In contemporary Afghanistan, the only ethnic group other than the Pashtuns to have adopted Salafism en masse are the Nuristanis, the last population to have been converted to Islam at the end of the nineteenth century. Africa today is a centre of Christian traditionalism, both for Anglicanism (Churches of Nigeria and Kenya) and Catholicism (Cardinal Hyacinthe Thiandoum, who succeeded Marcel Lefebvre as Archbishop of Dakar before he broke away from Rome). Tahitian evangelicalism is much more fundamentalist than the Protestant tendencies of metropolitan France.

Is Christianity Still Western?

Catholicism's centre of gravity has moved south: should this be seen as a cultural change, a different Catholic culture (as proposed by Philip Jenkins), or on the contrary, the height of deculturation? There has been a remarkable "third-worldization" of Christianity, and particularly of Catholicism, as a result not only of the demographic vitality of the South (and the plummeting birth rate in the traditionally Catholic countries like Spain and Italy), but also because those with a religious vocation are growing in number. In 1990, the Society of Jesus had 25,000 members: the leading country was the United States, with 4,724 followers, but the second was India (2,997); in 1990, the Société des missions de Lyon in France numbered 190 applicants, seventy-nine of them African, thirty-two Irish and four French.[14] Authors such as Philip Jenkins speak of "African Christianity" and foresee a reverse acculturation of Christianity: "As Christianity moves southward, the religion will be comparatively changed by immersion in the prevailing

155

cultures of those host countries".[15] But the question is whether this is indeed acculturation, since the Christianity of the South has re-exported to the North an orthodoxy that no longer fits there. In terms of norms, the Catholicism of the South does not represent different cultural norms but on the contrary, a resistance to changes in morality that are taking place in the West (the acceptance of homosexuality, for example). How can we explain the winning over of an Episcopal parish in a wealthy white suburb of Washington, hardly likely to dance to the sound of the tom-tom, by a Black Anglican bishop from Nigeria?[16] How should we understand the conversions carried out by the "dominated" among the "dominators"? The new religiosities are not specifically African: the use of music and emotions was already a feature of Western "awakenings". It is not the religious folklore that attracts recruits, but the central issue of orthodoxy and the place of religion in a person's private life.

The establishment of Christian Churches, or offshoots of Christianity in Africa (African Initiated Churches), has been described as a phenomenon of Africanization typical of Christianity, that is, of reverse acculturation.[17] This was perhaps the case initially, for these Churches were effectively born from breakaways from the white missionary Churches. On the one hand, the missionary Church became indigenized and, on the other, the "African Churches" like Aladura and the Celestial Church of Christ became globalized and exported themselves to the West. Experts (including Harold Turner) who prefer to avoid speaking of acculturation or syncretism, since the two terms are ethnocentric, have successively used the terms "African Independent Churches", to demonstrate their independence from the foreign missions, and to show their determination to be rooted in African culture, and recently "African Initiated Churches", as Africa is only a starting point and the Churches in question have the intention of becoming globalized.[18] These Churches gained a foothold in Europe in the 1960s, recruiting initially among African immigrant communities, using English and French, and then spreading into a sphere that was no longer that of immigration, either because they were reaching the second generation or those of Caribbean origin, or because they broke through among the "whites". These Churches are Protestant and charismatic, but multidenominational; they ignore traditional religious affiliations. They define themselves as religious communities, and not as the expression of an ethnic group.[19] Today, their strategy is to recruit in non-African areas, as do the major neo-Sufi brotherhoods and the Buddhist and neo-Hindu movements. But they also represent an interesting boomerang effect that completely clouds the issue of hybridization and acculturation. This phenomenon also affects the "new religions": the head of the Lukumi Babalu Aye, the first incorporated Santeria church (a religious movement born among Cuban slaves) in the USA is a "white", Ernesto Pichardo, whose bourgeois family in Cuba was converted by a black servant.

Here the separation of cultural and religious markers is particularly striking with regard to norms. One of Rome's traditional criticisms of the African clergy is of its laxity on the issue of sexuality: the Vatican excommunicated the Zambian Archbishop Emmanuel Milingo, who in 2001 married one Maria Sung, a Korean member of the Moon sect. But the "African Churches" do not claim to be more tolerant on issues of sexuality; on the contrary, today they claim to be closer to traditional Christian norms that are gradually being abandoned in the West, as evidenced by the controversy over homosexuality. It is interesting to see that nowadays there is talk of the homophobia of the "blacks" (or the Russians, etc.), as if tolerance towards homosexuality was a Western virtue, whereas it is a very recent phenomenon in the West. In fact, the question of norms should not be thought of in terms of "culture": the very rapid development of the debate on norms in contemporary Western law illustrates clearly that these norms are not specific to "Western culture". This is what the case of Pym Fortuyn, the gay activist sociology teacher who was assassinated in the Netherlands, illustrates; when he embarked on a political campaign opposing Islam, it was not in the name of defending a Christian Europe, but rather the Europe of the 1960s sexual revolution.

The new religious leaders from the South are often much more critical than their European colleagues when it comes to inculturation or the dialogue of civilizations. The criticism of inculturation as paganization comes not only from the traditional sectors of the European clergies, but also, increasingly, from religious representatives of these indigenous cultures, who argue for the universality of the dogma. The Reverend Fabien Ouamba states:

Inculturation is a poor disguise for a real desire to return to paganism for a category of Christians or a revenge strategy by this same paganism against Christianity from within. For a certain number of Christians, opening the Gospel to African culture amounts to allowing the African Christian to go back to his idols, incorporate his gods in the faith, go to the soothsayer, make sacrifices to his ancestors' skulls, get boozed with a clear conscience and to go and be purified by the priests of the traditional religion. It is, in short, to have permission to practice paganism in Christianity and in the Church under the guise of inculturation.[20]

Likewise, in 2008 in Great Britain, whereas Rowan Williams, the Archbishop of Canterbury, defended greater tolerance towards Islam, two of his Anglican colleagues (bishops in England but originally from the South), the Bishop of Rochester Michael Nazir, from the Indian sub-continent, and the Archbishop of York, John Sentamu, born in Uganda, could not have been more vehement in their criticism of the dialogue between civilizations and refusal to compromise.

Therefore, the South's move to Christianity does not signify the emergence of a new cultural hybridism, but quite the opposite, i.e. a greater divide between cultural and religious markers.

6

THE RELIGION MARKET

The Market: Metaphor or Fact?

The concept of a "religion market", more recent than that of acculturation, is now well established, at least in Anglo-Saxon academic circles.[1] In 2008, a leading international research organization, the Pew Forum on Religious and Public Life, published a survey on religious practice in the United States entitled *A Very Competitive Marketplace.* The concrete experience of a number of those involved in religion also prompts them to speak in terms of a "market":

So what have I observed? In terms of societal environment, it is clear that the religion 'market' is not flourishing for the historic Churches. It is very volatile, disparate, contrasting and indefinable, etc. Of course, there are 'niches' which are doing well, like that of Taizé, but they are not big enough to be significant in terms of growth ... The figures are there, and very much so. The laws of the market do indeed exist for everyone, and particularly for our parishes. It is up to us to recognize that for many of our contemporaries, our 'spiritual church products' seem either unappealing or inappropriate, or obsolete.[2]

In contrast to the theories of acculturation (which see religion as an offer that is imposed), this concept of a market, borrowed from the economy, postulates that first of all there is a demand for religion (invoking a human nature that, in any case, has a religious "need") which seeks out what is available on the market.[3] But globalization has led to a global religion market. We now speak of "consumers", in other words people who have spiritual needs to be fulfilled and who find themselves confronted with a choice of products that are varied and accessible, wherever they may be in the world, or almost. Globalization has opened up a market once controlled by one or several mainstream groups.

Today's "consumers" of religion have choice. The political constraint, which demands that subjects share the religion of the sovereign *(cuius regio eius religio)* has either disappeared or has become devoid of meaning as a result of the development of virtual spaces (Internet, satellite television). The social constraint, bound up with peer pressure, is seriously challenged by the loosening of social ties, the individualization of behaviours, access to information, and the crisis of the denominational Churches. The "products" are standardized, the marketing languages are either the vernacular languages or the major languages of globalization (notably English). In particular, the separation of religious and cultural markers means that people can "consume" a religious product without having to be familiar with the culture that has produced it. Products circulate via universalist technical media: radio, Internet, television networks. They are promoted through marketing campaigns: shows, star appearances, use of stadiums and advertising techniques; televangelists and imams (Amr Khalid) reach an audience that no pulpit or *minbar* could give them. Each individual can adapt the "belief kit" on the market to suit his or her needs, or almost: at the same time there is a customization and standardization of the products.

Market deregulation leads both to a homogenization of the products and increased competition. Religious freedom is not only an abstract right: it helps religion to evolve. Contemporary globalization therefore echoes the general extension of the market and places all religions in competition with each other, despite local attempts at closing in. The spread of religion goes hand in hand with democratization, as we witnessed with the collapse of the Soviet Empire. Of course, there are protectionist tendencies which attempt to reterritorialize religion (Algeria, Russia), by restricting conversions, or by dubbing any new product a "cult" especially if it is imported. In France in recent years the tendency of parliamentary missions has sometimes been to combat sectarian drifts—a tendency widely encouraged or boosted by the mass media.

But the opening up of the market presupposes the constitution of an individual player, more or less freed from ethnic, cultural, social and historical constraints, freely choosing the product on the religion market that best suits him or her. The market theory is vindicated by the phenomenon of free, voluntary mass conversions, carried out at the individual level, not collectively—a phenomenon that is probably typical of the modern era. We are no longer talking about the socially or politically inspired mass conversions which characterized the expansion of the major religions, but of a circulation of individual players who sometimes change "denomination" while remaining within the framework of the same religion (people switch from Sufism to Salafism or vice versa, or from Anglicanism to evangelicalism, very often as born-agains), or again by changing religion (from Islam to Christianity, or vice versa).

The use of the word "market" is nevertheless more metaphorical than truly conceptual. An interpretation that merely attempts to transpose economic theories, like those of Rodney Stark and Laurence Iannaccone,[4] soon comes up against its limitations: the idea that first of all deregulation is necessary (total religious freedom), followed by a rich and varied offer in order for religious practice to flourish (that is the theory of supply-side stimulation—the more there is of a religion on the market, the more people will consume), does not take into account either the disparities in religious practice or the fact that new religions can develop in hostile environments, like Christianity in Muslim countries (Algeria, Morocco and especially Central Asia).[5]

The market theory is diametrically opposed to the theory of acculturation. It is interesting to see how the debate on religion is modelled on, or apes, the debate on the economy in general, caught between a neo-Marxist theory of alienation, which sees religion purely in terms of domination strategies, and a neo-liberal theory of the rational individual acting within the transparency of a globalized market, which implies that the individual has absolute freedom. Advocates of the neo-Marxist viewpoint take a protective stance (defending sovereignty, territory, national tradition, established Churches, etc.), thus treating religion similarly to an identity issue, a line taken by conservatives and right-wingers until now, but becoming more prevalent among the left too. Suffice it to mention the role the secular left plays in France in the battle against sects, accused of being "submarines" of American influence. Typical is the attitude of Jean-Pierre Brard, the mayor of Montreuil who, in February 2005, interrupted an evangelical Protestant service where the worshippers were, incidentally, chiefly black. Today, this supposedly "republican" left is "territorialist": it is opposed to delocalization of the economy, wants to re-establish national sovereignty and is obsessed with the battle against foreign sects and missionaries, from Salafism to evangelicalism.

By contrast, exponents of the market approach defend marketization as inevitable and positive; the American Department of State has set up an office for the purpose of protecting religious freedom. Each year it publishes a report naming and shaming the countries which do not respect it, including France when it comes to the Islamic headscarf and cults. And so it follows that the upholders of "national" authenticity see Protestant proselytism as an avatar of American cultural imperialism and evidence of the desire to reduce "national markets"; authoritarian regimes all over the world also try to pass laws against proselytism (Russia, Algeria, where converts were prosecuted in 2008). On the other hand, supporters of the theory of the religion market see in it a sign of adaptation, of a marketing capacity and the exercise of freedom. The experience of conversions and of the expansion of some religions shows that, as always, "protectionism" is a rearguard action. The global religion market actually exists.

The question is, how does such a market work? How can religious goods circulate? Precisely because they are separated from their cultural origin. Culture makes the commodity unconsumable outside its cultural sphere, unless of course the indigenous culture itself is attacked. The creation of a uniform religion market presupposes the deculturation of religion, in other words the separation of the two markers. But this separation is enforced by the market and mobility, because the consumer can choose (this is the concept of availability for export). The market supposes the weakening of the social constraint and even the loss of its embeddedness. It gives people the freedom to choose and means that religious authorities cannot impose their will, at the risk of losing their customers. The current "religious revival" is not a revival at all, but a consequence of globalization.

But what makes the product marketable, apart from its ability to circulate? Effectively, the market in itself does not transform a religion into a product: the religion must have an ability to adapt to the market. It is the disconnect between cultural and religious markers that makes the product marketable. The market does not create the phenomenon, but it multiplies its effects by sanctioning the religions that have best adapted. The process of severance between religious and cultural markers is even more pronounced with globalization: in fact it becomes the norm and "crushes" traditional religiosities.

Secularization comes in not because it marginalizes religion, but because it isolates religion from culture and makes the religious object independent. Nevertheless, the detachment processes are not only linked to secularization, but also to the development of fundamentalisms which reject culture. Fundamentalism has always existed, but in globalization it finds a new space and a means of enduring. The separation of the religious marker from the cultural is both essential and unstable, the "fallout" for culture is unavoidable when fundamentalism (and all religious charismatism) appears in a real society. But globalization offers a virtual space which seems to make it possible to ignore both social and political constraints. Fundamentalism is therefore both a contributory factor and a product of globalization. It offers it a new space and it contributes to the deculturation of existing religions.

In separating religion from culture and autonomizing it, secularization and fundamentalism turn it into an export product. Free, individual conversion then becomes the proof of a religion's capacity to become globalized. The proliferation of laws against proselytism is the proof that the number of conversions rises in situations where conversion was perceived as marginal, even unthinkable (Algeria). Furthermore, even when conversions are not significant statistically, they always are symbolically, since they break a taboo and therefore help undermine a religion's social embeddedness (which is what is happening in Malaysia and Turkey).

Market Conditions

a) Circulation

The market assumes a common space for the circulation of products, operating outside any state controls. This free religion market exists today. It has not eradicated the national "markets", any more than in the economic sphere; national and ethnic religions are holding out. There are still protected markets, where laws attempt to restrict changes of religion or, to be more exact, the abandoning of national religions in favour of globalized religions. But on the other hand, religions closely linked to a group, a territory or a culture can suddenly put themselves on the global market and become universal.

Clearly, the circulation of religion is accentuated by migration and demographic shifts, but it goes much further. Religions can circulate independently of people, Neo-Buddhism, neo-Hinduism and a number of Sufi brotherhoods are spreading in the West independently of any mass migrations, since it is enough for the master or a few disciples to move around from place to place. There is also the increasingly frequent case of self-conversions as a result of reading or the Internet, or through fascination for a religion often evoked in the media and in some cases given a bad press (Islam in the West, Christianity in Muslim countries, but also Judaism). An interesting case is that of the African-Americans who converted to Judaism having had no contact either with a rabbi or with the local Jewish community, but from a Protestant biblical culture, as is also the case for a Ugandan community (*Abayudaya*) and a Burmese tribal group, which self-converted to Judaism declaring themselves to be the Bnei Menashe, one of the ten lost tribes of Israel.[6] In these last three instances, the leaders who self-converted to Judaism started out as Protestants: so it seems that the choice of Judaism stems from the promotion of Israel in a evangelicalist-type Protestant culture combined with the wish no longer to identify with Christianity; but the state of Israel does not encourage these conversions and generally refuses to grant citizenship to "self-converts", especially if they are black.[7]

While migration movements automatically result in a deterritorialization (and possible reterritorialization) of religions, this can just as easily happen *in situ*. But new technologies are obviously absolute deterritorialization factors. In his excellent study *Internet et Religion*, Jean-François Mayer shows how the Internet offers a non-territorial space to people who never leave their own homes. He cites the case of a virtual parish that was also "real", since its patron was the Anglican bishop of Oxford, which only accepts parishioners who are duly signed up and active on the website; in 2007, this i-church had 258 registered followers, some of them living in New Zealand.[8]

The emergence of the Reform Jews from the ghetto in the nineteenth century is an example of circulation without migration: it was the end of a territorial segregation associated with a social, cultural and linguistic segregation. This emergence prompted the Jews of the Enlightenment (the *Haskala* movement) to think of Judaism as "pure religion" and not as a culture (replacement of the concept of Jewish by that of Israelite). Hinduism "for export", which developed from the late nineteenth century (with the stream of Sris—or gurus—flocking to England), was not the outcome of a migration of Hindus, even if a few individuals did move around, masters going to the West and disciples going to India to study. Hinduism is traditionally the epitome of a territorialized religion: the role of the Ganges is central, and the social stratification of the caste system has difficulty surviving population movements. But Hinduism succeeded in becoming deterritorialized precisely by leaving aside the Ganges and caste and reconstituting itself as a religion for export, either to immigrant Indian populations (Jamaica), or to Western converts.

A recent example of a rapidly globalizing territorial religion is Mormonism: associated with a specific place, Utah in the United States, after a migration wave in 1847 modelled on the exodus of the Jewish people seeking a Holy Land where the Temple would be built, and victims of a persecution which served to reinforce the sense of community, highly endogamous (a tendency strengthened by the fact that the Mormons were initially polygamous), overtly racialist until the 1970s (blacks were not admitted to the priesthood), Mormonism seemed to have become the equivalent of a neo-ethnic religion through the establishment of a quasi-ethnic group around a religious identity. And then, within a few decades, swept along by an intense missionary movement (it was mandatory for young people to devote two years of their lives to preaching), Mormonism became deterritorialized[9] and gained a foothold among the black community, who were only allowed to become priests in 1978, following the civil rights movement.[10] Paradoxically, it was the civil rights movement that pushed a very conservative Church to abandon the chief obstacle to its expansion, i.e. its racial differentialism. Nowadays, the Mormon Church is one of the world's fastest-growing religions, especially among the black population. Jamaica and Africa both now have autochthonous Mormon Churches. The Church reportedly grew from 1.7 million members in 1960 to around 13 million by 2007, 7 million of whom are outside the USA.[11]

Today's missionary movements do not start from a centre and reach out to a "periphery". The prime movers do not necessarily come from countries associated with the religion they are spreading. The figure of the white Western Christian missionary is dying out to be replaced by a redistribution of roles. There is movement in all directions.

We have already mentioned the case of the Muslim Indians of Chiapas converted by white Spanish missionaries, themselves self-converts to Islam; the latter, the Murabitun, set up an organization in Spain made up solely of converts, the Junta Islamica, with Mansur Escudero as Chairman, Yusuf Fernandez as spokesman and Abdennur Prado as head of the Catalan branch. Meanwhile the Spanish Muslims of Arab origin are united under the umbrella of the Islamic Council of Spain. The Murabitun have also set up an organization in Dubai to mint gold dinars in order to bypass the global banking system (the company's chairman is Umar Ibrahim Vadillo). This represents a double cultural inversion: in Spain the Murabitun seem to be an Arab fifth column, albeit more culturally than ethnically, whereas in Mexico they are the expression of a Western-style deculturation.

Another reversal is the driving energy of an African Christianity which, in different guises, has set out to conquer the white West. A Protestant Pentecostalist Church, The Embassy of The Blessed Kingdom of God for All Nations, founded by a Nigerian minister, Sunday Adelaja, in Ukraine, sends missionaries to Western Europe and to the United States.[12] WASP American Episcopalians have joined the Anglican Church of Nigeria. Similarly, the Anglican Church of Kenya ordained two (white) American priests who are opposed to the ordination of gay priests; a participant in the ceremony, the Caribbean Drexel Gomez stated: "The Gospel ... must take precedence over culture".[13] In Denmark, a minister from Singapore, Ravi Chandran, is drawing those who feel let down by the Lutheran Church; the Lutheran bishop of Copenhagen reckons that more than a quarter of the capital's Sunday morning Protestant services are held in "foreign" Churches.[14]

In July 2007, twenty-three Korean Protestant missionaries, the majority of whom are women, were taken prisoner by the Taliban in Afghanistan, suddenly drawing attention to the huge Korean presence in Protestant missionary networks (particularly in Central Asia and West Africa). There are reportedly 16,000 Korean missionaries overseas, a figure which puts Korea (population 44 million, including 8.7 million Protestants) just behind the USA when it comes to the absolute number of Protestant missionaries abroad, and above it when it comes to the percentage of nationals with a missionary vocation.[15] It is as if Korean Protestantism were primarily an export product, like cars: the Protestant community is barely growing within the country (and, quite logically, Protestants are over-represented in the Ministry of Foreign Affairs). This is definitely an export religion.

Conversely (but the word barely has any meaning now), Westerners go to the East to become priests in Oriental religions to which they have converted in the West. The best-known examples are the members of Hare Krishna, various Zen schools and adherents of Sufism.

A young American Buddhist moved to Japan and wrote: "Early next morning we do *zazen* [meditation], joined by two board members. They are obviously unaccustomed to it". Suddenly young Japanese people are going to the United States to learn Buddhism: "Influenced by his long stay at Doshin-ji [Buddhist monastery in New-York, Ed.], the younger Suzuki plans to build an 'American-style' zendo at Unsen-ji next year. It is ironic, perhaps, that a revitalized Zen Buddhism in America is being carried back to influence the ancient, but weakened, practice in Japan. This morning's sitting is a rare event at the temple".[16] Extending the metaphor, we could speak of delocalized religions re-exporting themselves back to the countries of origin.

The Hare Krishna movement, a regular feature of Western street life since the 1960s, is also a good example of this "Hinduism for export": devoted to the worship of the god Krishna, it does indeed derive from Hinduism, but it was founded in New York in 1966 under the name of the International Society for Krishna Consciousness (ISKCON), by Bhaktivedanta Swami Prabhupada, and it recruited essentially among the Western hippie community. Missionary and egalitarian (rejection of the caste system), it breaks with the territorialist Hinduism of India. And yet, at the close of the twentieth century, it became re-Hinduized in two ways, while at the same time maintaining its missionary and anti-caste aspects. Numerous Indian immigrants to the United States joined the movement because it enabled them to reconcile their two identities, Hindu and American, in a synthesis that was virtual, since it was based on the use of floating religious markers (saffron robes, repetition of a mantra in a language they generally did not speak).[17] But the movement also became established in India, from the West and thanks to Western "priests" (the Vridavan temple founded in 1975, and New Delhi, at Raja Dhirshain Marg, built in 1998): an information panel at the Delhi temple informs us that "In the temple there are beautiful paintings by Russian artists on the different past times of Radha-Krishna, Sita-Ram, Laxman, Hanuman and Chaitanya Mahaprabhu. Special programs like kirtan, aarti, pravachan and prasadam are held every Sunday".[18] There are two noteworthy points here: the paintings in the temple are the work of Russians (the icon tradition?), and the "religious service" offered by the temple is modelled on the Sunday-morning Protestant service held at a specific time. Even the board giving details of the type of services and times of the services offered has a distinctly American flavour.

The Rastafarian movement targets "globalized blacks": it emerged in Jamaica and worships Haile Selassie, the emperor of an Ethiopia which was the only black country to hold out against colonialism. But in the 1960s, the movement crystallized around reggae with the musician Bob Marley as its figurehead, to become established in Nigeria.[19] A mythical Africa—Ethiopia—was re-invented in the West, subsequently to become rooted in the real Africa: the journey was made from West to East.

Another example is the radical Islamist movement Hizb ut-Tahrir. Founded in the early 1950s in Jordan as an Islamist movement to free Palestine, it spread throughout Europe from its London base. Recruiting among second-generation and converted Muslims, it advocated the establishment of a non-territorialized caliphate (in other words having jurisdiction over all Muslims wherever they are in the world). From London, it re-exported itself to Central Asia (Uzbekistan), Pakistan and Australia, and, from Australia to Indonesia where it is becoming increasingly influential. In 2002, three British citizens were arrested in Cairo, accused of attempting to establish Hizb ut-Tahrir there: one of them, from a Pakistani family was born in the UK, another, Ian Nisbet, was a convert, and the third, Reza Pankhurst, had an Iranian father and an English mother. This is an example of Islamic radicalism being exported to Muslim countries from the West.

Sufism is another instance of this delocalization of religion. A certain number of brotherhoods exported themselves by playing on two complementary factors: immigration and conversion. Among the first are the Tijaniya and the Mourides of Senegal, which themselves are relatively recent brotherhoods (late nineteenth century). These brotherhoods operate in a "glocal" manner: initially the group has a specific territorial base which will remain its global headquarters, i.e. the town of Touba for the Mourides. Immigrants from the brotherhood to Europe and the United States, who set off in search of work and not to proselytize, create very supportive networks: they send money back to Touba, they welcome and assist young migrants, while dignitaries circulate from one immigrant community to another. And so these networks become transnational networks for the movement of goods and people and become part of a globalized economy. But at the same time, the group converts outside its ethnic, migrant base; newcomers also find the path to Touba.

One of the best-known brotherhoods whose expansion is due to conversions rather than to emigration is the Haqqanya: originally it was a branch of the Naqshbandi family, established in the Caucasus and then in the Middle East; in the second half of the twentieth century, their Sheikh was Mawlana Shaykh Nazim Adil al-Haqqani, an Arab of Syrian origin living in the North of Cyprus. One of his disciples, Lebanese-born Muhammad Hisham Kabbani, moved permanently to Chicago in 1991. The American branch saw a meteoric growth, far surpassing the number of disciples in the Middle East. A Bosnian branch grew out of the American branch. The language of the brotherhood's websites is therefore English (with a Bosnian version).

But Sufism in the West has an older history. In 1910, Inayat Khan, an Indian musician, visited Europe with his brother. A member of the *chestiyya* Sufi movement, he founded his own order in the West, with converts. In 1923, he set up the International Sufi Movement in Geneva, with a constitution and a transnational hierarchical structure.[20] This framework is far removed from the Sufi traditions in the Muslim countries. This brand of Sufism is purely Western and is what I term "neo-Sufism", even if the word is used in various ways. Other Sufi movements transplanted in this way include the Qadiriya Boutchichiya, which came from Morocco, spread in France via converts who tended to be from the middle and upper classes, (a description from the inside can be found in the book *Self-Islam* by Abdennour Bidar).[21] The brotherhood of the Fethullahci, led by Fethullah Gülen, is a typical case of a globalized neo-brotherhood, even if it has difficulty spreading beyond the Turkish-speaking sphere. Familiar to experts on Turkey, it found new prominence when its leader was "elected" the most influential intellectual in the world through an Internet survey carried out by the magazines *Foreign Policy* and *Prospect* (June 2008). It was of course the followers of the brotherhood who voted collectively (probably under instructions), but, as there were 500,000 online voters, this reflects the globalized nature of the brotherhood (members are connected to the Internet and capable of following instructions in English). And then there are examples of more or less imaginary "brotherhoods", like the one founded by the prolific author Idries Shah who claimed to recruit among the leading figures of the Muslim world.[22]

The development of international religious networks from local groups is not confined to Sufism but is often linked to a charismatic figure who founds a religious school of thought. These "glocal" net-

169

works can also be strengthened as a result of splits, conflicts, the reformulation and autonomization of local branches, each one affirming its authenticity. The ultra-orthodox Jewish movement has also spawned networks similar to brotherhoods since they are essentially identified with schools of thought headed by charismatic rabbis; they are all the more deterritorialized in that they are originally non-Zionist—they do not convert but are entirely globalized.[23]

b) Export Religions

Successful religions all have an export formula. They are founded on the complete separation of the religious marker from the cultural marker, and on a formatting that enables them to appear as a universal religion adapted to the new forms of religiosity, such as self-realization. This does not mean they reject the cultural marker: on the contrary, they can exhibit some cultural markers, rather like supermarket loss leaders, but detached from any real society, in a context where a certain exoticism is seen as positive, like advertising designed to appeal to floating markets: exoticism (French names for US bakeries), the assumed permanent connection (pasta and Italy) that is found in the link between Zen and Japan (from the kimono to karate terms). The saffron robes of the Hare Krishna or the *shalwar kamiz* (long white shirt and baggy trousers) of the Salafis function as imaginary references. Deculturation does not mean abandoning cultural markers, but manipulating them outside any social reality. Proclaiming the autonomy of the faith community involves a certain exhibitionism, like the headscarf. That does not mean that any religious symbol is a sign of exhibitionism, but that it is interpreted as such. Visibility is characteristic of contemporary religion.

In the strict sense, we shall term "export religion" those that exist solely in their exported form: neo-Buddhism, neo-Hinduism, neo-Sufi brotherhoods. They are utterly cut off from their roots, and when they return to them, it is in the form of a re-exportation and not the revival of a local tradition.

Hinduism is deeply rooted in a society (castes) and a territory; it is very diversified and does not really refer to a body of precise, standardized doctrines. It can only become missionary if first of all it transforms itself into something new: it is hard to imagine Hindu missionaries explaining the need to adopt the caste system. It therefore requires an explicit reformulation of the belief system, detached from its original culture and society while preserving the exotic Oriental "touch" that is its appeal (especially the gurus' dress). Beliefs also need to be standardized, simplified and formatted so that they can operate in Western environments. In short, to export Hinduism, it must be transformed into a religion.

This reformulation process was implemented by Hindu thinkers in India, generally those with a dual culture, writing mainly in English but ultimately only finding an audience in the West. As with Buddhism, they emerged at a time of religious and political reform, at the close of the nineteenth century, as a reaction against the English hegemony of which they were nevertheless also a product—but this pre-dated exportation (it is not immigration in itself that changes a religion).[24] For them, the West was a means of affirming the universalism of their thinking. These were not Western intellectuals seeking an imaginary Hinduism, but Indian philosophers and gurus who went and "sold" a spirituality presented as universalist, as a reaction against Western materialism; but their approach also implies a critique of colonialism, which is very pronounced in thinkers such as Sri Aurobindo. The colonial background is fundamental, but it acts in both directions: the reciprocal reformatting of religion resulting in a competition to bring comparable if not similar products face to face.

The Ramakrishna Mission developed in India in the late nineteenth century; it targeted Anglicized Indians, and its first publication was in English. One of its members, Swami Vivekananda, gave a paper which attracted a great deal of attention at the 1893 World's Parliament of Religions in Chicago, one of the first examples of attempts to transcend religions in favour of spirituality and shared values (no Muslims were present at this gathering however). The most renowned case is that of Sri Aurobindo (1872–1950), who helped popularize yoga. He instigated the Auroville project, near Pondicherry. It is interesting that these movements adopt modern legal norms (registering their organizations under legal statutes), refuse to define themselves as a religion and prefer to be known as philosophies. They also emphasize the importance of meditation techniques that can be acquired outside their original host cultures and are often seen as providing access to an "Oriental" culture based on silence and the rejection of discourse, i.e. of the Word, thereby escaping the need for language learning and studying literature. Again, a little holy ignorance!

Other examples include the Sri Ram Chandra Mission (established in 1945 in the United States), the guru Swami Prakashanand Saraswati (whose centre is in Austin, Texas), Maharishi Mahesh Yogi (the Beatles' guru), and the Divine Light Mission, founded in 1970 by the guru Maharaj Ji and established in Denver, Colorado.

A number of similarities have been observed in Buddhism. In exporting itself, Buddhism loses two fundamental characteristics: its monasticism and the division into "vehicles" or schools of religious thought. As Raphaël Liogier points out, we are witnessing both a simplification and standardization of ideas, and a proliferation of transnational bureaucratic organizations claiming to be Buddhist but which are far removed from tradition.[25] British Buddhists have tried to re-establish Buddhism in India, as did the "Untouchables", or Dalits starting with India's first president, Bhimrao Ramji Ambedkar, who eventually converted. So in Buddhism this "deculturating" choice derives from the rejection of the caste system.

Some forms of Buddhism have prospered better in the West than in their countries of origin. Japanese Shin Buddhism began in the late nineteenth century within Japan's sphere of influence, but it quickly became established in Hawaii, and took off with "Bishop" Yemyo Imamura, between 1900 and 1932. Imamura switched to English and built a dharma school, as did the Hindus. Then he took on as his deputy a convert, Shinkaku Hunt, a former British Anglican priest. At the same time, in San Francisco, the Dharma Sangha of Buddha was established by "whites". Self-converts can also appropriate Buddhism in this way, as in Germany.[26] But generally, as with Hinduism, there is a master, in this instance from Japan, like the famous Teitaro Suzuki (1870–1966), whose master, Shako Suen, was also at the World's Parliament of Religions in Chicago in 1893. And so it is clear that the desire for internationalization (and not only to defend an existing religion) was evident in different milieus.

But this Western poaching takes on a different dimension when a movement like the Soka Gakkai appears. Here we are not dealing with a religion formatted for export: the transformation happened *in situ* in Japan where the movement has considerable influence including at a political level (embodied in a party, The New Komeito). But, as Lorne L. Dawson writes, it very consciously Westernized its organizational structure, not in order to export itself, but because it was fashionable to do so.[27] In this instance, the change is linked not to an export strategy, but to a transformation of religion setting it on a course leading to globalization.

Movements derived from Hinduism and Buddhism frequently adopt non-religious legal forms (foundations, NGOs), like the Brahma Kumaris World Spiritual University, a spiritual organization of the eponymous sect, which, as an NGO, was given consultative status to the United Nations Economic and Social Council in 1983, and then to UNICEF in 1987. It is also associated with the United Nations Department of Public Information. In 1986, it launched its "Million Minutes of Peace" appeal. The objective of the programme was to emphasize that "peace begins with the individual and the peace process therefore must start with the individual". This trend is probably a way of escaping the religion paradigm, which demands compliance with the mainstream model of religion, the concept of "religion" as it happens. Religions for export therefore challenge not only the relationship between the religious marker and the cultural marker, but also the nature itself of the religious marker.

The circulation of religions has possibly led to the erosion of religion by new forms of synthesis between belief, law and power, in other words, tending towards humanitarian action. NGOs are akin to modern-day foreign missions. But that is another story.

c) The Deterritorialization of the Local

Another form of deterritorialization is that of the local community: the disappearance of the territorial parish in favour of a choice of place of worship depending on affinities. The Catholic Church was a territorialization factor: in many countries, the "parish" became an administrative body (as is still the case in Louisiana) and, traditionally, worshippers were obliged to frequent their parish church; they married in it and were buried there. Jesuit missions in Quebec, Paraguay (on the colonial model of the *encomiendas*) and China established indigenous Christian villages; the Reductions of Paraguay were a sort of forerunner of the *kolkhoz* or the *kibbutz*.[28] The monasteries, often linked to an agricultural estate, were also forms of religious territorialization. The Catholic practice of worshipping local saints or associating one saint with a number of sites (Our Lady of Lourdes, our Lady of Lorette, our Lady of Guadalupe) helped to sanctify a territorial division and endow particular places with their own religious identity. Similar phenomena are to be found in Islam: the Afghan *zyarat*, the Moroccan *zawwya* and *mulud*, and the Azerbaijani *pir* are ways of pinning down sometimes nomadic tribal groups to a territory associated with a saint's tomb, or to mark the identity of local communities.

Moreover, in Islam, the identity of a neighbourhood is traditionally marked by a mosque; in Central Asia, the sudden mushrooming of mosques after the collapse of the USSR was more to do with the desire of each *mahalla*, or neighbourhood, to have its eponymous mosque than with a sudden surge of religion. Judaism, especially in North Africa, also has a long history of local "saints". In all the major religions, pilgrimages create a network across the territory which help shape it. There is a close link between religious practices, socialization and territorialization which the move towards "faith communities" breaks.

Effectively, in a number of today's religions, the notion of a "parish" or a territorial community is being eroded in favour of the community of affinities. The same place of worship might see not only different generations of believers passing through (newcomers who live as a diaspora, a second generation for whom culture and religion are separate), different categories of believers (in an American Buddhist temple immigrants from South-East Asia mix with white converts), but also different religions as upward social mobility disperses communities (synagogues or churches converted to mosques).[29] These days "ethnic neighbourhoods" resulting from immigration seem to last for a shorter time than at the beginning of the twentieth century; there is no longer a "Little Italy" in the United States, and upwardly mobile groups do not seek to reconstitute ethnic neighbourhoods (the Jews of New York who settle in Florida no longer form neighbourhood communities). On the other hand, people form groups on the basis of religious affinity rather than ethnicity (orthodox Jews like the Lubavitch and the Satmar in Montreal and New York).[30] But these groupings are precarious, as for different reasons (upward mobility of their members, housing conflicts etc.) the re-territorialization at local level remains fragile. In 2008, there was a neighbourhood conflict surrounding a Hindu temple in Fairfax county, near Washington, owing to its popularity there was insufficient parking and the neighbours demanded that the temple be moved. But the priests had just completed the slow ritual process of "territorializing" the gods, which made moving difficult from a religious point of view. The gods (and the worshippers) were sent away, through the power of real estate considerations, to wander in an endless "wilderness".[31]

People now move to be near the place of worship that suits their religious sensibility. There is no longer an automatic correspondence between the social bond and the religious bond. New religious movements favour mega churches, stadiums, assemblies in secular venues (including the gatherings of young people organized by Pope John Paul II). We are seeing congregations of affinity rather than of proximity. In France, the Catholic parish is often in decline as a result of competition from new, non-territorialized congregations, in other words not under the jurisdiction of the bishop. Many parishes prefer to call themselves simply a "community" rather than a parish. Priests are increasingly asking those who come asking for a religious service, such as marriage, to demonstrate commitment and a personal link with the community; it is not enough just to be included in the register of baptisms or to reside in the parish. To be married, for example, it is no longer sufficient to have been baptized or to reside in the parish; increasingly priests are asking that the couple be members of the local community and not simply "Catholic". What is vanishing, for the Church, is the notion of the "sociological Catholic" or "nominal Catholic": people must prove their faith, one can assume no longer that subjects are believers.

The decline in the number of priests has strengthened the role of the community to the detriment of the parish, since priests are now mobile. But the Vatican is resisting this development. Sunday Assemblies in the Absence of Priests (SAAP) were curbed if not prohibited, as increasingly the priest was being replaced by lay members. In France, 10 per cent of serving priests are of foreign origin—African, Polish, Lebanese etc. Priests are being replaced by lay people for all sorts of things. Only two sacraments are reserved for priests, the Eucharist and confession, in addition to their role of community leader. Lay communities are being established, not through the will of Rome, but quite simply because the priest is being marginalized. Alpha Groups, for example, are religious and theological formations set up by a fundamentalist Anglican, with special methods and a zealous proselytism, but these are rapidly being emulated by Catholics. Their aim is to bring back or bring in all-comers in the cities in particular, based on a very modern form of conviviality: people share an apartment and day-to-day life while working on a group project.

175

The ultimate stage of the process could be the i-church. There are already a number of websites for all the major religions which offer religious services: liturgical moments (the equivalent of hours of monastic prayer), prayer moments, guided "retreats", sermons, confession, and also conversion, or even matchmaking to find a spouse of the same religion, since people now have only sporadic, even virtual contact with their chosen community.

This is one of the reasons for the success of Protestantism and evangelicalism: whereas the Virgin Mary is territorialized, The Holy Spirit is anywhere and everywhere. There is no need to have a real rock on which to build the Church. You can pray in a garage or a stadium. The sacredness of the place is no longer important (whereas a church is traditionally consecrated, then purified if it is desecrated). Pentecostalists and evangelicals place the emphasis on the Holy Spirit; they do not attach any importance to the sacredness of the place of prayer, and nor do they go on pilgrimages. The Holy Spirit is everywhere, place no longer matters, except perhaps the Holy Land. The Catholic Church has the same theological conception of the Holy Spirit, but it plays no part in popular religiosity, which is chiefly devoted to Mary (hence often territorial), whereas it is essential in the evangelicals' worship. This confirms that the issue is less to do with theology than with religiosity.

This refusal to sacralize places of worship, geographical places and territories is just as evident in Salafism, which does not celebrate *mawlid* and *ziyarat* (respectively Moroccan and Central Asian local pilgrimage centres), the worship of local saints and the sacralization of tombs (even that of the Prophet). Only Mecca escapes this deterritorialization, and only just. Salafism picks up on the idea that a mosque is simply a place of prayer only for the duration of the prayer (*masjid*, the place of prostration [*sajd*], which no longer has any meaning when the rites are not being performed).

But Catholicism also has its own ways of globalizing its symbols. The "transportation" of territorialized saints is interesting. A local saint, in the context of migration, becomes either a sort of tribal "totem", or is transposed to the space of a broader section of the population. For example the Virgin of Guadalupe, greatly revered in Mexico, moved to Los Angeles with refugees from the *Cristero* rebellion of the 1930s and the clandestine Mexican immigrants of today. Although she was purely Mexican in her original context, since the other Latin American countries had their own holy places, the Virgin of Guadalupe gradually became the "saint" of all the Latinos in the United States, even of all the Catholic immigrants in Los Angeles, including the Vietnamese and the Koreans. This has gone hand in hand with the creation of neo-ethnic groups, followed by de-ethnicization.[32] On Saint Patrick's Day, all of New York is Irish. Here, the totemic function of the Catholic saints (being the emblem of a corporation, a parish, a group, an ethnic group or a nation) is also able to become globalized: the totem remains, but it becomes nomadic and its audience changes.

This is not to say that the Internet has replaced territory. There is a definite trend in this direction, but the notion of place still makes sense. However, territory is being eroded, or rather the new territories are virtual. Deterritorialization goes along with the quest for imaginary territories (*ummah*, Holy Land, Ganges, Lhasa etc.) and with the apocalyptic second-coming brand of millenarianism that announces the end of the world. Sub-cultures are becoming globalized, but they each bring their "map" of the world with a centre and specific places of pilgrimage. Beyond these pilgrimages which territorialize by drawing on historical roots—what I call "identity pilgrimages" (such as the Chartres pilgrimage)—what we are seeing is pilgrimages that have become deterritorialized. Paradoxically this applies to the Muslim *hajj*. There is indeed a place, Mecca, but it has been cut off from its context; the pilgrim, supervised, isolated, merged into the abstract mass of Muslims from all over the world, standardized by the clothing and the rite, does not go to Saudi Arabia, but to Mecca (which is even specified on the visa). The journey is no longer 'real', as pilgrims travel by air: they no longer journey by land. Apart from the Iranians (the riots of 1987) and the Saudis themselves (the storming of the Grand Mosque in 1979), no radical movement has shown an interest in Mecca. It is not an issue for political Islam because Mecca has only a virtual reality.

What is at issue in the pilgrimage is very much the territorialization of religion. For example, a controversy is currently raging in the Hassidic world. Rabbi Nachman of Breslau (1712–1810), is buried at Uman, in Ukraine. His tomb attracts tens of thousands of pilgrims every year, particularly at Jewish New Year, to the extent that special airline charters have been set up.[33] As mentioned earlier, the Nachman group puts the emphasis on "joy" as a factor in transmitting faith, and attracts followers from far beyond its traditional religious school. Historically, the group is not Zionist, like many Hasidim, and so feels non-territorialized (although that does not make it anti-Zionist). But an appeal has been launched in Israel to repatriate the rabbi's ashes to the Hebrew state, the effect of which would be for these religious, ethnic and political maps to coincide. So here we observe the territorialization of a religious Jewish identity in favour of an Israeli identity. But then what happens to the diaspora? Either it is perceived as having a vocation to make *aliyah* (which is the official Israeli position), or it is seen as a non-territorialized political Israel (in 2008 the Chairman of the Jewish Council of Europe demanded that all Jews have the right to vote in Israel), or as a religious community living in a space other than that of political territorialization.

Territorialization is the revenge of politics.

d) The De-Ethnicization of Religion

There is a to-ing and fro-ing in the separation of religious and cultural markers: ethnic religions become universalized, but, as a result of immigration among other things, new connections between ethnicity and religion are appearing, and new ethnic groups are even emerging, like those now called the "Muslims" of Europe, irrespective of the extent of their religious practice.

But this ethnicization is often purely transient, particularly with regard to immigration. Ethnic Churches are characteristic of the first generation, such as the "white Russians" in France after 1917. The Orthodox Churches of Paris are divided between Russian, Armenian, Ukrainian, Coptic, Syriac, Greek, Chaldean, Romanian, Georgian, etc. Paris had, and still has, Polish, Vietnamese and Tamil Catholic churches. The African Muslim brotherhoods, Vietnamese Buddhist temples after the immigration of the boat people, the Tamil Hindu temples of Reunion Island and the Iranian Shia mosques of Los Angeles—in all these cases a religious marker and a cultural marker (either national or linguistic) are closely interlinked. But this seeming ethnicization is often merely a transitional stage before a new separation. The moment (the transition) is taken for the essence of the phenomenon.

Let us take the case of the ethnically Chinese Protestant Church in the United States, the Chinese Christian Church (CCC) of Greater Washington, analyzed by Fenggang Yang. At first glance, it may appear to be an ethnic Church which recruits primarily among the Chinese immigrants keen to integrate, who convert to Christianity while holding onto Chinese cultural markers. But the author shows that things are more complex than that: first of all, unlike the traditional immigrant Churches (Italian, Polish and Irish for Catholicism), but like all the modern-day evangelical Churches, the CCC does not have any social integration activities (such as support or mutual aid). It devotes itself solely to preaching and worship (the only exception being that it gives Chinese classes). Furthermore, the ministers refuse to recognize any ethnic dimension (which would certainly not have been true of an Italian or Irish Church a century earlier). The congregation is made up of people of Chinese origin who are completely assimilated, who do not need a stepping stone to integration or a refuge. So why travel miles to be with others from the same background? Because here, that background is primarily religious: "Chinese Christians have chosen evangelical or fundamentalist Christianity and subsequently have formed non-denominational ethnic churches. They see themselves as a minority, not so much in the ethnic but in the religious sense. They say that, although many Americans claim to be Christian, only a few are true Christians—those who are born-again".[34] And the author goes on, emphasizing that for today's Chinese, Christianity is no longer an "imperialist" religion, but a universalist faith. In other words, it has broken away from its historical image, because it has become de-nationalized and de-ethnicized. This is an argument that I have heard among the Taliban: in answer to the question of why, if they claim to represent "true" Islam, do they define themselves (and particular why do they act) as Pashtuns, they reply: "Because the Pashtuns are the best Muslims in Afghanistan".

Another example is that of the reconstruction of Hinduism among migrant Indians. The first stage is the ethnicization of the religion, in other words the identification of an ethnic group with a religion. The fact that in India there is a large Muslim minority and that the state is officially secular means that, except among the nationalists of the Bharatiya Janata Party (BJP)—only just—there is no strict identification between Hinduism and being Indian. The diversity of castes, languages and regions is too enormous.

But with emigration, the socio-cultural basis of the castes disappears, even if the memory of them remains alive. Muslim Indians then tend to identify with other Muslims from the Indian sub-continent (for example, on Reunion, the *Zarab* Muslims from Gujarat define themselves as Muslim first, as opposed to the Hindu Tamils, who in this case stress their Tamil identity; and yet both groups come from India). Many expatriate Hindus then reconstruct a Hinduism common to all the groups, irrespective of caste, standardized and formatted according to the prevailing concept of what a religion is. Steven Vertovec has studied the phenomenon in depth and shows how, in the Caribbean, Hinduism becomes the ethnic religion of Indians.[35] This ethnicization process is often only the first step towards deculturation—separation of religious and cultural markers—since "ethnic" religions are formatted along the lines of the religions of the host countries. Once the religion is autonomized, it can become de-ethnicized and operate outside its original cultural environment. In fact, the deculturation of Hinduism among Indian migrants, or in the context of "religion for export", analyzed above, relies on processes that have much in common: challenging the caste system, standardization, simplification and professionalization of the protagonists.

Therefore, ethnicization can be a stage in the deculturation process, because we are dealing with a neo-ethnic group, like the "Muslims" in Europe who manufacture "pure religion" which is better equipped to emancipate itself from culture than the complex constructions rooted in the original cultures. In the case of reconstructed Hinduism in Jamaica, reformulation goes hand in hand with the influence of reformist groups. The Arya Samaj movement, which was founded in 1875 by Swami Dayanand Saraswati, who rejected the caste system, promoted monotheism and placed great importance on the Vedas, or sacred texts. Universalism, monotheism, revealed book: this is clearly a theological and "ecclesiological" formatting process based on the Christian template.

Paradoxically, the ethnicization stage can also be a route to the deculturation of a religion. Ursula King shows how Hinduism cannot function outside India unless it becomes deculturated.[36] But even in India, the process of deculturation by transformation is apparent in the way in which the nationalist BJP reconstructs a homogeneous Hinduism, also overlooking the caste system. In this instance, the invention of a Hinduism modelled on a Western religion, Christianity as it happens, is not the product of postcolonial alienation, but on the contrary, of a nationalist identity claim seeking to assert itself in the global religion market, to avoid being subjected to the influence of foreign religious paradigms that are better suited to the new market.

The fabrication of European Muslims as a neo-ethnic group also has a deculturating effect, since the lowest common denominator uniting them can only be defined in opposition to concrete cultures, which means that Salafism is often the best-placed strand to define this universalist religion.

The following stage is the transition from ethnic community to faith community. It is the faithful who no longer want to be seen as "ethnic", either because their personal identity is now religious, or because the group has ceased to have an ethnic base. Karen Chai studied the transformation of a "denominational" Korean Protestant Church in the United States into a multi-ethnic Church, using English as its working language and becoming evangelical to some degree.[37] The parents are Korean, speak Korean and want their children to marry Koreans; in the "bourgeois" Protestantism of the established Churches they are seeking a way of reconciling integration, social advancement and maintaining their ethnic and cultural identity. The younger generation, however, are born-again evangelicals for whom faith is more important than ethnicity when choosing a marriage partner. Here too the shift to evangelicalism works in favour of deculturation. It is often in the choice of minister (must he belong to the ethnic group?) that tensions become evident.

In Tahiti, one of the Chinese Pentecostalist Churches was initially explicitly "ethnic" (of the Hakka group), but it became a multi-ethnic Church as a result of a split: the Hakka community leaders of the Alleluja Church sacked the (French) minister because he was recruiting particularly among non-Chinese communities; so he left the Church to found a new one, and 80 per cent of the Chinese congregation followed him.[38] At the same time, in 1997, in an apparently unconnected move, the dances and other cultural expressions of the Bonne Nouvelle Tahitian Pentecostalist Church were rejected by the United States-trained clergy. This reflects a complex shift in the articulation between Tahitian identity, evangelicalism (which operates on the political level) and deculturation.

When the Russian Patriarch Alexis II visited France in October 2007, he requested that French Orthodox communities that are not linked with other national non-Russian Churches (Greek, Serbian etc.) be placed under his jurisdiction. But there was a great deal of protest from the French Orthodox community, since they did not feel, or no longer felt, "Russian" and they wanted to sever the link between ethnic group, nation and Orthodoxy. Michel Sollogoub, the secretary of the Council of the Archdiocese of Russian Orthodox Churches in

Western Europe, wrote in *Le Figaro*: "This revival of the Church in Russia should not eclipse the modest but real presence of Orthodoxy in France. A noteworthy effect of the history of the twentieth century is that the Orthodox Church stepped outside its traditional geographical boundaries. Russian and Greek, and later Serbian, Romanian and Lebanese migrations have resulted in a firmly established Orthodox presence on French soil, even if these communities maintain strong ties with their original Churches. After eighty years of history, Orthodoxy in France is no longer a foreigners' Church. The awareness of a common responsibility in the witnessing of Orthodoxy and the desire to overcome the divisions between ethnic dioceses led to the setting up of an Inter-Episcopal Committee in 1967. Following the recommendations of the pan-Orthodox meeting of Chambésy in 1993, this body was renamed the Assembly of Orthodox Bishops of France (AEOF) in 1997. The aim was to create, in the long term, and with the support of the different original Churches, a unified synodal structure, admittedly temporary, but in line with Orthodox ecclesiology".[39]

Christian Orthodoxy became established in France as a result of ethnic immigration, but it became de-ethnicized. Those who are interested in the subject can visit the chapel of Saint Gregory the Athonite and Anastasia the Roma at Bernwiller in the Sundgau (south of Alsace). The icons were painted by an American convert and the chapel is looked after by Dr Louis Schittly, a Mount Athos convert and one of the founders of Médecins sans frontières.

e) Deculturation

These "marketing" processes therefore assume the deculturation of religion and, once again, some religions are in a better position than others to become deculturated. People sometimes wonder why Pentecostalism is the religion that is experiencing the strongest expansion. Pentecostalism places the emphasis on emotion, healing and speaking in tongues. Under the influence of the Holy Spirit, emulating the apostles, some believers start "speaking in tongues", and people with whom they have no shared language are able to understand what they say. But the Pentecostalists who preach in "tongues" do not preach in any real language: glossolalia is purely a succession of sounds. The "message" gets through all the same: the Word of God no longer needs to be set down in a specific language and culture. It is precisely because the spirit is dissociated from the Word that the message is universal. The Holy Spirit is beyond culture, even if Christ took on a human form.

However, independently of religion, we are currently witnessing a reduction of the "substance" of languages in favour of the transmission of a message which, in order to be univocal, must be simple. Therefore, Pentecostalism sits alongside the improvement of automatic translation systems and the decline of languages of communication. English, which is now dominant, turns into pidgin, or rather "globish", the term coined by Jean-Paul Nerrière in his excellent book.[40] Now it's the era of "goddish".

José Casanova eloquently summarizes this link between the local and the global made by Pentecostalism:

But how can it [Pentecostalism] be de-territorialized and local at the same time? Because it is an uprooted local culture engaged in spiritual warfare with its own roots. This is the paradox of the local character of Pentecostalism. It cannot be understood in the traditional sense of Catholic 'inculturation,' that is, as the relationship between the Catholic, i.e. universal and the local, i.e. particular. ... Pentecostalism is not a translocal phenomenon which assumes the different particular forms of a local territorial culture. Nor is it a kind of syncretic symbiosis or symbiotic syncresis of the general and the local. Pentecostals are, for instance, everywhere leading an unabashed and uncompromising onslaught against their local cultures: against Afro-Brazilian spirit cults in Brazil; against Voodoo in Haiti; against witchcraft in Africa; against shamanism in Korea... It is in their very struggle against local culture that they prove how locally rooted they are...[41]

One could cite many more signs of this trend towards deculturation, even when the Pentecostalist Churches identify closely with a particular people; for instance, the Pentecostalist Assemblies of God, dominant in Tahiti, do combat traditional beliefs and advocate the use of French. Christian ministers of Pakistani origin return to their homeland and behave like the Christian version of the Tabligh: "This was part of Arif's mission: to infuse a fundamentalist faith and literalist understanding of Scripture in Pakistani 'nominalists', a word Martin and Shehzad spoke with disdain, a word damning those who were Christians in name only, Christians by lineage but not practice, Christians who conformed to Pakistani culture rather than biblical teaching".[42] All the literature on Pentecostalism is in a similar vein: there is both an affirmation of identity and a negation of traditional identity-markers. This dual logic is taken to extremes in one particular movement: Youth With a Mission. Taking the very classical view that Jesus will only return when the Gospel has been preached the world over, the movement's aim is to identify the "unreached people", those who have never heard the preaching of the Gospel, and to enable them to be evangelized in their own language. The movement has identified 8,000 ethnic groups and proposes that young Christians adopt these groups and possibly volunteer as missionaries (see http://www.ywam. org). The anthropological knowledge which the young people are taught is then used against the cultures to be "saved"—though not in the anthropological sense.

From Market to Huge Bazaar of Rites and Signs

Once again, the separation between religious and cultural markers does not mean that one disappears in favour of the other, but that they disintegrate and recompose themselves in a loose and random manner. That enables religions to create their market and compose *à la carte* menus connecting elements from different sources. This "customization" annoys both the cultural and the religious purists, who see it as syncretism or, worse, as a profound ignorance as to the specific nature of each religion. Ultimately, the "customers" here are simply learning the lessons of a real homogenization of the religious arena, which makes it so difficult to grasp what, in a given religion, is irreducible both with regard to other religions and to culture itself.

We end this section with two examples that mean nothing from a statistical point of view but which are typical of this dance of markers. The first is the story of an "emblematic" song entitled *"e-o" nigun* (the *nigun* is a traditional Hassidic "humming tune") which spread among American Reform Jewish students in 2003 during Shabbat retreats for young people. Now this chant had been brought over from South Africa and there is nothing Jewish about it; but, according to the author, that is precisely why it was adopted: because it allows a universal Jewish identity that is not connected to the traditional markers (Yiddish, religious or Israeli songs). It is the same principle as the "Torah-yoga" which appeared in the 1970s, where verses and prayers are recited accompanied by movements, which is traditional, but this time the movements are based on yoga.[43]

And one last anecdote: young Chinese girls adopted by American Jewish families are given a Jewish religious upbringing and a Chinese cultural one: "Olivia R., a girl in Massachusetts who celebrated her *bat mitzvah*[44] last fall on a day when the Jewish harvest festival of *Sukkot* coincided with the Chinese autumn moon festival, said she saw no tension between the two facets of her identity either. 'Judaism is a religion, Chinese is my heritage and somewhat my culture, and I'm looking at them in a different way,' she said. 'I don't feel like they conflict with each other at all'".[45] But in this description of a celebratory moment, nothing makes sense, either in terms of religion or in terms of culture. What "Chinese culture" had this young girl received apart from a calendar? What dual culture beyond a set of *kosher* chopsticks? How can kinship and adoption be reconciled within Judaism, *bar* and *bat mitzvah*, Chinese New Year and *Sukkot*? But that is precisely what is happening nowadays.

7

THE STANDARDIZATION OF RELIGION

The Formatting of Religions

The market and ease of circulation help standardize religion. But what are the criteria governing this process? Once again, it is clear that there are prevailing models (Christianity to be specific), but this model is itself transformed by the process. While Buddhism has become "Protestantized", and not only the export version, Christianity has "gone Buddhist" with numerous followers developing an interest in meditation and self-improvement techniques and becoming less concerned with traditional dogma based on an omnipotent, transcendent God the creator. People no longer believe in Hell. A taste for ecumenism, dialogue between religions, shared ceremonies and communion during festivals of world sacred music (such as that of Fès, Morocco) are resulting in a relativism that undermines Christianity's established hegemony.

I prefer to call this process of standardization "formatting" rather than "acculturation", since the word "acculturation" presupposes that all religion is embedded in a culture and does not take account of the separation of cultural and religious markers. The concept of acculturation assumes that there is harmony between the markers, hence a lack of understanding of the complexity of the phenomena at work in the integration process, which is seen as a power struggle between mainstream society and minorities trying to preserve their "authenticity". This is how the controversy over the headscarf in French schools was perceived, both in Muslim countries and in the United States, as a

187

desire to crush the Muslim community. Many outside observers felt that a multiculturalist policy would have made it possible to embrace both citizenship and the preservation of cultural traditions.[1] But as we have demonstrated throughout this book, multiculturalism is in fact an illusion, as it targets communities where the separation of religious and cultural markers has already taken place: it is an artificial way of redefining as cultural things that are no longer part of culture.

Formatting can be operated or perceived as a constraint (banning the wearing of the headscarf or polygamy) or, conversely, as simply a formal concession which does not affect the fundamentals (for example, Tariq Ramadan, the academic and President of the Brussels-based think tank European Muslim Network (EMN), is criticized for wearing Western dress and speaking excellent French to help promote his message). Marriage is a typical example of formatting: when a Muslim couple living in the West marries in a mosque, bride and groom hand in hand, the bride dressed in white and carrying a bouquet as in a Christian church wedding, is this merely a superficial adaptation, a change in the conception of the couple or is it a redefinition of the religious value of Muslim marriage?[2]

In fact, formatting is very often a process of interaction, reciprocal adjustments and reformulation of norms from very different cultural fields (Islam and Christianity define "lust" differently), into a new set of norms aiming, if not to create a consensus, at least to make the different norms and beliefs compatible and acceptable. Consensus is an ideal that often harks back to a mythical past ("Al Andalus", "the school of the Republic" in France) purportedly a casualty of a historical event (Crusades and *Reconquista*, immigration and globalization) the effects of which those seeking to create consensus are deliberately seeking to avert. Take, for example, the insistence in France on "Republican consensus" or on "Republican values" which are allegedly under threat from the arrival of Islam, whereas neither corresponds to historical fact: France has effectively been a republic since 1789, against a permanent political backdrop of undeclared civil war, where revolutionaries and reactionaries, the lay population and clerics, communists and anti-communists continually brand their adversaries "enemies of the nation". This illusory consensus is not the legacy of the good old days that never were: it is the prospect on which the formatting of Islam is focused.

What is the new shared "format"? There are three dimensions to it:

– *A Convergence of Religiosities*: in other words, similarly defining way faith and the believer's relationship to his/her religion, often expressed in terms of a spiritual quest. The market offers a range of products to fulfil one demand. This demand thus tends to be standardized by the market, which reflects consumers' image of what they are supposed to be. Nowadays, religion is no longer defined by anthropologists or philosophers, and decreasingly by the "professionals"— clerics or preachers—who are chasing after the convert/customer. Individual conversions often illustrate this itinerant, nomadic even eclectic characteristic of the new believer.

– *A Convergence of Definition*: the notion of "religion" becomes a normative paradigm with no specific content. It is the designation of any system as a religion, without taking account of its content, which makes it a religion: currently, it is the courts that decide in the event of dispute, even though they claim not to deal with matters of theology. Even, and perhaps especially, in countries where there is a strict division between religion and state (France, the USA) which prohibits the state from defining what a religion is, it is still necessary to say who is entitled to the label of a "religion", even if it is only to permit religious freedom (exemption from tax, chaplaincy, definition of places of worship, dietary exemptions, religious holidays etc.). Democratization and human rights theory tend to standardize the definition of religion (like that of any minority), in order to treat everyone equally. Secularism thus constructs religion since, in order to maintain it at a distance, it must assign religion a place and therefore define it as a "pure religion".[3] Formatting also aims to standardize the manifestation of religion in the public sphere: "religious practice" is thus overseen, from the wearing of the headscarf by Muslim women to the erection of an *eruv*[4] around an orthodox Jewish neighbourhood, the right to smoke hashish (or its prohibition)—a demand by Rastafarians in the United States, which was rejected—or to drink wine (during mass in prohibitionist countries) as part of religious practice.

– *An Institutional Convergence Between Religions*: the figure of the "priest" or of the "minister" tends to define all religious practitioners or professionals; *ulemas* (religious scholars) become theologians, imams and rabbis "parish" leaders. In the name of equality between believers, the law, courts and also institutions tend to format all religions in the same way. For example, in extending the principle of chaplaincy to Islam, the army and the prison authorities reinforce the institutional alignment of Islam with Christianity. In this sense we can speak of the "churchification" of religions by courts and states.

Formatting then can occur as part of various strategies, both top-down and bottom-up: integration for Reform Jews, exportation for Buddhism or Hinduism, construction of a national identity (Hinduism in India, Buddhism in Sri Lanka), a concern for law and order on the part of the state, political trauma (missionaries turning against coloni-alism, civil wars), or more simply conversion practices in a totally dif-ferent cultural environment. Formatting can be voluntary and explicit, as, for example, with the establishment of Reform Judaism in the United States, where it was very much a question of Jewish immigrants creating their own Judaism to fit in with American norms. It can take place within a "liberal" or conversely a "fundamentalist" perspective, since, and once again this must be emphasized, fundamentalism can also be the expression of modernity through deculturation: Salafism among immigrant communities, for example.

Formatting, even if it is experienced as a desecration, takes place according to a criterion of acceptability that has been negotiated to some extent. What appears as barbaric (cutting off thieves' hands) or simply weird (the Muslim headscarf, the Sikh turban and dagger) is either rejected from the outset, or negotiated, acclimatized (Sikh police officers in Great Britain are permitted to wear turbans). Over and above ostensible religious signs, formatting aims to draw out the simi-larities between religions rather than the differences. But this conver-gence can also result both in the emergence of a "religious front" defending conservative values (opposition to Gay Pride in Jerusalem), and in the extolling of "small differences", going hand in hand with the wearing of ostensible emblems of religious affiliation (headscarf, skullcap, cross).

Formatting is more part of a dialogical process, aiming to define through interaction an orthopraxy, a relative consensus on the expres-sion of religions in public life. Within globalization, orthopraxy, which up until now has been the sign of the culturation of religion, becomes an autonomous process aiming to compensate for deculturation and to place the emphasis on explicit norms for cohabitation, increasingly endorsed by the courts and lawmakers. But this process cannot occur as a result of a strictly religious debate, in other words based on theology and dogma. In fact, the acceptability of a religion has nothing to do with dogma; it leaves the existence of specific normative systems open (dietary, for example). The norms can effectively differ, but it must be possible for them to be conceived of in a common horizon of meaning. To say: "I don't eat pork" does not introduce a radical sense of otherness, but can be said in a context where the idea that dietary choices can vary from one person to another is recognized. On the other hand, "I don't drink Budweiser" sounds like a refusal to socialize in the context of micro-societies where alcohol consumption is seen as a social rite, as in the armed forces or among football fans.[5]

Otherness here is understood as foreignness in the sense of barbarity, weirdness, eccentricity or the unthinkable. By dialogical, we mean a process where the combination of confrontation and dialogue ends up by creating a new, relatively consensual equilibrium, because the actors, far from defending closed, preconceived systems, reformulate their own position in the debate with the other. The minimum consensus develops outside stances of principle and the original starting position of those concerned; for example, the redefinition of *sharia* as a system of voluntary norms allows Muslims to think of themselves as still being within the framework of Qur'anic law and "secular" Muslims to consider that unacceptable punishments (the *hudud*) have been consigned to oblivion. But, of course, such a compromise cannot be envisaged within closed ideological systems. The systematic hostility towards the Islamic headscarf in French secular society excludes any possibility of a consensus. Interestingly, it is the courts which are gradually defining, through a series of rulings, not a consensus, but a balance between the right to wear the headscarf and intolerance of the headscarf in the public sphere. The first example is the French courts' refusal, during the 1990s, to rule that the headscarf be banned on principle in state schools, which put the ball in the lawmakers' court, resulting in the setting up of the commission headed by Bernard Stasi and the law of 2004. Then it was the courts' job to define in what circumstances the headscarf could be worn: at work, if the wearer is not in direct contact with customers, if she was not informed of the dress restrictions when she was hired and if there is no health and safety issue (order of the Paris Court of Appeal, 19 June 2003), in public spaces, including hotels and rural self-catering accommodation (conviction of Mme Truchelut for discrimination in October 2007 for having cancelled the booking of a customer who wore a headscarf in the communal areas of her self-catering accommodation).[6]

In fact, as all the studies on this issue show, the French courts are careful to guard against applying the principle of secularism in an ideological manner and endeavour to find, if not a consensus, at least a reasonable balance in conflicts involving religious norms not recognized by the Republic, be it the wearing of the headscarf, the *guet* (authorization to remarry given by the husband in Jewish law), employment contracts involving compliance with religious norms or convictions, funerals, marriage annulments, etc. Can a female teacher in a Catholic faith school be sacked for being divorced? Can a slaughterer in a ritual Jewish abattoir be fired for unauthorized absence if he was keeping a religious holiday?[7] The courts are well and truly involved in a dialogical process of creating an arbitration space, and not in that of imposing an abstract norm of secularism.

But there is an astonishing gulf between the terms of the debate and the practice of confrontation/integration. People think they are discussing ideas whereas it is the process of discussing, in other words the interaction, that puts in place the formatting conditions. Formatting occurs before it is formulated, which explains the permanent gap between ideas and reality (there is still a debate over the integration of Muslims, whereas it has happened, albeit with sometimes unexpected outcomes). The content of the public debate is ideological and theological: is Islam compatible with Western values? Is the Confucian culture of China and Singapore compatible with democracy? Is the concept of a modern democratic state inextricably bound up with the history of Christianity? What does the Qur'an say? And so on. This is at the root of the clash/conflict of civilizations. It is pointless saying that these debates cannot contribute anything to the rolling out of a real policy: as Nicolas Sarkozy said, when he was Interior Minister, in response to the demographer Michèle Tribalat, if we come to the conclusion that Islam is incompatible with democracy, then what do we do with the millions of Muslim French citizens?[8]

The case of the Stasi commission, analysed by Nadia Marzouki, is illuminating: far from weighing up existing political and ideological discourses, the commission endeavoured to seek a consensus by bringing together discourse, personal experience, stakeholder positions and snippets of expertise. It was not a matter of developing new scholarly knowledge, a theory that would speak the truth and enable policymakers to act on a scientific basis, since expertise cannot create a formatting process; it claims to note facts and trends, but does not admit to being a party to the process of constructing the facts.[9] The commission, like any political stakeholder, was tasked with instigating a process, and not with establishing whether the conditions for the viability of this process can be scientifically proven in advance.[10] A sort of "government wisdom" was thus constituted, not so much to define a specific policy (only one of the commission's proposals has been implemented, i.e. the banning of religious symbols in schools) than to fit into the ideal, voluntarist framework of building a consensus, hence the gentle pressure on the only member of the group who did not approve the report, Jean Baubérot. He was criticized not for thinking differently from the others, but for damaging the consensus process.

But the context of the debate clearly differs according to political culture: multiculturalism in Great Britain and Canada, ideological secularism in France, separation of Church and state combined with the omnipresence of religiosity in public life in the United States, etc. We are witnessing a reciprocal reformulation of religion and the public sphere of which it is part; it is neither a constraint imposed on the "new" religion, nor a subversion of society by this religion. Time plays an important part: Judaism and Catholicism experienced teething problems when they were in the process of establishing themselves in the United States and it took them over a century to become part of the American landscape, whereas the formatting of Islam is being carried out hastily, for a variety of reasons (including 11 September).

On analyzing three historical cases: Judaism's emergence from the ghettos of Europe, the establishment of Catholicism in the United States and the integration of Muslims in Europe, it transpires that the conditions are similar. But it is misguided to make comparisons between Muslims and previous immigrant populations (Italian, Polish), for whom religion was not an issue. The real comparison is between religions that explicitly define themselves as such—Judaism, Catholicism and Islam.

In all three cases, as a result of the presence of a specific ethnic group, a "new" religion has appeared on the market which demands to be recognized in the public sphere on a par with the others. "New" religion, because it has arrived belatedly in this public sphere (even if its territorial presence dates back much further, in the form of Jewish ghettos in Europe, for example), and because the mainstream culture is associated with a particular religion (Protestantism in the United States, Christianity in general in Europe). In all three cases, there is

both suspicion on the part of the host society and a willingness to integrate on the part of at least a section of the religious community. So
there is both pressure and a demand. As Deborah Lipstadt writes:

For at least two decades after the termination of World War II, American Jews,
often unconsciously, designed their educational, communal and religious institutions as well as their private life so that they replicated the Christian world
in which they lived (...). Jewish parents were intent on having their children
retain their Jewish identity, but the intensity, nature and substance of that
identity was recast and restructured (...). Actions and behavior which Jews
believed would appear 'strange' in the eyes of non-Jewish neighbors were
eschewed.[11]

This self-formatting is embodied by the two major American reform
movements: the so-called "conservative" Jews, who are in fact reformist (they claim to abide by Jewish law but accept mixed marriage, the
transmission of Jewishness through the man and conversions, and they
eventually came to accept women rabbis), and the Reform Jews, who
are extremely liberal (they consider the letter of the law obsolete in
favour of the spirit, and are tolerant towards homosexuality).

Even though the American Catholic Church was established by the
English in the seventeenth century, it fast became an "ethnic" Church,
in other words non-English, and remained so for a long time; from the
first half of the nineteenth century it defined itself as the Church of the
new immigrants—Irish, Italian, and then Polish and lastly Latinos.
First of all it pledged political allegiance to the American system, while
at the same time defending its specificity. In an address to Congress in
1826, Bishop John England of Charleston implicitly endorsed the separation of Church and state and the distinction between being a citizen
and being a believers.[12]

However, the Syllabus, promulgated by the Pope in 1864, firmly
rejected the separation of Church and state. And yet Bishop England
was not a "progressive"—quite the opposite: for him, separation was
the best way of protecting his flock from the surrounding Protestant
culture. For the same reason, the American bishops opposed morning
prayers in schools and giving prominence to Christian references in
public life;[13] they did not want a "civil religion" presenting itself as a
boiled-down Christianity, the lowest common denominator of all the
Churches and denominations, since for them this was synonymous
with Protestantism. The Catholic Church had another vested interest
in separation, which would place it on an equal footing with Protes-

tantism. Incidentally, the *ulemas* (religious scholars) in colonial French Algeria took the same line when they asked for the law of 1905 on the separation of Church and state to be extended to Algeria. Their request was denied.

But in America, Catholics gradually internalized this separation and practised their faith in private, becoming "Protestantized" anyway. A so-called "Americanist" trend—for which adaptation to American values is not only a matter of opportunism, but an ideal in itself—emerged in the late nineteenth century and included the senior clergy: the separation between Church and state, far from being the lesser evil, was seen as positive, and the laity wanted to play a more prominent role. As Storch writes of Cardinal John Ireland, "He was growing ever more certain that American Catholics had a special mission, a unique duty, to demonstrate to the world that the freedom of democracy was congenial to the teachings of the Catholic Church. He believed that the entire world was moving rapidly towards the social and political conditions that existed in America".[14] American Catholics had integrated themselves into American political culture and found themselves in the same orthopraxy as the Protestants.

Pope Leo XIII first condemned "Americanism" in 1899 (Apostolic letter *Testem benevolentiæ*), and then the modernists, in 1907. At the heart of this debate is far more than the simple respect for local specificities (as in Gallicanism). It is very much the question of the universalist and positive dimension of American values that is at stake; but these values were established within a Protestant culture. It is interesting to note that a memorandum was circulating at the time in Rome to encourage Catholic immigrants in the United States to remain members of their national Churches of origin (keeping to the rites and languages of origin).[15] The Moroccan, Algerian and Turkish religious authorities adopted exactly the same attitude towards Muslim immigration in Europe, as did the patriarchate of Moscow towards the French Orthodox. The ethnicization of religion is seen by the conservative ecclesiastical authorities as a means of maintaining the link between religious and cultural markers and, in so doing, to remain within the traditional dogmatic framework. But globalization always wins out, and de-ethnicization leads to the recasting of orthopraxy, no longer in relation to tradition but to the new environment.

The formatting of American Catholicism is not simply the adoption of a new political framework; it translates as the internalization of new democratic norms that will be applied to the faith community, questioning the authority of the bishops and the Pope, and this is far more subversive. However, "Protestantization" does not affect dogma: the Eucharist, the worship of the Virgin Mary and the saints, confession, the principle of the papacy, etc., remain unchallenged. Acculturation would have meant conversion, or a breakaway from Rome, but this is not the case. On the other hand, modern American cultural values based on the freedom of the individual and promoting that as an end in itself are entering the religiosity of non-Protestant believers (Catholic, Jewish and Muslim). Feminism and the democratic spirit (people will not blindly accept the principle of authority) have changed "parish" life.

Self-Formatting

But where does this "form" of religion come from? How far do states borrow from mainstream anthropology to define religion? Anthropologists have often been accused of imposing Western classifications onto very different belief systems. A classic example is the construction of Hinduism. "The notion of a Hindu religion, I suggest, was initially constructed by Western Orientalists based upon a Judaeo-Christian understanding of what might constitute a religion. This construct, of course, was subsequently adopted by Hindu nationalists themselves in the quest for home rule (*swaraj*) and in response to British imperial hegemony", writes Richard King.[16] We have already touched on this recurrent argument, particularly with reference to the critique of Clifford Geertz by Talal Asad (see page 25).

But the reconstruction of religions based on a "Western" template has been taken up by newly independent states, precisely because standardization allows a better political management of religion, notably deploying it as an instrument of homogenization for the benefit of a national project. Therefore, the paradox is that formatting, in the form of "Westernization", occurs as much in a territorial, nationalist project as in the export form. This means that two antagonistic aims (one tending towards exportation and the other rootedness in the national), result in the same process. This concurs with my interpretation in *Globalized Islam*: it is not intrinsically immigration or deterritorialization that change religious paradigms. The changes (in religiosity, format, etc.) also take place *in situ*, either in an explicit national project, or as a spontaneous construction of a new identity in a context of immigration.

An example of a national project is that of Hinduism reconstructed by the Indian nationalist BJP party, whereas in Sri Lanka, it was Buddhism that was subject to formatting, particularly under the influence of an English convert, Henry Steel Olcott (1832–1907). While on the one hand it was a matter of countering the Christian missionaries, on the other, the Buddhists borrowed the latter's conceptual and institutional tools to make Buddhism a religion along the same lines. Experts disagree as to what extent it is fitting to speak of Protestantization. In Obeyesekere's view, it is definitely a form of emulation and the setting up of a Weberian model of Protestantism.[17] Stephen Prothero, however, argues that the analogy is not theological: it is not the Calvinist vision of God that structured this Buddhist reformation, but a form of "Creolization"—the mixing of cultures.[18]

I did not carry out field research in Sri Lanka, but it seems clear to me that it is not a question, either here or elsewhere, of the adoption of an external theological model or of acculturation, but definitely a case of formatting, since Buddhism takes on the form of a Western religion (transcendence of the divine), and in particular the faith is defined as a moral code. The reference to Max Weber is pertinent here, not so much because Weber revealed the "true" intellectual roots of Protestantism, but because in constructing the model of the Protestant ethic he himself helped to format Protestantism, to make it a model for exportation. It is fascinating to see Buddhists and former Islamists singing the praises of the Protestant ethic, whereas they have read neither the Bible nor Calvin, but only Max Weber. Rather than speaking of a Protestant influence on Islam and Buddhism, it is more appropriate to speak of a common orthopraxy, legitimized not so much by Protestant writings as by the links which the scholar Max Weber established with capitalism. Ultimately, in defining a "Protestant ethic", instead of producing a work of history, Weber ended up formatting Protestantism for exportation within the framework of capitalist globalization. This Protestant ethic could now be adopted just as easily by the Soka Gakkai Buddhists of Japan as by the Islamists of the Müsiad, the Independent Industrialists and Businessmen's Association in Turkey, since it does not oblige them to recant or to deculturate themselves, but allows them to defend both a modernity endorsed by reference to Protestantism and an authenticity guaranteed by their own theological references. In short, it is not so much Protestantism that prevails here (since this ethic contributes to the development of post-Islamism and of neo-Buddhism) as capitalism.

When the Secular State Defines Religion

The first element of formatting and standardization is that of classification as a "religion". The process is two-fold: being recognized as a religion offers the considerable advantage of having a seal of legitimacy; it also offers the assurance of being able to practise freely, and lastly it is a way of benefitting from the privileges granted to religions. These privileges differ considerably from one country to another: they can simply be reduced to the right to practise freely, especially when practice involves behaviour that is at odds with mainstream cultural or legal norms (communion wine in Iran, *halal* slaughter in Great Britain). In the West, the privileges are generally fiscal (exemption from corporation tax, even the possibility of levying taxes through the state, as in Germany or Spain); they also include obtaining exemptions (for ritual slaughter, for example). Above all, in the event of conflict, it is the courts that decide and define who is entitled to call themselves a religion: Jehovah's Witnesses in France and Wiccans in the United States owe their recognition as a religion to the courts. But there is another side of the coin: this recognition can result in the religion in question relinquishing some of its specific characteristics, or seeing them banned.

In France, a central issue is that of defining the difference between a cult and a religion. Officially, the distinction has no legal basis, but it plays an important part in the political debate. The government's setting up of the Miviludes (interministerial mission for tracking and countering sects), shows that it is determined to establish a clear distinction. The courts do not follow the Mission's lead, precisely because the principle of secularism prohibits the state from defining what constitutes a religion. The Council of State agreed to exempt the Jehovah's Witnesses from paying corporation tax, which *ipso facto* is tantamount to recognizing them as a religion. It is therefore not the practice or the beliefs that make a religion a religion, but the legal classification used to describe its fiscal status.

In the United States, recourse to the courts is even more frequent, and it is the legal system, under the control of the Supreme Court, which is the instrument of formatting. In 1961, the municipality of Boca Raton in Florida enacted a ruling prohibiting the erection of structures over the tombs in the municipal cemetery. In 1997, noting that over the years, tombstones, sculptures and vaults had been erected over many of the tombs, the municipality set about removing them. A number of families, essentially Jewish and Catholic, filed a complaint for infringement of their religious practices (invoking the Religious Freedom Restoration Act, adopted in 1998, which states that the authorities "should not substantially burden religious exercise"). The hearing therefore focused on whether erecting tombstones is classified as a religious practice. The court ended up ruling against the plaintiffs by making a distinction between the "high tradition" of a religion (the theology) and a "little tradition" which includes religiosity, folklore, customs, beliefs (the culture) which can be ignored without infringement of religious freedom—a Protestant vision of the relationship between culture and religion. The court imposed a Protestant definition of religion on Catholics and Jews, the consequence of which is explicitly to distinguish cultural markers, considered as non-essential, from religious markers.[19]

Without entering into the theological argument, a standard theological form was thus indirectly produced and will be applied to everything calling itself a religion. In this sense it is fitting to speak of a "Protestantization" operated by globalization.

Conversely, "religions" which do not come within the theological frameworks of the major revealed religions are recognized as such under the principle of equality, thus making this Christianization of religion a hollow form which is applied to everything, or almost everything, dissolving Christianity's specificity. A typical example is the recognition of the Wiccans in the United States. Wicca is a neo-pagan religion, inspired by Druidism, shamanism and the world of witches, which appeared in the 1950s and equally claims to be a philosophy. So it does not necessarily seek recognition as a religion, but has been pushed into doing so by the institutional process. Once again it is a cemetery that is at issue, this time a military cemetery. The widow of Sergeant Patrick Steward, killed in Iraq in 2005, wanted to place a Wiccan symbol on his grave, but the American Defense Ministry pointed out that it only recognized thirty-eight religious symbols (all forms of the cross, the crescent, the star of David, the Buddhist wheel, the Mormon angel, the nine-point Bahai star and the Atom of atheism!), but not the Wiccans' five-point star. The widow won her case in December 2006.[20]

Here again, it was never a question of "content". Religion is a form. Clearly it is not a matter of "anything goes" either: a group of students at Georgetown University, who had rented a house in an upmarket neighbourhood where more than five people were not allowed to share a house except for religious communities, therefore invented themselves as a religious community, the Apostles of O'Neill, and applied to be recognized as a congregation, their worship essentially comprising libation. Their request was eventually dismissed, but the proceedings took a year: in the United States, religion is no joke, nor is the price of real estate for that matter.[21] Some "religions" are created purely as a result of a "me too" effect. One example is the "Kwanza" formed in the 1960s by a group of African-Americans who defined it as an "observance", with symbols, rites, holidays and greeting cards which sit alongside Christmas and Hanukkah cards in stationers' shops. And each year, the US President sends a greeting to the community.

The United States exports this formatting of religion via the legal system. The State Department has set up an agency to monitor religious freedom in the world, following the passing of the International Religious Freedom Act by Congress in 1998. The formatting effect is obvious: this agency regularly accuses France of not considering the Church of Scientology as a religion. It does not recognize the "cult" classification. This is an attempt to create an international legal norm that would be imposed on other nations.

Formatting by Institutions

a) From Parish to Congregation

Religions tend to adopt the prevailing model, in this case that of the "congregation" (the local association of individuals) with a view to practising worship, which occurs less according to a principle of territorialization than as a result of affinities; worship takes place in a specific building, under the leadership of a "minister" (whatever his designation). The "place of worship" also houses related social and cultural activities. Religious groups can organize services, ceremonies and meetings there; these can be parties, meals, community activities for different age groups, but also, very often, matrimonial practices (they try to enable young people to meet each other within the framework of their religious community). The social purpose goes far beyond what is customary in a traditional place of worship, precisely because the separation of the cultural marker and the religious marker means that ordinary social practices, such as seeking a marriage partner, no longer have any cultural or social support structure and have to be taken care of by religion if the religious community wants young people to marry within the community. It is a recurrent problem for orthodox Jews, for example: how can young people be encouraged to marry their fellow Jews? Evidently by maintaining socialization within the group. But how can this be done when there is no longer territorialization? As is often the case, the formatting of the religious group goes hand in hand with the group becoming more inward-looking. Rather like Leibniz's theory of monads (a monad being an unextended, indivisible, and indestructible entity that is the basic or ultimate constituent of the universe and a microcosm of it), the religious community changes as the world changes, it absorbs the changes but remains closed in on itself and restricts interactions to the bare minimum.

Modern forms of ambient sociability (men and women mixing, the setting up of cultural, social or charity organizations, neighbourhood gatherings—festivals, fairs—leisure activities aimed at enabling young people to meet) force religious communities to rethink gender and intergenerational relations and relations with society at large.

Even though the Scout Association was founded by Baden Powell as a Christian organization, the Muslim scout movement is growing. This is not a consequence of immigration, since the Iraqi Baathists and the Muslim Brotherhood also established a scouting organization. But for both the Baathists and the Islamists the aim was the political mobilization of the youth, whereas nowadays the aim of the Muslim scout movement in France and in the United States is to involve youths in "healthy" activities importing new educational practices but under a Muslim marker. Scouting is about holidays and extra-curricular training for young people, not political activism.[22]

Traditional charity practices such as giving money are also changing and have become collective. Humanitarian activities are replacing charity: Muslims are adopting the "NGO model" of the 1980s, first of all as a form of militancy (support for the Afghan mujahedeen) then as an institutional framework for the fulfilment of a religious duty. But it is also a question of having a market presence along the same lines as other religions. Often one of the aims is to improve the brand image of the religion in question. Suddenly, humanitarian activities are carried out beyond the faith community. The standardization effect impacts on the humanitarian side. In France, Secours Islamique, set up in 1992, defines itself as a humanitarian NGO with a universal vocation.[23] In the United States, the movement spread after 11 September.[24]

This denotes a shift from a model of social pressure and cultural visibility, where practice is bound up with the follower's immediate environment (territorial parish, neighbourhood mosque), to voluntary membership of a community that is not necessarily territorial. This effect is accentuated by the proliferation of places of worship, corresponding not only to various different religions but also to different sensibilities within each religion. People attend a particular mosque or church because they like the preacher, the style, the ideas, even the music. So we are dealing rather with a juxtaposition of communities that are all minorities, or feel themselves to be. The range of choices assumes that people will rethink their membership, that they will explain why they have joined one community rather than another: the criteria become more explicit; "ministers" offer formulae that are successful, or, conversely, ask themselves why their flocks are deserting them.[25]

In the West, the mirror effect with Christian parishes often leads to a "Christianization" (or at least a "churchification") of forms in other religious groups. For example, synagogues in Germany adopted the organ in the nineteenth century. American synagogues resemble Protestant temples.[26] The arrival of Buddhists in California at the end of the nineteenth century is described as follows: "Temples were called 'churches' and priests, 'reverends'. Architecture also reflected Buddhism's new surroundings as most congregations opted for rather plain, non-traditional buildings. Inside, pews and lecterns created the aura of a Protestant church. An individualized, less regularized format gave way to a communal, scheduled worship on Sundays. Attending a morning adult service, one would typically find a format that included meditation, reading or chanting of Buddhist scripture, a sermon, *gathas* (songs), the burning of incense, and announcements. Sunday School programs for children, the Young Men's and Women's Buddhist Associations (YM/WBA), and Boy Scouts added further to what sociologist Isao Horinouchi has called the 'Protestantization' of American Buddhism". But the author immediately goes on to say: "Casting religious adaptation in Protestant terms, however, is misleading because it obscures the ways in which Shin Buddhism maintained its integrity".[27] This is an important comment, for it poses the problem of the relationship between standardization and theological transformation.

Suddenly, in this new environment, women, who may have been excluded from the place of worship (mosques, synagogues) started demanding access, which was granted to them or not, depending on whether the community tended towards the liberal or the fundamentalist. Reform and traditional Jews have opened synagogues to women, as have many Muslims in places where they are a minority, but often after making special adaptations to the place of worship.

b) The Professional "Religious Minister"

The professionalization of "religious ministers" goes hand in hand with a modification and a standardization of their functions along the lines of the Catholic priest or of the Anglican minister. The figure of the monk, which is central to Buddhism, is eroded in the export version: the Soka Gakkai, for example, does not have monks.[28] In the countries of origin, Buddhist monks are not disappearing, but tend to become involved in political activism, which is perhaps also a form of formatting through the practice of public and collective action, witness Sri Lanka, Vietnam, Thailand and Tibet. The rabbis and *ulemas* are no longer judges, either because there is no longer any social coercion (how can you make people appear voluntarily before a religious court?), or because the judicial function is taken care of by the state. The rabbi becomes a synagogue administrator, a role that formerly fell to the *hazzan;* the same is true of the imam in his mosque, often accompanied by a customization of the mosque. Imams, rabbis and Buddhist priests become "rectors" or simple performers of rites rather than judges trained in the application of the law.

The spiritual and the ritual blend into a broader function, that of "spiritual leader", of community representative and social facilitator—a new synthesis which appeared among Catholic priests in France while the secularism quarrel was simmering. The "social priest" emerged in the nineteenth century, with "patronage", also to promote the chaplaincy outside the school environment, but it flourished in the twentieth century. The new generation of religious leaders, especially Muslim, is often presented by the press as a "cultural oxymoron", but it is a consequence of the visibility of the recasting of religions in the public sphere.[29] They must therefore fulfil market demand and are no longer imposed on their congregation by their own institutions. This customization, which is at odds with Catholic ecclesiastic discipline, is nevertheless also apparent in the Catholic Church: in authorizing non-territorialized religious communities (like the Community of the Beatitudes) and two sets of rites (according to the Council of Trent or those of the Second Vatican Council), Pope Benedict XVI's Vatican automatically endorses believers' right to choose, thus stimulating competition between places of worship.

This standardization of the profession of "religious minister" is increasingly expressed by "clerical dress" which has little in common with traditional religious garments or with the dress code applying to all the members of a closed community (like perhaps the clothing of the Amish or the Hasidim—which is that of the general follower, and not that of the rabbi in particular), since it identifies the religious "professional" in modern public life. The creation of a religious "uniform", in the countries of origin too, is striking; only Protestant evangelicals are immune. In Europe, rabbis and imams dress in black or grey suits, with a black waistcoat and a little skullcap (plus a beard). Elsewhere in the Muslim world, the costume of the official imam of Turkey is emulated (Bosnia, Egypt): a red fez surrounded by a small white turban and a grey cassock. These uniforms are a consequence of secularization; thus in countries such as Afghanistan, the mullah has no distinguishing signs. In Iran, when Reza Shah imposed Western dress (shirt, jacket, trousers), mullahs were exempted and that was when the concept of religious dress appeared (and this is reflected in the contemporary vocabulary: *mo' amman*, "turbaned", *khal-e lebas*, "action of defrocking", words which would have had no meaning two centuries ago). Once again the formatting process is not a consequence of immigration, but is also happening *in situ*.

Religions' organizational structures are becoming more bureaucratic, as the state and international interlocutors are demanding that religions become institutionalized. Interestingly, institutions that are more bureaucratic than strictly clerical are being set up with boards of management, general assemblies, elections or co-options, various committees and a press office. That is the Soka Gakkai model. But even movements headed by charismatic leaders, like Fethullah Gülen's Turkish movement, tend to take on a bureaucratic form (with a hierarchy of salaried officials) which becomes stronger after the death of the leader. The bureaucratization of Islam in the form of centralized hierarchical national institutions is a major innovation which perhaps began with the institution of the *Muftiyya* (official clergy) by Catherine the Great in Russia (1783). But the model prevails today, both in Muslim countries, with the establishment of national grand muftis (Egypt, Bosnia), the Dyanet in Turkey (the directorship of religious affairs, a state administration under the First Minister), and exemplified in the West by the establishment of the French Council of the Muslim Faith (CFCM). Rarely considered centres of spirituality, these bodies are in charge of administrative affairs and the supervision of religious practice. They too have a homogenizing effect which tends to standardize religious practice and eliminate marginal practices (Sufism, Alevism, Shi'ism in Sunni countries, other forms of Sunnism by Saudi Wahhabism).

Naturally this bureaucratization of religion is partially a consequence of secularization, in other words due to the isolation of religion, which, in order to exist, must now secure representation, even if only in the form of a legal status either of the faith community or of local congregations, without evading the question of the status of the religious minister according to employment law. It is the separation of Church and state, either officially or unofficially, that prompts the state to seek, and if necessary to create, an interlocutor, because religion is no longer part of it or under its aegis. Thus, the bureaucratization of religious institutions occurs as part of a process of state control, as well as one of separation from the state. It is reinforced by employment law (the requirement to exist as a legal and moral entity), by the real estate issue (a legal existence is required to own property), by fiscal status and the need to use the courts if necessary. Whatever the choices (whether to act as a church or to go through *ad hoc* foundations or associations, often at local level), religions cannot avoid legal formatting.

c) Chaplaincy

The setting up of chaplaincies is a prime example of formatting by the institution, even when it claims not to influence religious dogma in any way. The chaplaincy is based on three assumptions: the recognition of the religion, that there is an orthodoxy specific to this religion and the existence of a "religious minister". Effectively, it recruits a category of professionals, religious officials, who are assumed to be "orthodox" in relation to the religion they represent. But the Defence Ministry (and also prisons and hospitals) cannot define what orthodoxy is, even though it has to refer to this concept. Furthermore, while defining each religion in contrast to the others (and to "deviations"), the chaplaincy principle implies a standardization of the notion itself of "religion". It assumes that all chaplains fulfil the same tasks and have the same remit (looking after the spiritual needs of members of their confession). So the demand for a religion to provide chaplains is a badge of recognition and legitimacy, but at the same time it imposes a sort of uniformization (in every sense of the word).

In 2007, Shareda Hosein, a Muslim and reserve officer in the American army, applied to be recruited as a Muslim chaplain. The army replied that, since the majority of Islamic religious authorities do not allow women to lead men's prayers, in other words fulfil the role of imam, it felt duty-bound to refuse her application. But she pointed out that being an imam was neither a permanent function nor a priesthood; and that prayers could be led by a man, whereas she would fulfil all the other roles of the chaplaincy. On a formal level she was absolutely right: there is no function of imam in Sunnism and any pious man can lead the prayers. But the army saw things in a different light, for it demanded that the chaplain fulfil all the ritual functions of the religion in question: that is why it accepts only Catholic priests and not nuns or deacons. This is formatting in the guise of respect for religious beliefs: the professional practice of the religious rites must follow the same model in all religions, that of the Catholic priest in this particular instance.[30] But, at the same time, it constitutes a recognition of Islam as a religion on a par with the others and marks the end of the pre-eminence of Christianity in the army.[31] A similar controversy raged when Keith Ellison, the first Muslim member of American Congress (2006), was sworn in on the Qur'an (but a Qur'an once owned by Jefferson); a conservative commentator, Jewish incidentally, requested that he use the Christian Bible, arguing that it was not a question of religion, but of political culture, the Protestant Bible being "the most important text of American history".[32] For there to be equal recognition for different religions they need to be formatted according to a matrix that is predominantly Christian, but also their own legitimacy needs to be recognized. This is not part of the culturalist view of religions, which separates faith and religious culture, as did French political thinker and founder of Action Française, Charles Maurras.

Formatting Through Social Practice

The moment religious and cultural markers are separated, people's wish to share the same cultural markers as their neighbours also has a homogenizing effect. The same cultural marker can apply to different religious contents: for example, the introduction of religious "festivals" along the lines of Christmas, with a holiday, when people do not work. The idea of not working during some religious festivals is typically Judeo-Christian. Furthermore, the "festive" side is not necessarily religious: there is nothing festive about Easter or *Ashura*—they are times of mourning. But we are witnessing a construction of the "religious festival" on the same model: holiday and festive (for cultural "Christians", Easter is about bells and chocolate, not death and resurrection). The homogenization of religious festivals is bolstered by their respective secularization, especially as there is a desire to share them with everyone, but also to underline small differences: "I'm just like you but my festival is on a different day". The spiritual dimension is superseded by a sort of folklore, which is both shared and placed in competition.

In one way, Christmas has been de-Christianized, but in another, the format of Christmas is borrowed to celebrate other religious holidays. The first cards to celebrate the Jewish festival of Hanukkah were printed in the United States in the early 1940s, but nowadays there are hundreds of types of such greeting cards.[33] As mentioned above, Hanukkah commemorates the victory of "orthodox" Jews over the Greeks and Hellenized Jews, in other words the restoration of the link between the cultural marker and the religious marker, whereas nowadays the festival identifies with new forms of cultural interconnections. These days it is possible to find cards celebrating the end of Ramadan sold in the same shops, with a message echoing Christian greetings: *Eid Mubarak*— Happy Eid.

The Homogenization Effect

The formatting of religions by the market and by institutions results in a double uniformization: internal uniformization, towards an often fundamentalist normalizing orthodoxy, and external uniformization, towards a common orthopraxy between different religions (which promote similar values), a shared religiosity and a similarity in "form" (clergy, institutions). Formatting has not always operated in favour of fundamentalism, as we have seen for liberal Jews in the United States, and it is probable that the West today is witnessing the emergence of an Islam that is "liberal" in its practice if not in its theological thinking. But clearly the globalization effect encourages fundamentalism—albeit temporarily—because it fits in with deculturation. Suddenly, the importance of "small differences" between religions takes on significance (since their real difference is less visible to the public), even if this uniformization is the result of an optical illusion as opposed to a theological convergence.[34]

Paradoxically, a growing conservatism within religions is accompanied by a proliferation of ecumenical events, inter-faith dialogues and religious coalitions against secularization in general or on specific issues such as gay marriage and evolution theory, This is because, in the face of secularization, religions which are no longer anchored in a culture are recast as "faith communities" and seek to redefine a common religious arena. The opposition is not between religions based on antagonistic cultures, but between religion and the secularization process.

The homogenization of religion by the spread of a normalizing "orthodoxy" absorbs and marginalizes sub-groups, multiple identities (including ethnic), sub-cultures and popular religions. In the nineteenth century, the Deobandi school played this role on the Indian sub-continent, combating "Hinduized" Islam and introducing a dividing line between what was Muslim and what was not; alongside British policy, it thus helped to define the political category of "Muslim". A century later, Wahhabism, Tablighism and Salafism all set themselves the same goal: to standardize the practice of Sunni Islam around an orthodoxy that is completely divorced from local cultures. On the Shia front, the clericalization of Shia communities in the Middle East has been ongoing since the 1950s, whereas many of these communities were either not very observant or practised a form of popular, local Islam. From South Lebanon to the Afghan Hazarajat, observers have noted the arrival of young mullahs from Najaf or Qom: they have ties with transnational clerical networks revolving around chief ayatollahs and are endeavouring to establish uniform orthodox religious practices, as well as to rebuild local identities around a transnational Shi'ism; and so they are opposed to ethnicity or localism in all its forms (tribal, regional, clan, feudal, etc.). In this sense, Iran's Islamic Revolution is only one aspect of a transnational Shia revivalism; it both benefits from it and encourages it. Television is also responsible for uniformization: the Iranian way of celebrating *Ashura* is spreading, because it is the one seen on television. The city of Qom has a special centre for foreign students, which has seen a huge expansion since 1979.

This homogenization policy, embarked on both by Sunnism and Twelver Shi'ism (the majority school which is dominant in Qom, Najaf and Karbala), places dissident Shi'ites (in other words non-Twelvers, such as the Ismailis, Yemen's Zaydites, the Alevis of Turkey and the Syrian Alaouites) in a difficult position: should they declare themselves as Twelver Shi'ites and bring clerics from Najaf and Qom (which is what the Syrian Alaouite regime sometimes urges), switch to Sunnism (like Sheikh Muqbil of Yemen), or declare themselves as a specific religion (the position of many Turkish Alevis)?[35] Another consequence is the escalating tension between Shia and Sunni, since both are the subject of an orthodox normalization which can only describe the other as "heretic" or traitor. These strains are apparent today in the rising community tensions between the two, beginning in Pakistan around 1982 and culminating with the American military intervention in Iraq and the execution of Saddam Hussein in 2007. The homogenization of religion can therefore lead to violence.

The Catholic Church set about the unification of the liturgy by defining a "Roman Rite" in 1850, followed by the affirmation of the infallibility of the Pope and the reduction of the autonomous spheres that Gallicanism could bring—even if with Vatican II Rome briefly opened itself to diversity. Despite the semblance of diversity (total lack of institutional unification), Protestants do not escape the homogenization phenomenon, but there is a permanent tension between the fundamentalists at one end of the spectrum (the origin, incidentally, of the term fundamentalism), who concentrate essentially on the strict definition of the articles of faith, and the liberals at the other, who have been losing ground since the second half of the twentieth century.

The bureaucratization of religions also stimulates the development of a normalizing orthodoxy. "Representative" Islam refuses to recognize the diversity of religious schools other than the major legal schools. The Turkish Dyanet (religious affairs directorate under the aegis of the First Minister) does not recognize Alevism or Sufism and publishes solely orthodox Sunni manuals and sermons; it has the monopoly over religious school textbooks. It has even gone so far as to normalize popular religion: it effectively publishes a list of superstitions *(bos inanç)*, like that of lighting candles on saints' tombs.[36] The courts frequently endeavour to define what is "orthodox", even in countries where there is a separation between Church and state.

A normalizing orthodoxy is spreading in very different contexts. This is also occurring at local level. Muslims from very different backgrounds who came to populate the island of Mauritius defined themselves according to their "sect", in other words by the branch of Islam they belonged to: Hanafi, Shafeite, Ahmadi, Shia or *bohra* (Ismaili). But later they joined forces in order to wield greater influence, and particularly to benefit from public subsidies given to religions. After the census of 1962, Muslim Mauritians gradually stopped mentioning their "sect", keeping only the generic term "Muslim", which led to a process of "Sunnitization" and the expansion of a normative orthodoxy to the detriment of diversity and popular Islams; and this development favoured the Tablighis. Furthermore, in Mauritius and Reunion Island, there has been increased interaction with the outside Muslim world: missionaries come to preach orthodoxy, but numerous imams from the two islands also embark on missions, making good use of their multilingualism (English, French and sometimes Gujarati).[37] On Reunion Island, most of the mosque imams are members of the fundamentalist Tablighi movement, whereas sociologically the Muslims now belong to the middle and upper classes and tend to be "liberal" in their outlook.

The same applies to Hinduism in the United States, where a uniform Hinduism is developing.[38] Raphaël Liogier has shown how the development of different movements in Buddhism actually corresponds to a homogenization: when exported, Tibetan, Vietnamese and Japanese Buddhism all present the same theology.[39] The same phenomenon occurs in Judaism. The founding of the State of Israel was a considerable contributory factor both to religious homogenization in favour of orthodoxy and to stifling Jewish cultural pluralism: *aliyah* to Israel eroded cultural Judaisms (Judeo-Spanish, Judeo-Arab). This does not mean that Israel is a homogenous society for the Jews—far from it. But diversity is no longer—or is decreasingly—linked to a particular connection between religion and culture. The Judeo-Arabs have disappeared: the Sephardim are no longer Arab at all; their specificity expresses itself in their own forms of religiosity and they occupy a specific socio-cultural dimension in national Israeli life. There are of course new fissures appearing, but these are between the religious and the non-religious, between secular and religious, Zionists and non-Zionists, diaspora Jews and Israeli citizens.

External Uniformization

Followers of different religions find themselves linked by a common religiosity comprised of both individualism and identity communitarianism, based on religion rather than on ethnicity or culture. Religious markers become identity markers according to a standardized range since, once again, formatting pushes religions to be defined in identical ways. Symbolic markers, dress, food, festivals are all put on the same level. The army demands that each religion be identified by a specific symbol to be inscribed on gravestones. Airlines offer a list of menus according to religion. Governments seek to come up with a coherent policy regarding the authorization or banning of external religious symbols; in France, the Sikh turban, which bothered no one, was suddenly transformed into an ostensible religious symbol by the law which sought to ban the Islamic headscarf in schools. The Education Minister, Luc Ferry, had to rack his brains to find a Christian equivalent of the headscarf and ban it, so as to prove that the law was not singling out Islam (he referred to the sudden appearance of huge Assyro-Chaldean crosses around the necks of high-school students).

But this standardization effect is also accentuated by borrowings between religions. A certain very trendy Buddhist vision is spreading to other religions.[40] Meditation techniques are swapped (transcendental meditation, Zen, Torah-yoga etc.). New combinations of religious markers are formed, with no links to their cultural origins: the (Protestant) work ethic has also been claimed by both Islam and Buddhism. Fascinated by Hindu spirituality, Catholic priests in the first half of the twentieth century went off to live in ashrams in India. Henri le Saux, the French Benedictine monk known as Swami Abhishiktananda, and "Bede" Griffiths even set up Christian ashrams in South India in the 1950s. The spiritual nomadism common to all, where people "try out" different religions, reinforces this similarity effect.[41]

The close of the nineteenth century saw the first interreligious congresses where the aim was not to argue about the Truth, but to affirm the unity of religion, reduced of course to the lowest common spiritual and ethical denominators. The first such conference was the world

211

Parliament of Religions held in Chicago in 1893:[42] a large contingent of "Eastern" religions attended but no Muslims. More than a century later, the same city hosted the interfaith Thanksgiving service.[43]

Confusion is rife. In July 2006, Don Larsen, a Pentecostalist chaplain with the American forces in Iraq, announced that he was changing religion after he had discovered the Wicca during the Chaplain's Basic Training Course at Fort Jackson, where all religions were presented in a "neutral" way. He therefore asked to be re-classified as a Wiccan chaplain at the end of his stint as a Protestant chaplain. But, as the new contract could not come into effect until 1 September, he asked to remain a Protestant chaplain until that date. The army consulted the ecclesiastic authorities who demanded the chaplain's immediate suspension.[44] But at the same time, to save money, some institutions ask their chaplains to be multi-faith. In 2004, Father Henry Heffernan, a Jesuit, was sacked from his post of chaplain to the Warren Grant Magnuson Clinical Center, near Washington, because he refused to deal with other religions. He won his case, but as a victim of discrimination (the Center wanted to impose duties on him that went against his religious beliefs).[45] The community of Taizé in France, founded by Brother Roger (Roger Schutz, the son of a minister and former theology student in Lausanne) aims to be non-denominational (in 1976 its name was removed from the directory La France Protestante, and Catholic monks joined it in 1969). But Taizé could be said to be Protestant (there is no Eucharist in the liturgy), while having the visibility of a Catholic monastery and practising a liturgy of a partially Orthodox inclination and inspiration.

Ultimately, this does not imply a uniformization of theologies, but an emphasis on the religious experience to the detriment of religious knowledge. That too is holy ignorance. Speaking of the new American Protestantism, Donald Miller writes: "This Reformation, unlike the one done by Martin Luther, is challenging not doctrine but the medium through which the message of Christianity is articulated" and he cites a preacher: "we sing not religion tonight, we talk about a relationship with Jesus".[46] Religiosity supersedes religion, and therefore knowledge is no longer a salvation factor.

This allows one to grasp an apparent contradiction: how can the spread of standardizing theologies within each religion go hand in hand with the general uniformization of religion? It is because the lack of differentiation between religions concerns religiosity and not dogma, which conversely is reaffirmed with increasing vehemence by the religious authorities, precisely because of the confusion between religions. The Charismatic Catholic movement began in 1967, when at the Catholic University of Duquesne in the USA, a group of Catholics claimed to have been "baptized in the Holy Spirit" through the laying on of hands, a borrowing from the religiosity of Pentecostalist Protestant evangelicals. It places great emphasis on the Holy Spirit, but goes no further, or very quickly reverts to Papal obedience and worshipping the Virgin Mary, and it is this which marks the boundary with Protestantism.[47]

Religious authorities react against what they perceive as a risk of syncretism: they encourage the return to Latin for Catholics, the wearing of distinctive symbols, they are critical of an ecumenism that is too benevolent, reject religious relativism and reaffirm that there is only one truth. In different guises, the major religions—or perhaps we should say "the new believers", since it is a grassroots movement—attempt to reinforce their frontiers. So Christian ashrams are rejected by some Charismatic Catholics.[48]

But is this "reculturation"? The Catholic Church's return to Latin, advocated by Benedict XVI, is less akin to a classic humanist culture (which, incidentally, he defends) than to the use of a new mantra, which it is hoped will have a "magic" effect. It is the mystery of Latin that attracts new believers, and not its role as a vehicle for classic culture: they will not read Virgil or Cicero. Similarly, for the Tablighis, learning the Qur'an by heart does not mean learning Arabic so as to read other books: the Qur'an rather has a "magic" effect; learnt by heart, it transforms the soul of the believer who absorbs it; this is more a sort of Eucharist than the acquisition of knowledge. Holiness does not always need knowledge.

CONCLUSION

How to be Born from Born-Again Parents: the Challenge Facing the Next Generation

Nowadays, religions tend to set themselves up as "faith communities" that are completely separate from their surrounding culture. Some movements opt for isolation, encourage endogamy, and even seek to become territorialized to remain a closed community. Others, by contrast, are universalist and proselytizing.

But they all face the question: how does one transmit the faith? Particularly when the parents are converts or born-again, since transmission is no longer guaranteed by the social or cultural visibility of religion. Proselytizing religions are faced with a different problem: how does one become reconnected to culture? How does one reach out to the other, whose non-belief remains a challenge?

Religious revival movements have largely been generational phenomena, and so often break away from the parental religion. Evangelicalism and Salafism are associated with the Sixties generation, with evangelicalism finding California's hippie milieu fertile terrain.[1] Donald Miller shows how the new Churches piggybacked on the counter-culture wave: Churches are seen as "new paradigms" which attract the baby boomers.[2] The discourse of the born-again is also that of disillusionment—with sexual liberation, drugs or political activism; the same is true of Benny Lévy, the founder of the Gauche Prolétarienne (the Proletarian Left) in France. But this same scenario is also repeated among numerous Salafis, who originated among the ranks of the far left: former British pop star Cat Stevens who became Yusuf Islam also shows that it is not only Christianity that holds an attraction for the Sixties generation.

215

But how is the experience of a breakaway to be transmitted? How can one be born from a born-again? How does religion reach out to the new generations which have their own history and for whom the "return to God" is perhaps already "an oldies' thing", in other words that of their parents?

One solution is isolation and the establishment of a counter-culture by setting up a closed community (like the Amish, the Old Catholics, the Ibadites of Algeria and the ultra-orthodox Jews), with marriages in the community and the obsession either with reproducing, or with "dropping out", and in which young people are fascinated by profane culture (*shababniks*). Dogmatism finds it hard to hold out in the long term if it is not upheld within a closed community. Many pass through Tablighism, Salafism or Pentecostalism, but eventually leave. There is also the problem of those who have "cooled off",[3] those who, without leaving, stop playing a full part or are not "paid up". But Pentecostalism is a binding religion: God keeps his promise if man keeps his. It requires an ongoing commitment; a nominal commitment is not sufficient. And so it is hard to stay. Family problems (divorce, etc.) often result in the believer being out of step with the demands of the faith community. The sex scandals that regularly engulf American televangelists are also a clear indication of the difficulty in abiding by the norms. Particularly as one of the characteristics of modern fundamentalisms is to replace spirituality with a system of norms and codes. Sin is no longer part of the system: when it occurs, it breaks it.

When the adherence to new forms of religion also means retribution for the excluded (as often occurs in Latin America), the success of the evangelicals has often been bound up with the social advancement of many believers (and the lining of the pockets of numerous ministers, resulting in scandals in Brazil, Nigeria and Ghana). Suddenly, the breakaway effect is eroded and the new generations have a more "routinized" religious practice, losing the sense of revivalism.[4]

The American press recently echoed the concern of the ageing born-again generation at the departure of the younger generation.[5] Thom Rainer's *The Bridger Generation* (those born between 1977 and 1994) analyzes the problem: the author is a Sixties generation born-again who became a father in 1980. He wrote his book in 1997, on realizing that his teenaged children belonged to a culture that was neither that of his generation nor that of his faith. And it is this culture that he decided to investigate—in order to offer a Christian response.[6] But this only highlights the exteriority of religion in relation to cultural markers.

Thus the older generation attempts to woo the young through their own culture, using current social networking ploys; religious practice is presented as a form of community association, playing on "tribe" culture.[7] They put on Christian rock parties, use "youth" language, adopting the codes of the "tribe" to preach to its members. They pick from the floating cultural markers and pin them to religious markers: Christian rock, eco-*kosher*, *halal* fast-food. This is the recipe of the televangelists, Christian and Muslim (for example, Amr Khaled). But the cultures they are targeting are in fact sub-cultures, made up of codes and modes of consumption; they are transient, linked to a specific generation. They have barely any specific "content". Sub-cultures have always existed, but they can flourish today because it is possible to exist in a virtual space, outside the culture of society (websites, word-of-mouth book recommendations, chat). The conviction effect is reinforced because the group confirms itself and is not contradicted by external social practice. We live in "archipelagic" societies. We are in fact in sub-cultures that ultimately deny their affiliation to an encompassing and lasting culture. But it is also the end of "religious purity".

However, we are now witnessing a weakening of fundamentalisms. The 2008 American electoral campaign showed that the Christian right no longer has a united front. The new generations of believers are also concerned by global warming and social issues. There is probably saturation as regards the obsession with prohibitions (like abortion). Admittedly there is also a decline in feminist or libertarian activism, but this does not signal a return to family values. The achievements of the Sixties have become mainstream, and the decline in campaigning for emancipation and freedom does not mean that conservatism is back with a vengeance. In fact, many young conservatives, unlike the old Christian right, have internalized the changed practices. Many born-agains have not abandoned the new social practices. The family is no longer sacrosanct; opting for a family life is presented as an individual choice, a desire for self-realization and not as compliance with some natural law. The reaction is no longer what it was. Religion is constantly reformulating itself, even if it is probable that it has lost its original and perhaps incestuous link with culture. The crisis of religion is also a crisis of culture, but that is another story. Ignorance has a rosy future.

GLOSSARY

Acculturation	The process of adopting the cultural traits or social patterns of another group.
Arminianist	A view of salvation that believes God has granted sufficient mercy for the entire human race to be saved, if men so wish.
Ashura	The word *Ashura* literally means "tenth", as it is on the tenth day of Muharram, the first month of the Islamic year. In the year 680 A.D., Hussein, the grandson of the Prophet Muhammad, was murdered during a battle against the ruling Caliph on the tenth day of Muharram (Ashura) in Karbala (modern-day Iraq). Shia Muslims observe the day in mourning for Hussein and in remembrance of his martyrdom.
BJP	Bharatiya Janata Party (India). Hindu nationalist party formed in 1980.
Brit Mila	Jewish circumcision rite.
Deculturation	The loss or abandonment of culture or cultural characteristics.
Exculturation	Term coined by the French sociologist, Danièle Hervieu-Léger: the process by which a religious denomination becomes disassociated from the surrounding culture.
Falun Gong	Established in China in 1992 by Liongzhi, Falun Gong is a worldwide organization, whose members are trained in an ancient practice for refining

the body and mind, Falun Dafa, based on Qigong exercises and meditation. Li Hongzhi, Falun Dafa now has a worldwide following.

Great Sanhedrin The supreme Jewish legislative and judicial court in Jerusalem under Roman rule. Also the name of the assembly of Jewish religious leaders convened by Napoleon in 1807 to organize the Jewish community on a religious basis.

Hanafi Islam Within the Sunni Muslim tradition, Hanafi is one of four "schools of law" and considered the oldest and most liberal school of law. Named for its founder, the Hanafi school of Imam Abu Hanifa, it is the major school of the former Ottoman empire, central and South Asia and of the Iraqi Sunni Arabs.

Haredim Applied to non-Zionist and anti-Zionist ultra-orthodox Jews who generally wear clothing associated with Central and Eastern Europe of about 1600-1700 and follow one of several very strict rabbis.

Hare Krishna A religious sect based on Vedic scriptures, whose followers engage in joyful congregational chanting of Krishna's name: founded in the U.S. in 1966.

Haskala Enlightenment.

Inculturation The attempt to make a religious message accessible in and through a local culture.

Tablighi Jamaat A missionary movement founded by Muhammad Ilyas in India in 1927 to "re-Islamicize" the Muslim community.

Kibanguism Named after Simon Kibangu, the spiritual founder of a Christian-inspired African Church in Congo.

Latin Empire of Constantinople 1204-61, feudal empire established in the South Balkan Peninsula and the Greek archipelago by the Latin Catholic leaders of the Fourth Crusade after they had sacked Constantinople in 1204.

Lubavitch Lubavitch and Chabad are synonymous terms referring to the same organization. Embracing the philosophy of the Chabad Lubavitch Movement, which originated in the town of Lubavitch in White Russia during the eighteenth century, Lubavitch's underlying doctrine is *"Ahavat Yisrael"* (love for a fellow Jew). Lubavitch recognizes no differences between Jews; its goal is to serve the spiritual and physical needs of each Jew regardless of affiliation.

Manichaeism Religion founded by the Persian Mani in the latter half of the third century. It purported to be the true synthesis of all the religious systems then known.

Marrano A Spanish or Portuguese Jew who was converted to Christianity during the late Middle Ages, usually under threat of death or persecution, especially one who continued to adhere to Judaism in secret.

Melchite Melchites are the people of Syria, Palestine, and Egypt who remained faithful to the Council of Chalcedon (451) when the greater part turned Monophysite.

Millenarianism The belief that, before the final judgment of all mankind, Christ will return to the earth and, together with resurrected saints, will reign over a glorious kingdom which will last a thousand years.

Mithraism Ancient Persian religion in which Mithras was worshiped and a major competitor of Christianity in the Roman Empire during the second and third centuries.

Monophysitism A Christological heresy that originated in the fifth century. Its chief proponent was the monk Eutyches, who stated that in the person of Jesus Christ the human nature was absorbed into the divine nature, therefore, Christ had only one nature, the Divine (Greek *mono-* one, *physis*—nature).

Morisco A Moor of Spain, converted to Christianity more or less by force after the *Reconquista*.

Neo-Sufism A term which has different meanings according to different authors. Launched by Muslim scholars (notably Fazlur Rahman) who felt that a number

221

of important changes in the nature of Sufism had taken place in the late eighteenth and early nineteenth centuries. "Neo-Sufism" was claimed to distinguish itself by increased militancy, stronger orientation towards *sharia* law and rejection of *bid'a* (a negative term of religious innovation), and a shift from efforts to achieve unity with God to imitation of the Prophet. It has also been used by social scientists to describe contemporary forms of brotherhoods, which construct themselves as new-age sects and combine the role of the guru and a Western individualist form of religiosity.

Pentecostalism Pentecostalism is a form of Christianity that emphasizes the work of the Holy Spirit and the direct experience of the presence of God by the believer. Pentecostalists believe that faith must be powerfully experiential, and not something found merely through ritual or thinking.

Prevenient Grace Universal prevenient grace refers to the doctrine that there is a divine enabling grace extended to all mankind, prior to and without reference to anything they may have done. This grace purportedly restores man's free will, which was corrupted by the effects of original sin, and enables him to choose or refuse the salvation offered by God in Jesus Christ.

Salafism From the Arabic *Salafiyyah* meaning predecessors or previous generations. A name used to denote various branches of Islam, which have in common the notion that the earliest forms of Islam were the purest and most correct, and that Islam must be reformed by returning to those forms of Islam.

Soka Gakai Worldwide Buddhist network that promotes peace, culture and education through personal transformation and social contribution.

Tablighi Jamaat Founded in rural India seventy-five years ago, Tablighi Jamaat describes itself as a nonpolitical, and nonviolent, group interested in proselytizing and bringing wayward Muslims back to Islam.

Therevada Buddhism — Also known as Hinayana Buddhism: earlier of the two great schools of Buddhism, still prevalent in Sri Lanka, Burma, Thailand, and Cambodia, emphasizing personal salvation through one's own efforts.

Thomism — The name given to the system which follows the teaching of St Thomas Aquinas in philosophical and theological questions.

Ulema — The body of Muslim scholars trained in theology, Hadith (the tradition of the Prophet), Islamic law (*sharia* and *fiqh*) and interpretation of the Qur'an.

Uniatism — Uniatism is the rallying policy of the Eastern Christian Churches, usually Orthodox, to Rome. The Uniate Churches recognize the authority of the Pope, but retain their traditional oriental rites (language and liturgy).

Ultramontanism — A strong emphasis on papal authority and on centralization of the church. The word identified those northern European members of the church who regularly looked southward beyond the Alps (that is, to the popes of Rome) for guidance.

Voodoo — A polytheistic religion practiced chiefly in the Caribbean, deriving principally from African cult worship and containing elements borrowed from the Catholic religion.

Wahhabism — Muslim sect founded by Abdul Wahhab (1703-1792), known for its strict observance of the Qur'an and dominant in Saudi Arabia.

White Fathers — The missionary society known as "White Fathers", after their dress, is a Roman Catholic Society of Apostolic Life founded in 1868 by the first Archbishop of Algiers, later Cardinal Lavigerie, as the Missionaries of Our Lady of Africa of Algeria, and is also now known as the Society of the Missionaries of Africa.

NOTES

INTRODUCTION

1. Cécile Chambraud, "L'Église Catholique Espagnole perd sa dotation publique", *Le Monde*, 24 September 2006.
2. Stephen Bates, "Devout Poles show Britain how to keep the faith", *The Guardian*, 23 December 2006.
3. "Americans May Be More Religious Than They Realize", *Washington Post*, 12 September 2006, p. A12.
4. "Students flock to seminaries, but fewer see pulpit in future", *ibid.*, 17 March 2006.
5. There is of course a problem in defining religious practice objectively: it is easy in the case of Catholicism in which religious practice revolves around the administration of the sacraments by a priest (mass, confession, Eucharist), whereas for Protestants, and even more for Muslims, religious practice can be much more personal. But it seems that among the Muslims in France, observance of purely religious practices (praying five times a day) is low, whereas practices associated with a cultural and festive marker (Ramadan) are widely observed. See Sylvain Brouard and Vincent Tiberj, *Français comme les autres? Enquête sur les citoyens d'origine Maghrébine, Africaine et Turque*, Paris: Presses de Sciences Po, 2005.
6. Philippe Fargues, *Générations Arabes. La Chimie du nombre*, Paris: Fayard, 2001.
7. Richard Niebuhr, *Christ and Culture*, New York: Harper, 1996.
8. This subject was addressed by Michel de Certeau, who saw glossolalia as a "pure religious language": "Vocal Utopias: glossolalias", *Representations*, no. 56: "Special Issue: The New Erudition", Autumn 1996, pp. 29–47.
9. Neela Banerjee, "Taking their faith, but not their politics, to the people", *New York Times*, 1 June 2008.
10. They are called *shababniks* in Israel, cf. Daniel Ben-Tal, "Yeshiva dropouts walk on the wild side", *Jerusalem Post*, 17 January 2007.
11. Dana Clark Felty "Mega-church unveils youth facility", *Savannah Morning News*, 16 September 2006.

12. "Lourdes se lance dans le réveillon Chrétien", *Le Figaro*, 28 December 2006.

13. "The Offbeat Is Helping Some Jews Reconnect: Chabad Rabbis' Modern Outreach Methods Are Controversial but Forge Ties", Jacqueline L. Salmon, *Washington Post*, Sunday, 27 May 2007; C01. See also: "Playing with soul, at synagogue. More Jewish services are using bands during the Sabbath to appeal to young people", Deborah Horan, *Chicago Tribune* staff reporter, 16 March 2007.

14. See Thom S. Rainer, *The Bridger Generation, America's Second Largest Generation, What They Believe, How to Reach Them*, B&H Publishing Group, 2006, or Dick Staub, *The Culturally Savvy Christian*, San Francisco: Jossey-Bass, 2007.

15. Further on in this book are the cases of fringe groups which, under the influence of a charismatic local leader, very often Protestant originally, decide to declare themselves as Jewish, resorting, if necessary, to the myth of the ten lost tribes of Israel: the Ben Menashe (a Tibeto-Burmese group living in India), the Abayudaya (Uganda), and the "Black Hebrews" of Chicago who emigrated to Israel.

16. In an excellent documentary by Karim Miské, *Born again: The new believers* (2005), one of the young Salafis interviewed is a French convert called David, and one of the evangelicals who tells his life story in front of the entire community is named Mohammed. This was not the reason they were chosen by the director, who merely observed some born-again communities in the same city.

17. Harvey Cox, *Fire From Heaven*, Cambridge: Da Capo Press, 1995; R. Stephen Warner, Judith G. Wittner, *Gatherings in Diaspora*, Philadelphia: Temple University Press, 1998; Peter Berger, *The Sacred Canopy*, New-York: Random House, 1967; French studies include, Sébastien Fath, *Du ghetto au réseau: Le Protestantisme Évangelique en France (1800–2005)*, Genève: Labor et Fides, 2006 and Yannick Fer, *Pentecostalisme en Polynésie Française: L'Évangile relationnel*, Genève: Labor et Fides, 2005.

18. *Le Monde*, 4 June 2008. Several Catholic leaders protested against this position.

19. Two computer scientists, Rachid Mohammed Seghir and Jamal Dahmani, were gaoled; the trial of another convert, Habiba Kouider, was postponed. See "Condamnation de deux Algériens convertis au Christianisme", *Le Monde*, 3 July 2008.

20. Sudarsan Raghavan, "A clash of culture, faith; Latinas balance Catholic upbringing, adoption of Islam", *Washington Post*, 5 June 2006.

21. There are websites, generally Protestant, promoting conversion and reviving the old tradition of refuting "false religions", for example: www.answering-Islam.org.

22. Thesis by Oumar Arabov, *Les Mutations de la religion au Tadjikistan*, Paris, EHESS, 2005.

23. Below is a non-exhaustive list of people harassed for "illegal" religious activities between 2004 and 2006 (source *Forum-18*, www.forum18.org, Oslo, Norway).

   – *Uzbekistan*: Protestants: Bakhtier Tuichiev, Makset Djabbarbergenov, Nikolai Zulfikarov, N. Yermolayeva, L. Lankina, N. Tsoi, S. Tsoi, O. Usmanova, O. Saidaliyeva, R. Karimov, Bakhrom Nazarov, Khaldibek Primbetov, Kurbongul Yermanova, Nurumbetova, Ainur Tajikova, Aliya Sherimbetova, Shirin Artykbayeva, Sofia Mambetniyazova, Kural Bekjanov, Dmitry Shestakov;
   Jehovah's Witnesses: Khojbayev, Ajigilev, Alimardon Pulatov, Nikolai Kryukov, Artur Arsanov, Dila Safieva.
   Hare Krishna: Asa Bekabayeva.

   – *Azerbaijan*: Protestants: Novruz Eyazov, Khalid Babaev, Vahid Nagiev, Zaur Balaev; Jehovah's Witnesses: Mahir Bagirov.

   – *Kazakhstan:* Protestants: Rashid Turebaev, Pyotr Panafidin, Rustam Kairulin.

   – *Turkmenistan*: Protestants: Vyacheslav Kalataevsky.
   Jehovah's Witnesses: Bilbil Kulyyeva, Babakuly Yakubov, Shukurjan Khatamova, Rozyzhan Charyyev, Oguldurdy Altybayeva, Gulzhemal Allagulyyeva, Begench Shakhmuradov.

   – *Kirghizistan*: Protestants: Saktinbai Usmanov assassinated in 2006, Dzhanybek Zhakipov, Zulumbek Sarygulov.

   – *Tatarstan*: Protestants: Rafis Nabiullin, Takhir Talipov.

24. Issandr El Amrani, "The Emergence of a 'Coptic Question' in Egypt", MERIP, 28 April 2006.

PART 1: THE INCULTURATION OF RELIGION

1. WHEN RELIGION MEETS CULTURE

1. This is François Burgat's theory, notably in *Face to Face with Political Islam*, London: I. B. Tauris, 2003.

2. Talal Asad, *Genealogies of Religion*, Baltimore: Johns Hopkins University Press, 1993, p. 43 foll.

3. See Philippe Roger, *L'Ennemi Américain*, Paris: Le Seuil, 2004.

4. Granet, Marcel, *The religion of the Chinese people*, translated [from the French], edited and with an introduction by Maurice Freedman, Oxford: Blackwell, 1975.

5. Paul Veyne, *Les Grecs ont-ils cru à leurs mythes?*, coll. "Points-Essais", Paris: Le Seuil, 1992; Lucien Febvre, *Le Problème de l'incroyance au XVIe siècle: La religion de Rabelais*, Paris: Albin Michel, 1968.

6. Cf. the excellent book by Jean-Yves Château on Plato's *Euthyphron*, Vrin, 2005 (second edition), particularly p. 191 ff.

7. Richard Niebuhr, *Christ and Culture*, op. cit., particularly pp. 30 and 31. It is no coincidence that it is within Protestantism that the most powerful

expression of God's absolute transcendence is found, since Protestantism was born out of the rejection of Christianity's "paganization".

8. For a typical case see: http://observer.guardian.co.uk/uk_news/story/0,, 1973838,00.html (Catholic Church in new sex abuse row: The Catholic Church faces fresh allegations of turning a blind eye to paedophilia after an Observer investigation revealed that one of its priests was allowed to continue working despite warnings he posed a danger to children).

9. In modern Protestant religiosity, Jesus can equally be "The Lord" or "my friend".

10. Leo Strauss considers that philosophy and theology are founded on two radically different orders and that the operation carried out by Spinoza (excluding the "living God" from philosophy) prohibits positing the question of values ontologically. For him, as for Niebuhr, there is an inbuilt tension between religion as transcendence and everything that is of the order of the profane, including philosophy and culture, cf. "Progress or return? The contemporary crisis in western civilization", *Modern Judaism*, vol. 1, no. 1, May 1981, pp. 17–45.

11. Cf. Jean François Billeter, *Contre François Jullien*, Paris: Allia, 2006.

12. The first two terms derive from anthropology, the third was ratified by the Vatican Council II, and the last was coined by Danièle Hervieu-Léger, *Catholicisme, la fin d'un monde*, Paris: Bayard, 2003.

13. *Haskala*: Jewish enlightenment, a Jewish ideological movement aiming to modernize Jewish life and thought.

14. Charles Maurras (1868–1952), influential French political theorist and author, and one of the founders of the royalist right-wing journal *L'Action Française*. A supporter of fascism and collaboration with the Nazis he became one of the ideologists behind Pétain's Vichy regime.

15. *Le Monde* journalist Xavier Ternisien, the paper's then religious affairs editor, paid the price for this suspicion: the Israeli newspaper *Haaretz* of 6 July 2005, describes him, mistakenly, as an "Armenian converted to Islam".

16. See the affair of the Finaly children who were hidden during the Occupation by Catholic priests who then refused to hand them back to their families after they had been baptized.

17. A recent case is that of the Bnei Menashe, the Mizo-speaking Shinlung group living on the border between India and Myanmar. Converts initially to Pentecostalist Christianity in the 1930s, they claimed to be Jewish descendents of the tribe of Menasseh. A thousand of them were accepted in Israel after being "reconverted" by orthodox rabbis. See Shalva Weil, "Dual conversion among the Shinlung of North-East India", *Studies of Tribes and Tribals*, New Delhi, vol. 1 no. 1, 2003, pp. 43–57. It is an interesting example of the conversion from Christianity to Judaism in the modern-day world. For another example of a "lost tribe", see "Judaïsme : les Abayudaya de l'Ouganda enfin reconnus comme juifs", *Religioscope*, 18 March 2002 (www.religioscope.com/info). They too converted to Judaism by way of evangelical Protestantism.

18. Rodney Stark, *The Rise of Christianity*, San Francisco: HarperOne, 1997.

19. Vasiliki Limberis, "Religion" as the cipher for identity: The cases of Emperor Julian, Lebanonius, and Gregory Nazianzus", *The Harvard Theological Review*, October 2000.

20. An exhibition on the Roman Christians shows that it was possible to be wealthy and a Christian, and for a person to take a stand against the asceticism of their brothers who could disperse the family heritage; for example, in 400, a certain Valerius Severus fought the choice of his brother Pinianus, the husband of Saint Melanie the Younger, while at the same time having Christian inscriptions carved on his furniture. See Peter Brown, "The private art of early Christians", *New York Review of Books*, 20 March 2008, which reports on the exhibition: *Picturing the Bible: The Earliest Christian Art*, at Kimbell Art Museum, Fort Worth, November 2007–March 2008.

21. This is the common thread linking all the "*nouveaux penseurs de Islam*" (new thinkers of Islam)—according to the title of the book by Rachid Benzine, Paris, Albin Michel, 2003; it is echoed by Shirin Ebadi, the Iranian human rights activist and winner of the Nobel Peace Prize.

22. Cf. Bruno Dumézil, *Les Racines Chrétiennes de l'Europe*, Paris: Fayard, 2007.

23. This idea persisted until the beginning of the nineteenth century, among the Protestants too, as is illustrated by the success of a book such as *The True Nature of imposture fully displayed in the life of Mahomet; with a discourse attached for the full vindication of Christianity from this charge*, published by Humphrey Prideau in 1697 and reprinted up until 1808, with an American edition in 1798. It includes the following condemnation: "Muhammad was above all the great imposter, or, in Charles Wesley's phrase, 'The Arab thief, as Satan bold' whose doctrine should be chased back to hell".

24. Charles J. Halperin, "The Ideology of Silence: Prejudice and Pragmatism on the Medieval Religious Frontier", *Comparative Studies in Society and History*, vol. 26, no. 3, July 1984, pp. 442–466.

25. One of these congregations specifically bears the name of "Missions étrangères de Paris" (Paris foreign missions).

26. Eloquently summarized in Claude Prudhomme, *La Querelle des universels, Problématiques missionnaires du XIXe siècle*, Lyon: Université de Lyon 3, 2001. "The appeal to the state and the recommendation to maintain good relations does not mean the relinquishing of the independence of missionary action, which was the fervent wish of Colin, the founder of the Marists ('We missionaries are for God and for souls; we are not from any one country; we are from all countries'); of François Libermann ('may you be seen solely as the priest of the Almighty and the doctor of the truth'); of Marion Brazillac ('I beseech you, O my God, not to be French in matters of the Church, but Catholic, Catholic only, Roman Catholic'). But it must be acknowledged that on the ground, a de facto solidarity was

established. In the name of pragmatism and efficiency, the colonial solution took hold during the course of the century because it is generally in the best interests of the mission".

27. Jean-Claude Baumont, "La renaissance de l'idée missionnaire en France au début du XIXe siècle", in *Les Réveils missionnaires en France du Moyen Age à nos jours*, Lyon colloquium, 29–31 May 1980, Proceedings, Paris, Beauchesne, 1984.

28. Cf. Prudhomme, *La Querelle des universels*, op. cit.

29. http://218.188.3.99/Archive/periodical/abstract/A013F2.htm, by Patrick Taveirne. In brief: establish territorial divisions, appoint bishops, promote local priests to episcopal positions, not treat the local clergy as mere auxiliaries but as equals to the European priests, not get involved in politics or secular affairs, become involved in primary and secondary education for boys and girls, not forgetting pious and charitable works, devote oneself to everything that can help the Church root itself in local societies.

30. Uniatism is the rallying policy of the Eastern Christian Churches, usually Orthodox, to Rome. The Uniate Churches recognize the authority of the Pope, but retain their traditional Oriental rites (language and liturgy).

31. A line that would remain constant in Protestant thought, up to and including Karl Barth and Richard Niebuhr, despite the development of a theology of presence in the world.

32. Francis Higman, *La Diffusion de la Réforme en France*, Geneva: Labor et Fides, 1992, p. 170.

33. *Ibid.*

34. James Tanis, "Reformed Pietism and Protestant Missions", *The Harvard Theological Review*, vol. 67, no. 1, January 1974, pp. 65–73.

35. The title of a Protestant text from 1622 (the year in which the Vatican created the Congregation for the Propagation of the Faith) like *A prayer for Christians for the converting of the Heathens*, by Willem Teellinck, is proof that calls for converting were isolated and that the protestant community at that time was not interested in converting (cited in James Tanis, *ibid.*, p. 73).

36. Jean de Léry, *Histoire d'un Voyage Faict en la Terre du Brazil*, Paris: Le Livre de Poche, 1994, including a discussion with Claude Lévi-Strauss.

37. For a critique of the theory of the "Huguenot refuge", see John McGrath, "Polemic and History in French Brazil, 1555–1560", *Sixteenth Century Journal*, vol. 27, no. 2, Summer 1996, pp. 385–397.

38. Jean de Léry, *Histoire d'un voyage faict en la terre du Brésil*, Paris: Le livre de Poche 1994, featuring an interview with Claude Lévi-Strauss. English edition with translation and introduction by Janet Whatley. *History of a Voyage to the Land of Brazil*, Berkeley, CA: University of California Press, 1990.

39. See the writings of Frank Lestringant, *Jean De Léry ou L'invention du sauvage—Essai sur Histoire D'un Voyage Faicte en La Terre du Brésil*, Paris: Honoré Champion, 2005.

40. For an excellent analysis of Léry's religious thinking, see Andrea Frisch, "In a Sacramental Mode: Jean de Léry's Calvinist Ethnography", *Representations*, no. 77, Winter 2002, pp. 82–106.

41. Frank Lestringant, "The Philosopher's Breviary: Jean de Léry in the Enlightenment", *Representations*, no. 33, *Special Issue: The New World*, Winter 1991, pp. 200–211.

42. Andrea Frisch, op. cit., pp. 82–106.

43. William S. Simmons, "Cultural Bias in the New England Puritans' Perception of Indians", *The William and Mary Quarterly*, 1981.

44. Thomas S. Abler, "Protestant Missionaries and Native Culture: Parallel Careers of Asher Wright and Silas T. Rand", *American Indian Quarterly*, 1992.

45. James P. Ronda, "Generations of Faith: The Christian Indians of Martha's Vineyard", *The William and Mary Quarterly*, 1981; William S. Simmons, "Cultural Bias in the New England Puritans' Perception of Indians", *The William and Mary Quarterly*, 1981.

46. Rachel Wheeler, "Women and Christian Practice in a Mahican Village", *Religion and American Culture*, The Center for the Study of Religion and American Culture, 2003. It was a Moravian mission in the eighteenth century. But it was the exception: the Moravians were very different from the other denominations and systematically reached out to the indigenous population, with whom they shared the same suspicion of the Anglo-Saxon settlers (the Moravians were not Anglo-Saxon). The author stresses certain cultural similarities in the rites (blood, torture ritual).

47. Universal prevenient grace refers to the doctrine that there is a divine enabling grace extended to all mankind, prior to and without reference to anything they may have done. This grace purportedly restores man's free will, which was corrupted by the effects of original sin, and enables him to choose or refuse the salvation offered by God in Jesus Christ.

48. Cited in Neal Salisbury, "Red Puritans: The 'Praying Indians' of Massachusetts Bay and John Eliot", *The William and Mary Quarterly*, vol. 31, no. 1, January 1974, p. 28. See also Hilary E. Wyss, "Captivity and Conversion: William Apess, Mary Jemison, and Narratives of Racial Identity", *American Indian Quarterly*, 1999.

49. Annette Laing, "Heathens and Infidels? African Christianization and Anglicanism in the South Carolina Low Country, 1700–1750", *Religion and American Culture*, vol. 12, no. 2, Summer 2002, pp. 197–228. Other sources with similar arguments include: James Axtell, "Some thoughts on the Ethnohistory of Missions", *Ethnohistory*, The American Society for Ethnohistory, 1982, p. 38.

50. Annette Laing, op. cit., p. 2.

51. Dana L. Robert, "The Influence of American Missionary Women on the World Back Home", *Religion and American Culture*, Center for the Study of Religion and American Culture, 2002.

52. Patrick Taveirne, "The Nineteenth-Century Religious and Missionary Revivals: Liberal and Socialist Challenges", in *Theology Annual, The European Roots Of The Modern Missionary Enterprise*, 1993, pp. 155–188.

2. FROM CIVILIZATION TO MULTICULTURALISM

1. See the various articles by Jean-Louis Schlegel, in the special edition of *Esprit* of March-April 2007, "Effervescences religieuses dans le monde", and "L'eschatologie et l'apocalypse dans l'histoire: un bilan controversé", March-April 2008.

2. Instruction by the Duc de Montmorency in 1603, cited in Cornelius J. Jaenen, "Problems of Assimilation in New France, 1603–1645", *French Historical Studies*, vol. 4, no. 3, Spring 1966, pp. 265–289.

3. Founder of Quebec in 1605.

4. *Ibid.*

5. Cited in Claude Prudhomme, *La Querelle des universels...*, op. cit. (see: http://resea-ihc.univ-lyon3.fr/publicat/bulletin/2001/prudhomme.pdf). Cf. C. Prudhomme's thesis, 'Stratégie missionnaire du Saint Siège sous le pontificat de Léon XIII. Centralisation romaine et défis culturels', Lyon III, 1989, 1031 p. 1 vol. of annexes.

6. Claude Prudhomme, *La Querelle des universels...*, op. cit.

7. Born Jacob Libermann (1802–1852), a converted Jew from Alsace, founder of the Society of the Saint-Cœur de Marie, member of the Congregation of the Holy Spirit, he was the driving force for a series of missions to Sub-Saharan Africa.

8. Libermann, *Mémoire* of 1846, cited by Prudhomme, *ibid.*, p. c.

9. On China, see Wayne Flynt and Gerald W. Berkley, *Taking Christianity to China: Alabama Missionaries in the Middle Kingdom, 1850–1950*, Tuscaloosa: University of Alabama Press, 1999; this is a phenomenon which I regularly observed in the 1970s, particularly in the Ibb Baptist mission in North Yemen: the missionaries' house was built in the same style as the American officers' barracks in post-war France.

10. Wayne Flint and Gerald W. Berkley, *Taking Christianity to China...*, op. cit.; of course, this book talks of the Baptist missionaries from the Southern US states, which were much less open than the others (particularly, the author points out, no missionary returning from China evinced a more open attitude towards the blacks of Alabama).

11. Wayne Flint and Gerald W. Berkley, *Taking Christianity to China...*, op. cit., p. 91.

12. For example, in the book *Race et Histoire*, commissioned by UNESCO.

13. On the Protestants, see: http://www.eglise-reformee-mulhouse.org/el/eld2. htm, minister Fabien Ouamba, Institut de Théologie de NKongsamba, Ndoungue (Cameroon). We reference this document because it is both a good account and a critique of the limitations of the inculturation theory: "After assimilation, adaptation or incarnation, we now speak of the inculturation of the Gospel in Africa. By inculturation we should understand the introduction of the Gospel into the African's culture and actions. It is a process by which African culture is recognized, accepted and affirmed as being capable of welcoming and conveying the Gospel in the same way as

all the other so-called Christian cultures. Behind the problem of the inculturation of the Gospel into the African situation, there is the attempt to legitimize African culture. In this sense, this process becomes a gradual or sudden removal of the prohibition of the Africans' culture and its liberation in relation to Western culture. And lastly, it should be added that inculturation presupposes a more or less permanent, localizable and identifiable cultural space. The announcing of the Gospel then takes this cultural space seriously with its languages, its symbols, its rites and its vision of the world to allow the welcoming and the adoption of the Good News of Salvation in Jesus Christ. [...] Inculturation barely disguises a real desire to return to paganism for a category of Christians or a revenge strategy of this same paganism against Christianity from within. For a certain number of Christians, opening the Gospel up to African culture is tantamount to letting the African Christian go back to his idols, incorporate his gods into the faith, go to the soothsayer, make sacrifices to his ancestors' skulls, to harden himself without feeling guilty, and be purified by the priests of traditional religion. In other words, it is to have the authorization to practise paganism within Christianity and within the Church under cover of inculturation. [...] And so, the inculturation of the Gospel outwardly appears to be enabling the Gospel to penetrate a given culture, but then who needs this inculturation of the Gospel? [...] Inculturation becomes possible, productive and enriching when the Gospel does not seek to establish itself and shut itself up in a culture but to make that culture a vehicle and an instrument of God in the service of God for the wellbeing of man, the safeguarding and protection of the whole of creation. [...] Thus inculturation can be harmful if it contents itself with human culture, wisdom, tradition, custom and principles. Man, the producer of this culture being capable of the best and the worst, is in the process of breaking away from God. But if he becomes a man of God, he will produce a culture that will reflect and give a structure to his relation with God and the others in such a way that he may say: "Everything is done for the glory of God, it all depends what you do with it".

14. P. Mario L. Peresson, SDB, at: http://www.sedos.org/french/peresson. htm.

15. His Holiness Pope Paul VI, Apostolic Exhortation, *Evangelii Nuntiandi*, 8 December 1975.

16. *Dictionnaire des valeurs oblates*, article entitled *Inculturation* (at: http:// www.oblats.qc.ca/OMI/dictvalues/v_inculturation.html).

17. *Redemptoris Missio*: http://www.vatican.va/edocs/ENG0219/_P7.HTM, chapters 52–53.

18. I cite this text which defines "Indian theology" more extensively: "It is a Christian theological current which anchors its experience and thinking in the culture and the tradition of the native peoples. It is a superb example of the inculturation of the Christian faith, in other words of respecting and taking into account cultural concepts that are external to Christianity,

in which Christianity immerses itself and which it uses to reinvent itself. What is happening today with Native American theology is similar to what happened for the Christian faith and Greek culture: the birth of an original way of living and interpreting the evangelical message. [...] The earth is the Earth-Mother, the *Pachamama*. It is the origin of life itself. Man owes everything to the earth. He cannot live without her. To take away his land is to kill him. Man maintains a true relationship with the earth, like with a living being. We westerners have a relationship of control and domination with the earth. The Indian has a relationship of communion and gratitude. It is a question of living in harmony with the Earth-Mother and not of dominating her". Further on, we read: "It is not a matter of covering traditional Indian theology with a veneer of Christianity, but of showing its profoundly Christian sense in matters of life, man and woman, of the community, etc. It is a matter of the same God in Native American life and in the Christian conscience. [...] What does Indian theology say about Christ? I am struck by the fact that it says little, very little. Probably, the Indian theologians confess the faith of the Church on the subject, but I do not have the impression that their thinking is particularly oriented towards a Christology. [...] I can only cite this passage from a Credo written collectively by Indians during a lesson on Indian theology which took place in 1995 in La Paz, Bolivia: 'We believe in Jesus Christ who lives, dies and is resuscitated in those who fight to build a historic live project starting with the poor. We believe in Jesus Christ God of closeness and unity, who has given us life and strength through the sacrifice of Quetzalcoatl who has been, and will continue to be on our side, in the search for a new *pachakuti*, through the community, solidarity, reciprocity and brotherhood, for all this is the actualization of his vast love which directs us towards the new Earth and new Heavens'". Cf. Alain Durand, *Amérique Latine—La Théologie Indienne Latino-American*, DIAL bulletin (*Diffusion de l'information sur l'Amérique Latine*) of Thursday 22 June 2006. See: http://www.dial-infos.org/01_com/html01_com/cadre.html.

19. Maurice Barth, "Au Mexique, le Vatican met en question la pastorale indigène", *Parvis*, no. 12, December 2001.

20. Olivier Bauer, *La Christologie vue par un observateur particulier sur deux îles du Pacifique sud*, lecture given as part of the Université Theologique Libérale d'Automne, Lyon, September 2000 (see: https://papyrus.bib.umontreal.ca/dspace/bitstream/1866/779/1/Bauer_Christologie_Polyn%C3%A9sie_Lyon2000.pdf).

21. *Ibid.* See also *La théologie de la terre dans les Églises du Pacifique*, edited by Joël Here Hoiore, Alain Rey and Kä Mana, Yaoundé, Éd. Sherpa, 2000.

22. *Le Monde*, 9 May 2007.

3. RELIGION, ETHNIC GROUP, NATION

1. This is not to deny the very strong link between Catholicism and Irish nationalism after the English conquest of the sixteenth century, especially after the Great Famine that led to the decline of Gaelic and the quest for a new Irish identity in opposition to England, this time based on religion, see: John Newsinger, "I bring not peace but a sword: the religious motif in the Irish War of Independence", *Journal of Contemporary History*, vol. 13, no. 3, July 1978, pp. 609–628. The article nevertheless gives several examples of Protestants and Marxists aligning themselves with nationalists and also highlights the often ambiguous role of the Catholic Church, which on some occasions has had no hesitation in excommunicating radical nationalists. Conversely, so to speak, a Protestant leader of the 1916 Easter Uprising, Sir Roger Casement, converted to Catholicism before his execution. On 18 April 1918, the Church published a declaration outlining its stance: "The Irish people have the right to resist by all the means that are compatible with God's law"; which made it possible to assert a religious rule above nationalism, and to condemn the means used by the IRA, but not its aims.
2. As exemplified in a joke I was once told: "In Belfast, at the corner of two roads, one Protestant and the other Catholic, a Bangladeshi grocer opened a convenience store and served both communities. One winter evening, a hooded armed man held a gun to his temple and asked: "Catholic or Protestant?" "But I'm a Muslim!" he replied. "I mean a Catholic Muslim or a Protestant Muslim?"
3. David Martin, *Tongues of Fire: The Explosion of Protestantism in Latin America*, Oxford: Wiley-Blackwell, 1993, p. 35.
4. Hovann Simonian, *The Hemshin: A Handbook*, London: Routledge and Kegan Paul, 2006.
5. Although there are Syriacs of Kurdish mother tongue, they consider this to be accidental and claim their Syriac origins, proof once again that the religion/culture association is constructed rather than a fact. Identity construction can also operate through denial of the facts.
6. Personal interview, October 1996.
7. Personal testimony, village of Midin.
8. Olivier Roy, *The New Central Asia*, London: New York University Press, 2000.
9. Having already invoked my grandfather in the foreword, I would like to mention here my uncle, Roger Barraud, who set up the first white Gospel group in 1947, the "Compagnons du Jourdan", after having spent some time as the only white in an African-American regiment in Morocco in 1942–3 (as a simple "liaison soldier", since "liaison officers" were sent to white regiments, American segregation demanded it). Today the Gospel troops are often mixed, but that is possible because there was a civil rights battle in the United States in the 1960s. There has also been a certain secularization of African-American Gospel by left-wing American singers, although their inspiration comes more from country and folk music.

10. In 1896, the decision of the Supreme Court "Plessy vs. Ferguson" defined a Black as any person with a single drop of black blood, which erased the categories in-between (mixed race, mulatto) and thus the possibility of changing race through intermarriage and social advancement, which is characteristic of postcolonialism in Latin American countries.

11. See Theophus H. Smith, *Conjuring Culture: Biblical Formations of Black America*, Oxford: Oxford University Press, 1995. A major movement among African-American academics wants to rehabilitate an African genealogy of civilizations and religions that has supposedly been concealed by "white" historiography; the archetype is the book by Martin Bernal, *Black Athena: The Afroasiatic Roots of Classical Civilization*, New Brunswick: Rutgers University Press, 1985.

12. This qualification is recent: it dates from post World War II. In 1923, the Supreme Court refused to naturalize an upper-caste Hindu, arguing that, even if he was genetically descended from a white race, he did not physically resemble a white, "US v. Bhagat Singh Thind" (1923). It was very much one's visible colour that defined race and it was seen as a stark choice between being either white or non-white, i.e. black.

13. An article in the *New York Times* tells of the visit of a black imam from Harlem, a prison chaplain, to a much richer mosque in Long Island, recruiting among middle and upper-class Muslims from the Indian subcontinent and Arabs, in order to fundraise for his charitable works: Andrea Elliott, "Between Black and Immigrant Muslims, an Uneasy Alliance", *New York Times*, 11 March 2007.

14. See the very fine Canadian TV sitcom, *The Little Mosque on the Prairie* (2007).

15. Cf. Rodrigo Zayas, *Les Morisques et le Racisme d'État*, Paris: La Difference, 1992.

16. See Matthew Carr, *Blood and Faith: The Purging of Muslim Spain*, Hurst: 2010. The figure of the picaresque hero roaming the bleak landscapes of seventeenth-century Spain has been interpreted as the need for many *conversos* to uproot themselves in order to conceal their origins; Jean Vila, "Le Picarisme Espagnol", in *Les Marginaux et les Exclus de l'histoire*, Cahiers Jussieu, No. 5, Paris, 118 October, 1979.

17. Paul W. Werth, "The limits of religious ascription: baptized Tatars and the revision of "apostasy", 1840–1905", *Russian Review*, vol. 59, no. 4 (October 2000), pp. 493–511.

18. Conversely, but on the basis of the same presupposition (culture and religion are inseparable), when, at around the same time, some Hemshin—Armenian-speaking Muslims in the Ottoman Empire, asked to revert to Christianity, the local authorities' response was to force them to speak Turkish. Hovann Simonian, *The Hemshin : A Handbook*, op. cit., p. 76.

19. Christian Delorme, "Non, l'Algérie n'est pas anti-Chrétienne", *Le Monde*, 4 June 2008.

20. They replaced the incantation *"Sri Sri Iswar"* with *"Allah-O-Akbar"* and their Hindu names (Chand, Pal, Dutt) with Muslim names (Siddiqui, Yusufzai, Qureshi); cf. Francis Robinson, "The British Empire and Muslim Identity in South Asia", *Transactions of the Royal Historical Society*, 1998.

21. *Ibid.*

22. A Sunni Pakistani journalist, theologian, Muslim Revivalist Leader and political philosopher, and a major twentieth-century Islamist thinker. He was also a prominent political figure in Pakistan and founder of the Jamaat-e-Islami, an Islamic revivalist party.

23. See Nathalie Clayer and Xavier Bougarel (eds), *Le Nouvel Islam balkanique*, Paris: Maisonneuve et Larose, 2001.

24. See R. Stephen Warner and Judith G. Wittner (eds), *Gatherings in Diaspora: Religious Communities and the New Immigration*, Philadelphia: Temple University Press, 1998.

25. *Ibid.*, p. 301.

26. Even though this is the thesis of the book *Gatherings...*, *ibid.*

27. Personal observation.

28. In contrast, another "diaspora" people, the Roma, have systematically adopted mainstream religion, nowadays evangelical Christianity.

29. Peter Berger, *The Sacred Canopy: Elements of a Sociological Theory of Religion*, New York: Doubleday, 1967, p. 170.

30. This is not unique to the Jews; Christian customs are found among some groups of Christian converts to Islam, like the Syriacs to the West of the town of Midyat who became Arabic-speaking Muslims (known as *Mhalmoye*).

31. Stephen Sharot, "Minority situation and religious acculturation: a comparative analysis of Jewish communities", *Comparative Studies in Society and History*, 1974 (ed. by the Society for Comparative Studies in Society and History), p. 340.

32. Definitions often proposed by American Jews who supported the American civil rights movement (on civil rights, Rabbi Marc Shneier took part in the commemoration of the assassination of Martin Luther King. Cf. Shlomo Shamir, "Rabbi: Jews, more than anyone, helped black Americans achieve equality", *Haaretz* of 24 May 2008). On the definition of Jewish humanitarian values, cf. Anshel Pfeffer, "Jewish values can fight world poverty", *Haaretz* of 6 April 2008, interview with Charles Keidan, the director of the Pears Foundation, a private British-Jewish philanthropic fund that runs projects to empower civilians in Africa, "we want to redefine what a Jewish objective is. Fighting poverty and illness, helping the homeless, world social justice are part of Jewish values".

33. An author like Ahan Ha'am translates *Volkgeist*, "spirit of the people", litterally by *ruach ha-'am*, cf. Paul Mendes-Flohr, "Cultural Zionism's image of the educated Jew: Reflections on creating a secular Jewish cul-

ture" *Modern Judaism*, vol. 18, no. 3, *100 Years of Zionism and the 50th Anniversary of the State of Israel*, October 1998, pp. 231 and 240.

34. Lila Corwin Berman, "Mission to America, the Reform Movement's Missionary Experiments, 1919–1960", *Religion and American Culture*, vol. 13, no. 2, Summer 2003, pp. 205–239.

35. In religious anti-Judaism, the Jew is someone who does not want to see the truth; being Jewish is not a destiny, it is a choice. Hence adjectives such as "obstinate", "perfidious" (taken in the Latin sense of unbeliever, a person who does not want to know); so, once converted, he ceases to be Jewish. In racial antisemitism, a Jew is a person with Jewish blood. Hence the controversy over Cardinal Lustiger, who said he was Jewish (in the ethnic sense) and Christian, but who was considered Jewish and therefore an unlikely Christian in the eyes of the racist far right, and who was not accepted as a Jew by many rabbis, who, on the other hand, focused only on the religious aspect.

36. *L'Arche*, no. 538, December 2002.

37. Ofra Edelman, "Judge okays sale of leavened products during Passover", *Haaretz*, 4 April 2008.

38. Paul Mendes-Flohr, op. cit.

39. See the institute's website: http://www.iishj.org/about_iishj.htm.

40. Yair Ettinger, "Chief rabbinate upset over 'secular rabbi' ordination ceremony", *Haaretz*, 22 December 2006.

41. Craig Smith, "In Poland, a Jewish Revival Thrives—Minus Jews", *New York Times*, 12 July 2007.

42. The Jewish hero of *Portnoy's Complaint* faints on arrival in Israel and explains to his analyst his shock at seeing Jewish police officers.

43. Yannick Fer, *Pentecostalisme en Polynésie Française*, op. cit., pp. 30, 428: Turo Raapoto writes about a theology of indigenous culture.

44. Donald K. Swearer, "Lay Buddhism and the Buddhist Revival in Ceylon", *Journal of the American Academy of Religion*, vol. 38, no. 3, September 1970, pp. 255–275.

45. In 2007, the Federal Court of Malaysia refused to recognize the conversion of a Muslim Malaysian woman, Lina Joy, to Christianity.

46. A group of "reform" theologians from the Volos institute of theology, in Greece, attempted to define a non-ethnic orthodoxy. See Christos Yannaras, "The role of the Brotherhood of the Holy Sepulchre", *Kathimerini*, 10 April 2005: "Why should the patriarchate of Jerusalem continue to be Greek Orthodox?... since when has an ethno-phyletic designation constituted a necessity that determines the workings of the ecclesiastic institution?" See also Pantelis Kalaïtzidis, "The current situation of the patriarchate of Jerusalem: a form of ecclesiastic neo-colonialism?", *Thessalia*, 25 March 2005.

47. *Ibid.*

48. The F18 website lists numerous cases; for example, F18, 17 March 2004, "Georgia: will violent Old Calendarist priest now be punished?". Basil

Mkalavishvili, a priest belonging to the "Old Calendarist" branch, physically attacked Baptist converts.

49. Mazwin Nik Anis, "*Herald* can't use 'Allah' in its publications", *The Star*, 4 January 2008.

50. This authority was more recently justified by Pope Benedict XVI in the name of rehabilitating reason versus the emotion of pure faith: Address of Pope Benedict XVI "Faith, Reason and the University, Memories and Reflections", Aula Magna of the University of Regensburg, 12 September 2006.

51. More precisely, for the English translations, see Barbara Tuchman, *The Bible and the Sword*, New York, New York: University Press, 1956, p. 85.

52. Jean Delumeau, *Le Catholicisme entre Luther et Voltaire*, Paris, PUF, 1996, p. 74.

53. The first Hangul grammar was written by John Ross, a Scottish Presbyterian missionary, and the first dictionary by French missionaries.

54. See the praise for Breton popular culture, including its folklore side, by Monsignor Gourves (interview in the journal *Kephas*, January-March 2004). In the Catholic Church, inculturation is not a specifically "left wing" notion.

55. Yannick Fer, *Pentecostalisme en Polynésie Française*, op. cit., pp. 30 and 428.

56. Nicholas Omenka, "The role of the Catholic mission in the development of vernacular literature in Eastern Nigeria", *Journal of Religion in Africa*, 1986, p. 199 foll.

57. "By 1911 there were, for example, seven newspapers and monthlies published in Khasi, and in the previous decade thirty-seven books had been produced in the language. The result of the growth of a vernacular tradition was however to check the process of assimilation, conversion to Hinduism usually involving the abandonment of tribal languages. The effect of these developments was seen in the growth of the tribal population speaking the vernacular, in some cases a growth that exceeded their increase in population". J. H. Beaglehole, "The Indian Christians, a study of a minority", *Modern Asian Studies*, vol. 1, no. 1, 1967, p. 61.

58. In fact, this was a recent prohibition; the Church translated a lot in the first millennium, but after that less and less, to maintain its monopoly over interpretation. But in the sixteenth century, two new constraints appeared: evangelizing the new peoples and the counter-attack on Protestant soil itself.

59. B. A. Greene, "The influence of the Authorized Version on English literature", *The Biblical World*, 1911 (see website: http://www.jstor.org.gate3.inist.fr/journals/ucpress.html).

60. J.D. Benoît, *Les Prophètes huguenots*, thesis, Montauban, 1910; see also the writings of Ch. Bost, from his *Prédicants des Cévennes*, 1912, to the publication of his *Mémoires inédits d'Abraham Mazel et d'Élie Marion...*, (1931). Whether this is true or not is irrelevant, what matters is that the

"prophets" were supposed to prophecy in French, for that would be the proof that they were inspired by the Holy Spirit, and therefore that French was seen as being superior in status to dialects.

61. Abbé Grégoire, *Rapport sur la nécessité et les moyens d'anéantir le patois et d'universaliser l'usage de la langue Française.*

62. Robert Bonfil, Guglielmo Cavallo, Roger Chartier, *Histoire de la lecture dans le monde occidental*, Paris: Le Seuil, 2001, p. 309.

63. *Kephas* journal, January–March 2004. The entire interview with Bishop Gourves, the only Breton-speaking bishop in Brittany in 2000, is interesting as it encapsulates the theory of inculturation and justifies support for popular religion, as a merger of Christianity and culture, a merger maintained by the practice of the language and the communion in one and the same art (including music, in short what is perceived from the outside as folklore): "Since its beginnings, there have been two successful examples of the inculturation of Christianity in the world: the time of the Church Fathers and popular religion. Here, popular religion has permeated everyone. Not all have the faith, for certain; not all are convinced practicing Catholics, but all have been 'plunged into the cauldron of the Church'—Q: *Can there be a true Breton culture without the Catholic faith, in other words also open to the universal?*— Bishop Gourvès: That is a difficult question. I think that Breton culture can only find its full expression with the faith. There would be something lacking if the faith were not part of it, giving it another dimension, purifying it and perfecting it in a way".

64. Kaspar von Greyerz, *Religion et Culture: Europe 1500–1800*, Paris: Le Cerf, 2006.

65. On the fate of Yiddish, see Dovid Katz, *Words on Fire*, New York: Basic Books, 2004.

66. Dominique Avon, *Les Frères prêcheurs en Orient*, Paris: Cerf, 2005, p. 280.

67. Cited in the review of the book by Leila Lalami, *Dancing Arabs*, in "Native Speaker", *Boston Review*, September–October 2006.

68. Readers' letters, *Libération*, 6 October 2006.

69. See the successive UNDP reports (United Nations Development Programme), *Arab Human Development Report*, written by Nader Fergani in 2002 and 2004.

70. See Olivier Roy, *Globalized Islam*, London: Hurst, 2004.

71. As discussed in Dovid Katz, *Words on Fire*, op. cit.

72. In 2008, the publishing house Safa Brura, linked to the Satmar Hassidic movement, published a pamphlet entitled *Tohar Halashon* (The purity of language), advocating the return to Yiddish, cf. Yair Ettinger, "Language wars—round two", *Haaretz*, 28 March 2008.

4. CULTURE AND RELIGION: THE DIVIDE

1. There is a development of this same aporia in the work of Abdolkarim Soroush, who attempts to reconcile democracy and religion in defining a "religious civil society". The problem is: what happens if the citizen stops being religious? Either this hypothesis is excluded by law and there is no religious democracy, or society stops being religious and there is just democracy. That is presumably why Soroush has abandoned this concept.

2. Maurice Godelier, *Au fondement des sociétés humaines*, Paris: Albin Michel, 2007, p. 98ff.

3. Calvinism's "essentially congregational conception of government was wholly inadequate as a system to rule a whole nation" as wrote Harold J. Berman in "Religious Foundations of Law in the West: An Historical Perspective", *Journal of Law and Religion*, 1983, p. 14.

4. This is precisely what Foucault said about the Iranian revolution, and yet his writings were interpreted in the opposite way. It is the absolute negation brought by religious protest that fascinated him, and not at all some promise of a new, just order, in which he believed so little that he did not even elaborate on the subject; see Olivier Roy, "L'Enigme du soulèvement: Michel Foucault et l'Iran", *Vacarmes*, Autumn 2004, no. 28, translated into English as "The Enigma of the Uprising", *Truthout*, http://www.truthout.org /072809T.

5. Michel de Certeau, *L'Invention du Quotidien I*, Paris: UGE, coll. "10/18", 1990.

6. Yair Ettinger, "Chief Rabbi to revoke ruling which invalidates thousands of conversions", *Haaretz*, 4 May 2008. The President of the Supreme Rabbinical Court, Shlomo Amar, stated his disagreement with this decision, for reasons similar to those expanded on here.

7. Danièle Hervieu-Léger, *Catholicisme, la fin d'un Monde*, op. cit.

8. Jean-Noël Ferrié, *Régime de la civilité en Égypte*, Paris: Éditions of the CNRS, 2004.

9. Baudouin Dupret, *Le Jugement en action. Ethnométhodologie du droit, de la morale et de la justice en Égypte*, Geneva: Droz, 2006.

10. Danièle Hervieu-Léger, *Catholicisme, la fin d'un Monde*, op. cit.

11. CSA survey, December 2006.

12. Bishop Vingt-trois in *Le Figaro*, 23 November 2007.

13. Fanny Capel, "Le catéchisme en quête de nouvelles ouailles", *Le Figaro*, 25 August 2006.

14. *Le Figaro*, 10 October 2007.

15. Yair Ettinger, "Until ignorance divides us", *Haaretz*, 18 July 2007. The article repeats the words of a Jewish-American visitor who complains that his intellectual friends in Israel are not even aware of the existence of the *havdalah* prayer that marks the close of the Sabbath.

16. Jacqueline L. Salmon, "The Offbeat is Helping some Jews Reconnect, Chabad Rabbis' Modern Outreach Methods are Controversial but Forge

Ties", *Washington Post*, 27 May 2007; p. C01: "With ice cream sundaes, iPod giveaways, spa days and yoga classes, a group of Orthodox rabbis in the Washington area is employing decidedly unorthodox methods to address a growing problem: the fading involvement of Jews in local Jewish life".

17. Furthermore, it is interesting to note that in metropolitan France, swear words are essentially sexual or scatological, but in Quebec they are borrowed from the vocabulary of the Church—which shows how rooted Catholicism is in Quebecois culture.

18. Doug Struk, "Quebecers Turn to Church Terms, Rather Than the Sexual or Scatological, to Vent Their Anger", *Washington Post*, 5 December 2006, p. A21.

19. Richard Willing, "Christians protest actions that play down Christmas' religious nature", *USA Today*, 21 December 2004.

20. Candace Rondeaux, "Area Muslims Develop a Taste for Turkey, Distributors of Specially Prepared Birds are Catering to a Fledgling Trend", *Washington Post*, 24 November 2006, p. B03. For Hanukkah: Tami Abdollah, "Searching for genuine faith in an assimilated holiday. Although Hanukkah is marked with minor celebrations elsewhere in the world, it tends to be treated as 'Jewish Christmas' in the US", *Los Angeles Times*, 16 December 2006.

21. See above the challenging of a conversion to Judaism by a rabbinical court because afterwards the convert did not demonstrate regular religious practice.

22. "Rumeur confirmée pour deux curés pères de famille", *Le Figaro*, 7 September 2005.

23. This lack of understanding of the seriousness of the issue is clearly expressed, during the trial of a paedophile priest in France, in Rouen in 2005, by the two successive bishops who covered for the priest in question: "Denis Vadeboncœur had been appointed priest to Lieurey in 1988, by Jacques Gaillot, Bishop of Évreux. During his testimony, Bishop Gaillot stated that he 'regretted' having appointed him. He explained that he had listened to 'a cry for help' from the priest, adding: 'Now I admit I made a mistake', saying that at the time he was 'less aware of the problem of paedophilia than today'. His successor, Jacques David, the current Bishop of Évreux, who, incidentally, contradicted Bishop Gaillot on several points, also stated that 'like the average French person, he had only realized the seriousness' of the problem of paedophilia 'much later, 6 or 7 years ago'". cf. "Le procès d'un religieux prêtre Canadien", *FlashPress—Infocatho*, 19 September 2005 (see the website: http://infocatho.cef.fr/fichiers_html/archives/deuxmilcinqsem/semaine38/25nx38europeh.html).

24. On the controversy in the United States see Cathy Young, "The great fellatio scare. Is oral sex really the latest teen craze?", *Reason on line*, May 2006, see website: http://www.reason.com/news/show/36643.html.

25. "The Gospel… must take precedence over culture", said Archbishop Drexel Gomez of the West Indies, one of ten Anglican leaders or repre-

sentatives who attended the ceremony in Nairobi's All Saints Cathedral. "Homosexual practice violates the order of life given by God in Holy writ", cf. "Two US Priests Defect To Anglicans in Kenya", *Washington Post*, 13 August 2007, p. A11.

26. "Gays fear an influx of hate", *Los Angeles Times*, 16 March 2008.

27. The campaign was called *hojjum* (the assault), see Gregory Massell, *The Surrogate Proletariat: Moslem Women and Revolutionary Strategies in Soviet Central Asia, 1919–1929*, Princeton: Princeton UP, 1974.

28. Caryle Murphy, "Soldier of Faith", *Washington Post*, 20 January 2008, p. W16.

29. On the issue of the demand for mixed mosques in the United States, see: http://interfaithpathstopeace.org/2006/06/as-barrier-comes-down-muslim-split.shtml.

30. For example, in June 2006, the American Presbyterian Church convention agreed to consider the experimental use of liturgies using alternatives to the expression "The Father, the Son and the Holy Spirit", including two proposals: "Mother, Child and Womb" and "Rock, Redeemer, Friend". Bruce Schreiner, "Presbyterians Splintering Over Scripture, Conservative Congregations Break Away From Church", *Washington Post*, 13 October 2007, p. B09. There is evidence of the same debate in Hinduism: Rita M. Gross, "Toward a new model of the Hindu Pantheon. A report on twenty-some years of feminist reflection". Symposium "Gender and Religion", in *Religion*, vol. 28, no. 4, pp. 319–327 (October 1998).

31. Women from conservative backgrounds have begun to study the Talmud, without waiting for the authorization of the rabbis: Yair Ettinger, "Be pure or be fruitful", *Haaretz*, 11 December 2006. This goes hand in hand with other phenomena: development of a religious women's press (cf. Smadar Chen, "Changing times for Haredi women, Media developing women's supplements, features and columns to give voice to their needs—but no pictures", *Ynetnews*, 22 May 2005), edifying novels written by Haredim women, the arrival of Haredim women in the workplace (with frequent work conflicts when their employer is also Haredi, *Haaretz*, 26 June 2008).

32. Nicole Neroulias, "Gay Jews Connect Their Experience to Story of Purim", *Washington Post*, 24 February 2007, p. B08.

33. On the split of the Episcopal parish of Falls Church, see the abovementioned article, "Episcopal Churches' Breakaway in Virginia Evolved Over 30 Years", *Washington Post*, 4 January 2007, p. A01.

34. Bishop Roland Minnerath, "Politique Chrétienne ou Chrétiens en politique ?", University of Strasbourg, international symposium on the role of Christianity in the cultural identity of the peoples of Europe, Klingenthal, 27–30 May 1993.

35. Rosa Jiménez Cano, "Ataques a las políticas del gobierno en el acto por la familia Cristiana", *El País*, 30 December 2007.

36. Pope's homily at the Yankee Stadium in New York, 20 April 2008.

37. Jean-Louis Schlegel, writing in *Esprit*, May 2008, describes the Catholic "who no longer obeyed, no longer protested, but tiptoed away", in connection with a case that hit the headlines in 1967, when a Jesuit, François Roustang, wrote an article on similar lines in *Christus*, a spirituality journal.

38. "Lustiger ou l'intelligence de la foi", *Le Monde*, 11 August 2007.

39. Bernice Martin, "New Mutations of the Protestant Ethic among Latin American Pentecostals" *Religion*, vol. 25, no. 2, April 1995, p. 108.

40. Margaret Miles, "Living lovingly amid fear", *Harvard Divinity Bulletin*, Autumn 2006.

41. Donald Miller, *Re-inventing American Protestantism*, op. cit., p. 95.

42. Daniel Marguerat, *Les Actes des Apostles (1–12)*, Geneva: Labor et Fides, Geneva, 2007, devotes nearly 500 pages to a rigorous analysis of the first twelve chapters, which are less than twenty pages long. On the Latin literary dimension of the Vulgate: Catherine Brown Tkacz, "*Labor tam utilis*: The creation of the Vulgate", *Vigiliae Christianæ*, vol. 50, no. 1, 1996, pp. 42–72.

43. Which explains how an erudite Protestant like Jean-Claude Margot can write a book dedicated to the complexity of the translation of the scriptures, *Traduire sans trahir*, Paris, L'Age d'Homme, 1979, concluding that, ultimately, it is not inherently impossible to transmit the message in its entirety. He backs up his argument with Chomsky's generative linguistics and concludes that language is "transcultural"; he refuses the close link between language and culture posited by structuralist theories (see chapter 3: "Traduire la totalité du message"). This book is very interesting for he denies that there are cultural obstacles to communication, for example, the problem of Eskimos' understanding of metaphors relating to the Paschal lamb. We discover that no Bible in any Eskimo language has replaced the lamb with a baby seal, as a widespread culturalist myth would have us believe. Lastly, Margot insists on a fundamental point: the problem is not the precision of the translation but what the reader understands, and that is inseparable from preaching (p. 95), in other words, in the final analysis, from the Holy Spirit.

44. Bernice Martin, "New Mutations of the Protestant Ethic among Latin American Pentecostals", *Religion*, vol. 25, no. 2, April 1995, pp. 101–117.

45. Laurie Goodstein, "Evangelicals Fear the Loss of Their Teenagers", *New York Times*, 6 October 2006.

46. Patrick Haenni, *Islam de Marché*, Paris: Le Seuil, 2006.

47. Alan Cooperman, "Is there disdain for evangelicals in the classroom? Survey, bias allegation, spur debate", *Washington Post*, 5 May 2007, p. A03: "In an unprecedented lawsuit that opens yet another front in the nation's culture wars, an association of Christian schools, including Calvary, charges that the admissions policy at the university unconstitutionally discriminates against them because they teach from a religious

perspective ... The case offers a window into the deepening conviction of many conservative Christians that there is hostility to their faith in the public square and particularly in public schools". Christian associations are being set up to act systematically in the courts, like the American Center for Law and Justice.

48. Andy McSmith, "Fire and brimstone! College principal says we're all going to hell", *The Guardian*, 9 January 2008.
49. Shahar Ilan, "Reconciling conscription", *Haaretz*, 21 April 2008.
50. Noah Feldman, "Orthodox Paradox", *New York Times*, 22 July 2007.
51. For two interesting points of view criticizing Feldman's article: Jaimie Fogel, "Noah Feldman: A Lost Battle", *Yeshiva University Observer*, 26 August 2007, and Norman Lamm, "A Response to Noah Feldman", *Forward, Web Exclusive*, 2 August 2007.
52. *The Vanishing American Jew: In Search of Jewish Identity for the Next Century*, New-York: Touchstone, 1998.
53. "The greatest threat in the eyes of the Jews in France is assimilation", says the principal of the ORT school in Marseille, Maurice Cohen-Zaguri. "Fewer and fewer parents want to send their children to schools that are not religious, even though we too are strengthening our traditional side. The aim of 90 per cent of the parents is that their children should keep *kosher* and observe the Sabbath, and that Heaven forbid, they should not marry a non-Jew". Yair Ettinger, "A new Jewish Force", *Haaretz*, 4 May 2007.
54. Jean Sévilla, "Génération Jean Paul II", *Le Figaro Magazine*, 14 August 2004.
55. Card. Giacomo Biffi, Archbishop of Bologna, 16 January 2003 This article by Cardinal Biffi was published under the title: "Catholic Culture for True Humanism" (see website: http://www.va/roman_curia/congregations/cfaith/documents/rc_con_cfaith_doc_20021124_card-biffi-).
56. "The minister Leuliet states: "Nowadays only that which is visible exists. Evangelical culture must come out of the places of worship and impact on all spheres of society. This step enables us to combat prejudice and to show the world that we are neither followers of sects nor American agents!" *Le Monde*, 24 May 2008.
57. This right-thinking religious literature is often written by women, like the Islamists in Turkey and the Haredim in Israel, but also in Iran.
58. Like *The Love Verses* by the Indonesian Habiburrahman El-Shirazy, published in 2003 (*Ayat-ayat Cinta*, Kuala-Lumpur, Ar-Risalat Product), bestseller on which a successful film was based.
59. Tom Heneghan, "Thai Buddhists seek blasphemy law to punish offences against their faith", 25 October 2007, *Reuters*.
60. For example, on the subject of the Gay Pride march in Jerusalem in 2006: "The Rabbinical Court has held a special session and discussed placing a *pulsa danura* on those who have a hand in organizing the march", Rabbi Shmuel Papenheim, editor of the Eida Haredit's weekly magazine

245

'Ha'eidah told Army Radio on Tuesday. The curse could also be cast "against the policemen who beat ultra-orthodox Jews", Papenheim added. "If words can kill, *pulsa danura* is a weapon of mass destruction" *Haaretz*, 11 November 2006.

61. Adam Molner, "Rolling with the Na Nachs, the most high-spirited and newest Hasidic sect", *Haaretz*, 25 May 2008.
62. http://www.voxdei.org/nicolas/Indiax.php/2006/05/06/148–le-business-evangelique-a-jerusalem.

PART 2: GLOBALIZATION AND RELIGION

5. FREE MARKET OR DOMINATION BY THE MARKET?

1. See Nathan Wachtel's pioneering work, *The Vision of the Vanquished*, translated by Ben and Sian Reynolds, Hassocks, Harvester Press, 1977. Note that for the Native Americans of North America, the policy was different. No systematic conversions, but a gradual repression that led to the extermination or confinement to reservations, where the cultures declined. This is more a case of deculturation and ethnocide than of forced acculturation.
2. See Theophus H. Smith, *Conjuring Cultures: Biblical Formations of Black America*, Oxford: OUP, 1995.
3. Philip Jenkins, *The Next Christendom*, Oxford: OUP, 2007, p. 7.
4. T. H. Smith, *Conjuring Cultures*, op. cit.
5. The author adds: "Obviously, this brand of Christianity often lay very lightly on the surface of their lives, its acceptance largely expedient to ensure their Independence and group identity", Robert F. Berkhofer, Jr. "Protestants, Pagans, and Sequences among the North American Indians, 1760–1860", *Ethnohistory*, 1963, p. 39.
6. Luis Leon talks of "cultural oxymorons" (*mariachis* and psalms) in "Born Again in East L.A: The Congregation as Border Space", in Stephen Warner and Judith Wittner (eds.), *Gatherings in Diaspora, Religious Communities and the New Immigration*, Philadelphia: Temple University Press, 1998, p. 173. Each chapter of the book is written by a researcher of the ethnic group being studied.
7. This is taken to extremes in the writings of Pierre Bourdieu for whom, ultimately, all is domination and alienation, except of course the Chair of Sociology at the Collège de France, from which the truth about others' misfortune can be pronounced.
8. Pascale Chaput, "Castes, religions et sacré au Kerala (Inde du Sud): Des Chrétiens dans une société multi-castes et pluri-religieuse", *Revue Française de sociologie*, vol. 38, no. 2, April-June 1997, pp. 327–350. The Jews of India also adopt the caste system, see Stephen Sharot, "Minority situation and religious acculturation: A comparative analysis of Jewish communi-

jee, "Religion and its role are in dispute at the service academies", *New York Times*, 25 June 2008.

32. Frederic J. Fromme, "Group Asks Removal of Koran Swearing-in Critic", *Washington Post*, 5 December 2006, p. C08.

33. Tami Abdollah, "Searching for genuine faith in an assimilated holiday", *Los Angeles Times*, 16 December 2006.

34. Peter Berger, *The Sacred Canopy*, op. cit., pp. 142 and 149.

35. Élise Massicard, *L'Autre Turquie : Le mouvement aléviste et ses territoires*, Paris, PUF, 2005.

36. Benoît Fliche, "Les frontières de 'l'orthodoxie' et de 'l'hétérodoxie': *Türbe et églises à Istanbul*", in Valtchinova G. (dir.), *Religion, Boundaries, and the Politics of Divine Intervention*, Istanbul: ISIS, 2008.

37. Oddvar Hollup, "Islamic Revivalism and Political Opposition among Minority Muslims in Mauritius", *Ethnology*, vol. 35, no. 4, 1996, pp. 285–300.

38. Prema Kurien, *A Place at the Multicultural Table: The Development of an American Hinduism*, New Brunswick: Rutgers University Press, reviewed by Richard Cimino (Religion Watch, October 2007).

39. Raphaël Liogier, *Le Bouddhisme mondialisé : Une perspective sociologique sur la globalisation du religieux*, Paris: Ellipses, 2004, Introduction.

40. Kathleen Garces-Foley, "Buddhism, hospice, and the American way of dying", *Review of Religious Research*, 2003; the author emphasizes that this does not mean that people become Buddhists: it is a question of a change of attitude towards death, seeking to accept it rather than deny it.

41. Donald Miller describes a typical case: a cocaine addict, after a tragic experience, chants mantras, invokes Krishna and Buddha, but feels no "vibe"; but, as soon as he utters the name of Jesus, he has a positive hallucinatory experience; so he becomes a member of the Pentecostalist Church of Calvary movement: *Re-inventing American Protestantism*, Berkeley: University of California Press, 1997, p. 100.

42. Richard Hughes Seager, "Pluralism and the American mainstream: The view from the world's Parliament of Religions", *The Harvard Theological Review*, vol. 82, no. 3, July 1989, pp. 301–324.

43. Each one "performs" their service in front of the others and gathered together are, according to the article "Buddhist, Bahai, Catholic, Episcopal, Greek Orthodox, Hindu, Jain, the Church of Jesus Christ of Latter-day Saints, Muslim, Protestant and Sikh", Tina Shah, "Diversity of faiths, unity of followers", *Chicago Tribune*, 15 November 2007.

44. Alan Cooperman "The Army Chaplain Who Wanted to Switch to Wicca? Transfer Denied", *Washington Post*, 19 February 2007, p. C01.

45. Michelle Boorstein, "Discrimination Complaint: Federal Panels order NIH to Reinstate Priest", *Washington Post*, 2 March 2007, p. B03.

46. Donald Miller, *Re-inventing American Protestantism*, Berkeley: University of California Press, 1997, respectively pp. 11 and 29.

47. Andrew Chesnut, "A preferential option for the spirit: The Catholic Charismatic Renewal in Latin America's New Religious Economy", *Latin American Politics and Society*, 2003, cf. http://www.as.miami.edu/international-studies/.

48. A very interesting article on this subject is, *Les Ashrams en Inde: Catholicisme ou nouvel âge?* by Michael Prabhu, who is Indian and a Catholic Charismatic and considers that there is nothing Christian about these ashrams. Here, as is often the case, born-again Christians from the former colonies are vehemently opposed to inculturation theory. Cf. the journal *Métamorphoses* at: http://www.ephesians-511.org/.

CONCLUSION

1. Donald Miller, *Re-inventing American Protestantism,* op. cit.

2. For example, comparisons are continuously being made between the religious experience and the drug experience, the "trip", the "flash" (Miller, *ibid.*, p. 98).

3. Yannick Fer, *Pentecostalisme en Polynésie Française*, op. cit., p. 453.

4. B. Martin: "In practice, however, the evangelical body image has acquired the stigma of being lower class and old-fashioned. Many of the new middle class groups have simply jettisoned this sector of the rules and are indistinguishable, at least in terms of dress and appearance, from their secular peer", *Religion*, 1995, vol. no. 25, pp. 101–117.

5. Laurie Goodstein, "Evangelicals fear the loss of their teenagers", *New York Times*, 6 October 2006 and David Gonzalez, "A church's challenge: Holding on to its young" *New York Times*, 16 January 2007.

6. Thom Rainer, *The Bridger Generation*, Nashville, Broadman and Holman, 1997.

7. The social fragmentation into "tribes" based on individualization and self-realization is a theme that has been explored at length by sociologists such as Jean-Claude Kaufmann, *L'Invention de soi: Une théorie de l'identité*, Paris: Armand Colin, 2004.

INDEX

255

INDEX

ties", in *Comparative Studies in Society and History*, Society for Comparative Studies in Society and History (ed.), 1974.

9. See Christian Jaffrelot, *The Hindu nationalist movement and Indian politics: 1925 to the 1990s: strategies of identity-building, implantation and mobilisation (with special reference to Central India)*, London: Hurst, 1996; see also Ursula King, "Some Reflections on Sociological Approaches to the Study of Modern Hinduism", *Numen*, vol. 36, part 1, June 1989, pp. 72–97.

10. C. Jaffrelot, *ibid.*

11. Natascha Garvin, "Conversion & Conflict, Muslims in Mexico", *ISIM Review*, no. 15, Spring 2005, Leyden. This was also the case of African-American and Burmese converts to Judaism. The deculturation effect of Protestantism is evident.

12. Debate during the OSCE meeting on Islamophobia in Cordoba, in October 2007.

13. Fer speaks of syncretism, *Pentecostalisme en Polynésie Française*, op. cit., p. 10 foll. He describes the manipulation of religious markers by the ministers (p. 408 foll.).

14. Claude Prudhomme, *La Querelle des universels*, op. cit., see also Phili[p] Jenkins, *The Next Christendom*, op. cit.

15. Philip Jenkins, *The Next Christendom*, op. cit., p. 10.

16. Alan Cooperman and Jacqueline L. Salmon, "Episcopal Churches' Brea[k] way in Virginia Evolved over 30 Years", *Washington Post*, 4 Janu[ary] 2007, A01.

17. Philip Jenkins, *The Next Christendom*, op. cit.

18. For an overview, see Religioscope (www.religioscope.com): "Les É[glises] Africaines se développent en Europe", interview with Afe Adogame[, *Reli-*]*gioscope*, 19 January 2003; for a discussion on terminology, see[A.] Anderson, *Pluriformity and Contextuality in African Initiated Ch[urches]*, Selly Oak Colleges, Birmingham, http://artsweb.bham.ac.uk/aar[?] Publications/pluriformity_and_contextuality_i.html.

19. See A. Adogame, Religioscope, op. cit.

20. See http://www.eglise-reformee-mulhouse.org/el/eld2.htm. This i[s a] criticism, which echoes that of the Foreign Missions against the[...] the quarrel over rites, but it is interesting that it is voiced here [by an Afri-]can minister.

6. THE RELIGION MARKET

1. In French, see the various works by Danièle Hervieu-Lége[r...] Haenni's book *Islam de marché*, op. cit. For American sourc[es on the sub-]ject, see R. Finke and R. Stark, "Religious Economies an[d Sacred Cano-]pies", *American Sociological Review*, no. 53, 1988; P. Ber[ger...]

Canopy, op. cit., p. 138 and the Introduction to D. Martin, *Tongues of Fire*, op. cit.

2. Bernard Grosclaude, "Sortir des incantations" (on the Luthero-Protestant ministers of Montbéliard), *Reformation*, 14 February 2008.

3. This is a nagging question: why are humans religious? If religion is based on a quest for the sacred instead of it being part of a cultural or ideological system, then a link with "human nature" needs to be found. Scott Atran puts forward an original atheist viewpoint in *In Gods We Trust: The Evolutionary Landscape of Religion*, Oxford: Oxford University Press, 2002.

4. Laurence R. Iannaccone, Roger Finke, Rodney Stark, "Deregulating religion: The economics of Church and state", *Economic Inquiry*, vol. 35, no. 2, 1997.

5. For a critique see Steve Bruce, "1999 presidential address. The supply-side model of religion: The Nordic and Baltic states", *Journal for the Scientific Study of Religion*, vol. 39, no. 1, March 2000, pp. 32–46.

6. Shalva Weil, "Dual Conversion Among the Shinlung of North-East India", *Studies of Tribes and Tribals*, vol. 1, no.1, pp. 43–57, 2003.

7. "There are 2500 in Israel, spread across the entire country, essentially in Arad, Mitzpe Ramon and Tiberias; but Kfar Hashalom is located close to Dimona, the heart of the community of Black Hebrews. In 1969, these blacks from Chicago who claim to be from the tribe of Judah immigrated to Israel, after two years of wandering in Liberia. Their spiritual guide, Ben Ammi Ben Israel (born Ben Carter) tells how he saw a vision of the Angel Gabriel while he was lying on his bed, in Chicago, in 1966; he entreated him to set out for Israel with his nearest and dearest", cf. Nathalie Szerman, in collaboration with André Darmon, "Israël: une visite chez les Hébreux noirs", 9 October 2006, http://religion.info/french/articles/article_269.shtml.

8. Jean-François Mayer, *Internet and Religion*, Gollion: Infolio, 2008, Switzerland.

9. Jan Shipps, *Sojourner In The Promised Land: Forty Years Among The Mormons*, Illinois: University of Illinois Press, 2006.

10. There was indeed a Mormon mission in Tahiti and in the Pacific from 1844, but it was because they were looking for a lost tribe of Israel. This is indeed a case of racial exclusivity. Nowadays, 10 per cent of the population of Tahiti belongs to the Morman Church, cf. Yannick Fer, Religioscope, website http://religion.info/french/entretiens/article_314.shtml.

11. Mary Jordan, "The New Face of Global Mormonism: Tech-Savvy Missionary Church Thrives as Far Afield as Africa", *Washington Post*, 19 November 2007, p. A01.

12. Mara D. Bellaby, "Nigerian preacher runs Ukraine's first megachurch", *The Associated Press*, 4 August 2006. According to the article, the mayor of Kiev, Leonid Chernovetsk, is apparently a member of the Church.